Baptized into Christ

Baptized into Christ

A Guide to the Ecumenical Discussion on Baptism

DAGMAR HELLER

World Council of Churches Publications

BAPTIZED INTO CHRIST
A Guide to the Ecumenical Discussion on Baptism
Dagmar Heller

WCC Publications is the book publishing programme of the World Council of Churches. Founded in 1948, the WCC promotes Christian unity in faith, witness and service for a just and peaceful world. A global fellowship, the WCC brings together more than 349 Protestant, Orthodox, Anglican and other churches representing more than 560 million Christians in 110 countries and works cooperatively with the Roman Catholic Church.

Opinions expressed in WCC Publications are those of the authors.

Scripture quotations are from the New Revised Standard Version Bible, © copyright 1989 by the Division of Christian Education of the National Council of the Churches of Christ in the USA. Used by permission.

Cover design: 4 Seasons Book Design/Michelle Cook

Cover image: Mosaic of Christ's baptism in the Jordan, a copy of an 11th-century original from Daphne, Greece, offered by the Ecumenical Patriarchate to the chapel of the Ecumenical Centre, Geneva.

Book design and typesetting: 4 Seasons Book Design/Michelle Cook

ISBN: 978-2-8254-1577-1

World Council of Churches
150 route de Ferney, P.O. Box 2100
1211 Geneva 2, Switzerland
http://publications.oikoumene.org

Contents

Preface

THIS BOOK RESULTS FROM MY TEACHING IN ECUMENICAL theology at the Ecumenical Institute at Château de Bossey, Switzerland, during the winters of 2007-2011. Every year students of all the different confessional traditions and from all the continents come to Bossey for the sake of deepening their knowledge and discussing with each other how their churches could achieve unity. Most of them hear for the first time and meet for the first time people of certain traditions that do not exist in their countries. Thus, all of them are challenged to present and explain their own tradition to people who do not know anything—or who know very little—about this tradition.

Given the main task of introducing students to the ecumenical discussions on theological issues, the challenges for the teacher in this setting are manifold. It has become clear to me that in order for students to understand ecumenical discussions, it is first necessary that they understand the positions of the different confessional traditions. Thus the challenge is to present all the different traditions in such a way that representatives of those traditions sitting in the class would find appropriate. At the same time, the different confessional positions should be made understandable to people from different confessional and cultural backgrounds. The second challenge stems from the fact that ecumenical discussions have become an impenetrable forest through which students need guidance.

For the subject of baptism I was greatly helped by a German book written by the Baptist scholar Erich Geldbach,[1] in which the author gives an overview of the different confessional traditions and of the ecumenical dialogues, multilateral and bilateral. Because I could not find anything similar in English, and because time had progressed and further ecumenical work had been done since the publication of Geldbach's book in 1996, I felt I had to write a book myself.

The result is a book that is meant to provide an overview of the confessional traditions as they understand baptism, of the history which led to the ecumenical situation as it is today in regard to baptism, and of solutions proposed and agreements made. This book is written as a guide for students and other interested readers for their own reflection and for further research. For this purpose I have tried to quote as much as possible from primary sources.

I am aware of the fact that this book has its limitations. First of all, I tried to write from an overall perspective, but I cannot deny that my background is the Lutheran tradition. And this cannot be erased, although I tried to do justice to other traditions by giving the manuscript to colleagues from other confessional backgrounds for their feedback.

Another limitation is that I could only use literature which is available in English, German, French and to a small extent Russian, as these are the languages I can handle. This was especially regrettable for the first chapter, in which it would have been helpful to have access to some texts and literature in other languages. For example I could not find a lot of English sources for the Coptic understanding and practice of baptism. The same is the case for the African Independent Churches. Also, for the Orthodox positions, some Greek and Russian literature would have been helpful. In particular, especially the historical overview is limited to existing translations of the primary sources and does not discuss literary critical issues.

---

1. Erich Geldbach, *Taufe*, Ökumenische Studienhefte 5, Vandenhoeck & Ruprecht, Göttingen, 1996.

Nevertheless, I hope that this book will be a helpful tool for the study of ecumenical theology.

I would like to express my deep thanks especially to Thomas F. Best and Geoffrey Wainwright, who helped me with the English language, which is not my mother tongue. I also would like to thank all the students who have sat in my seminars during the last five years. Among those special thanks go to Dilene Fernandes (Brazil), Andrej Zuckowicki (Poland), Renata Nehring (Poland), Eva Guldanova (Slovakia), and Bruce Myers (Canada), who helped me to find some of the agreements between local churches on mutual recognition of baptism. I am also grateful for the help of Martin Junge (Chile-Switzerland), Christopher Dorn (USA) and Leo Koffeman (Netherlands). Thanks go as well to John Gatu (Kenya), Alan Varghese (India) and Christos-Filotheos Kolliopoulos (Greece), who looked at parts of the manuscript and made helpful comments and corrections. Jean-Daniel Plüss, a Pentecostal from Switzerland, also offered important comments on parts of the text, for which I am grateful. The same is true for Artem Borzov (Russia), Nang Kim Mang and Ram Din Puia (both Myanmar), who helped with the index. I am also grateful to the World Council of Churches for granting me a three-month study leave in 2011 in order to do research for this book. Finally, I would like to express my thanks to the publisher of WCC, Michael West, for his friendly and helpful collaboration.

Bossey, Palm Sunday 2012
Dagmar Heller

Introduction

"THROUGH BAPTISM, CHRISTIANS ARE BROUGHT INTO UNION WITH Christ, with each other and with the Church of every time and place. Our common baptism, which unites us to Christ in faith, is thus a basic bond of unity."[1] This bold statement was made about 30 years ago by the Commission on Faith and Order of the World Council of Churches (WCC) in the document *Baptism, Eucharist and Ministry*.[2] It includes two major aspects: that there is one, common baptism, and that this baptism is a uniting bond for Christians. The same conviction is shared by many others, from whom I quote just one statement, made by Roman Catholic Cardinal Walter Kasper: "Through our common baptism a fundamental unity is already given. The reflection on the common baptism and on the baptismal confession which we repeat at every Easter Vigil is the starting point and reference point of the ecumenism of life."[3]

During the last decades, however, there has been more and more a question whether this conviction reflects common ground for ecumenical conversations. Already the official responses of

---

1. World Council of Churches, Commission on Faith and Order, *Baptism, Eucharist and Ministry*, Faith and Order Paper No. 111, WCC Publications, Geneva, 1982, "Baptism," par. 6.

2. Ibid.

3. Walter Kasper, "Ökumene des Lebens," Vortrag auf dem Katholikentag 2004 in Ulm, published at www.foerderverein-unita-dei-christiani.com/ deutsch/index.htm, translation into English by the author.

the churches to the 1982 WCC document *Baptism, Eucharist and Ministry* showed that within some churches there are reservations about such statements. These reservations are related to the two different themes mentioned above: Orthodox churches question the emphasis on baptism as bond of unity because in their understanding unity cannot be based just on baptism. On the other hand, Baptists and other churches which baptize only persons who can speak for themselves question the idea that there is one common baptism because they do not see a possibility of recognizing infant baptism.[4]

Nevertheless, all churches know the words of the Letter to the Ephesians, which say: "There is one body and one Spirit, just as you were called to the one hope of your calling, one Lord, one faith, one baptism, one God and Father of all, who is above all and through all and in all" (Eph 4:4-6). The reality in worldwide Christianity reveals a different picture—and the churches are aware of the discrepancy between the biblical statement and their reality. As the Roman Catholic scholar Susan Wood puts it:

> We do not believe the same things about baptism. We have different notions of what constitutes a sacrament. We disagree on the relationship between the sign of baptism and the reality it signifies. We disagree about the effect of baptism. We engage in sometimes heated arguments about who can be baptized, some churches baptizing infants while others reserving baptism to adults. We do not necessarily baptize in the same way, some churches using *immersion while others sprinkle or pour water over the person being baptized. The very formula of baptism has become contested ... We have different practices of admitting the baptized to the Eucharistic table, thereby raising the question about the interrelationship of the three sacraments of initiation and the relationship between baptism and church membership.[5]

---

4. More details in Dagmar Heller, "Baptism into the Body of Christ : An Exploration of Its Ecumenical Implications," 2010, http://doc.rero.ch/record/20538?ln=fr.

5. Susan K. Wood, *One Baptism: Ecumenical Dimensions of the Doctrine of Baptism*, Liturgical Press, Collegeville, MN, 2009, 21ff.

The fact that these positions differ has a concrete and often painful effect when *converts (words with * are explained in the glossary) who have been baptized in their original church are baptized by the church they enter. Against the background that, according to common Christian tradition, baptism cannot be repeated, such baptism is often understood as re-baptism by the church which the convert has left, and thus as a manifestation that his or her first baptism is not recognized as such by the newly entered church.

Mutual recognition of baptism, therefore, is one of the most important goals for the ecumenical dialogue.

In the framework of the complex network of multilateral and bilateral dialogues on international, regional and local levels—mainly between the traditional churches which have engaged in the ecumenical movement during the last 60 years—various proposals have been made which would enable churches to mutually recognize their baptism. In some cases agreements for mutual recognition have been signed, in other cases this has not (yet) been possible. During the last 20 years new churches, such as Pentecostal churches and African Independent churches, have also begun to enter ecumenical discussions and have brought new perspectives and positions that need to be taken into consideration much more than has been the case until now.

All the material existing in this regard shows that the issue of baptism is more complicated than originally envisaged by many pioneers of the ecumenical movement. For the younger generation it becomes more and more difficult to keep an overview of the different discussions, the attempts at solutions and the agreements made. All these can only be understood if the problems and the issues involved are clear and their historical and systematic aspects known.

This book, therefore, offers an overview of baptism as an ecumenical issue. It begins with the general ecumenical situation concerning baptism and especially the attitude of the different confessional traditions toward mutual recognition. In order to understand the different positions, it is necessary to have a look into the history of baptism and its theological conception, as far as we know about it from historical documents; I undertake this in Chapter Two. Chapter Three introduces the reader to the ecumenical conversations on baptism in the multilateral and bilateral dialogues on the international level. A systematic view in Chapter Four offers some more insights into the nature of the ecumenical theological discussions and the doctrinal difficulties preventing mutual recognition. The final chapter presents the most recent work towards mutual recognition of baptism on the multilateral level as well as in bilateral discussions and agreements on national levels.

CHAPTER 1

Baptism in the World Church

The Different Confessional Positions

I N ORDER TO UNDERSTAND THE ECUMENICAL DEBATE ON
baptism, it is necessary to know the differences in the understanding of baptism existing in the various churches. This
chapter offers an overview of the different practices and theological views concerning baptism in the different Christian traditions
with a specific interest in their implications for ecumenical relations between the churches.

The main line of separation in the understanding of baptism
is the difference between churches which practice infant baptism
and those in which baptism is only possible for persons who can
express their own faith. Thus the following presentation is divided
into these two large groups of churches. Within each group the
presentation follows a mainly chronological order according to the
genesis of the respective church traditions.

Churches Practicing Infant Baptism
(*Paedobaptist[1] Churches)

This section of the chapter will present those churches which practice infant baptism. It has to be noted that all of them, in fact, practice adult baptism as well as infant baptism. The term "paedo-baptist" churches is used as a short form to distinguish them from those churches which practice exclusively the baptism of adults.

ORIENTAL ORTHODOX AND EASTERN ORTHODOX CHURCHES[2]

The reader should note that although the two church families of Oriental and Eastern Orthodox churches[3] differ in their historical

---

1. Words with * are explained in the Glossary.
2. My presentation on Orthodox churches is based in general on the following scholarly works (unless indicated differently): Alexander Schmemann, *Of Water and the Spirit*, St. Vladimir's Seminary Press, Crestwood, NY, 1974; Michael Pomazansky, *Orthodox Dogmatic Theology*, St. Herman of Alaska Brotherhood, Platina, CA, 1983; Karl Christian Felmy, *Orthodoxe Theologie: Eine Einführung*, Wissenschaftliche Buchgesellschaft, Darmstadt, 1990; Constantin Andronikof, *Des mystères sacramentels*, Editions du Cerf, Paris, 1998; and Boris Bobrinskoy, "Baptism: Sacrament of the Kingdom," in Thomas F. Best, ed., *Baptism Today: Understanding, Practice, Ecumenical implications*, Faith and Order Paper No. 207, WCC Publications, Geneva and Liturgical Press, Collegeville, MN, 2008, 3-14.
3. The term "Oriental Orthodox" refers to those churches which did not accept or were not present at the Council of Chalcedon in 451, and therefore have another way of expressing the relationship between the human and divine natures in Jesus Christ. They therefore are also called non-Chalcedonian churches and were in the past by their opponents sometimes called "monophysites" (mono= one, physis=nature), - a nomenclature which is to be avoided as it is not reflecting the self-understanding of these churches. These are today: the Syrian Orthodox Church of Antioch, the Armenian Apostolic Church, the Coptic Orthodox Church, the Ethiopian Orthodox Tewahedo Church, and the Malankara Orthodox Syrian Church (also called the Indian Orthodox Church).
"Eastern Orthodox" refers to the Orthodox churches which follow the Council of Chalcedon. They are also known as "Byzantine" churches. These are today: The Patriarchate of Constantinople, the Patriarchate of Alexandria, the Patriarchate of Antioch, the Patriarchate of Jerusalem, the Russian Orthodox Church, the Serbian Orthodox Church, the Romanian Orthodox Church, the Bulgarian Orthodox Church, the Catholicosate of Georgia, the Church of

and theological development, and consequently in their liturgical life, their theological standpoint regarding baptism is similar. Therefore they are presented here within the same sub-chapter. The presentation focuses on the Eastern Orthodox tradition in the first place, because the churches of this tradition have developed—especially in the 20th century—a more detailed baptismal theology.

The Baptismal Rite The Orthodox churches emphasize that theology is expressed in the liturgy, according to the principle *lex orandi lex credendi*.[4] Therefore, in order to understand baptism as it is understood in the Orthodox tradition, the most appropriate method is to look at the liturgical order and the liturgical texts for baptism.

The Russian theologian and liturgist Constantin Andronikof points out that the whole of the baptismal prayers and acts refers to the natural human being, living under the conditions of sin, as one whom baptism forms into a spiritually newborn person and leads to communion with the body and blood of Christ.[5] This is a way which proceeds in steps, following a dynamic process. Therefore, in the baptismal rite in the Orthodox Church the water rite is embedded in a series of other rites, so that baptism is one element in the *mystagogical process of *initiation.

The rite begins with a preparation, which starts with prayers for the reception of a *catechumen. This stems from the early church, when the *catechumenate was a preparation time which preceded baptism. After the reception, which is understood as the enrollment of the candidate in the "Book of Life,"[6] the catechumen first is directed towards the West, which is the seat of the "prince of darkness." The idea is that not only in words, but also by spitting

---

Cyprus, the Church of Greece, the Orthodox Church of Poland, the Orthodox Church of Albania, the Orthodox Church of Czech Lands and Slovakia, the Orthodox Church of Finland, and the Orthodox Church of Estonia.

4. "The rule of prayer is the rule for belief." This saying is attributed to Prosper of Aquitaine (ca. 390-463 CE; henceforth all dates in this book are CE unless otherwise indicated); see Alexander Schmemann, *Of Water and the Spirit*, 10.

5. Andronikof, *Des mystères sacramentels*, 93.

6. Ibid., 97.

at him, the catechumen rejects Satan three times. These *exorcisms are the preparation for the following "allegiance to Christ": the catechumen turns to the East, from where the "sun of justice" rises, in order to join Christ by answering three times the question "Do you unite yourself unto Christ?" with "I do." Finally, again, to the question "Have you united yourself unto Christ?" he or she answers "I have." The priest then asks: "Do you believe in him?" Answer: "I believe in him as King and God." What follows is the "Commitment to Faith,"[7] in which the catechumen recites—three times—the Niceno-Constantinopolitan Creed, whereby the knowledge *about* Christ becomes a knowledge *of* Christ.

After these preparatory rites the proper act of baptism takes place, beginning with the priest vesting in white garments, the lighting of candles, the incensing of the baptismal font and the introductory blessing. The baptismal water is blessed by an *epicletic prayer, after which the candidate, who has been anointed with the "oil of gladness," is immersed three times. This immersion signifies "the real death of the Old Adam and his resurrection in Christ, the new Adam."[8] The baptismal formula is: "The servant of God N. is baptized in the Name of the Father, Amen. And of the Son, Amen. And of the Holy Spirit, Amen." It has to be noted that the passive formulation expresses the idea that baptism is an act of God, in which the baptizing person as well as the baptized person are not the primary actors.[9] After the triple immersion the newly baptized person is vested in a white garment, in order to express the newness of life: the person is clothed with Christ. In the *chrismation immediately following, the candidate receives the Holy Spirit, which is Christ's spirit. It provides the fullness of baptism and involves an *anointing in the form of a cross on the forehead, eyes, nose, mouth, ears, chest and hands with *myron, which normally has been prepared and consecrated by the head of the church. With each anointing

---

7. Bobrinskoy, "Baptism: Sacrament of the Kingdom," 9.
8. Ibid., 10.
9. See Erich Geldbach, *Taufe*, Bensheimer Hefte 79, Vandenhoeck & Ruprecht, Göttingen, 1996, 28.

the priest says "Seal of the Holy Spirit. Amen."[10] Now the person is a full member of the Church as the body of Christ and can receive the *eucharist. But before this, there is a procession around the baptismal font—as Alexander Schmemann explains, the remnant of the procession from the *baptistery to the church in the early times, when the baptistery was in a separate building.[11] Today it is explained as symbolizing baptism as a "nuptial Covenant ... with the divine Bridegroom."[12]

The eucharist is the fulfillment of chrismation and the "culmination of baptism."[13] Nowadays it is often celebrated not directly after baptism, but on the following Sunday. The end of the rite—originally eight days after baptism—is the washing off of the Holy *Chrism, which means the sending into the world, and the tonsure, the cutting of a tuft of hair, symbolizing obedience and *sacrifice.

Baptism is normally performed by a priest. In case of extreme need, lay persons may also baptize,[14] but chrismation must always be performed by a priest. This means that an emergency baptism has to be confirmed by a priest.

Practice of Infant Baptism This liturgical pattern comes from the early church, where it was performed with adults. When infant baptism started to be practiced in the first centuries, the different liturgical elements were (and still are) used in the same form. Those parts which cannot be done by an infant are said or done by the parents and godparents instead. There has never been a doubt, according to Meyendorff, that children could be baptized, because baptism understood as new birth is independent of any decision on the part of the person being born.[15] But as Schmemann

---

10. Felmy, *Orthodoxe Theologie*, 185. For this understanding, the Orthodox refer to Church fathers such as Cyprian of Carthage, Clement of Alexandria and Cyril of Jerusalem. See Michael Pomazansky, *Orthodox Dogmatic Theology*, 270ff.

11. Schmemann, *Of Water and the Spirit*, 109ff.

12. Bobrinskoy, "Baptism: Sacrament of the Kingdom," 10.

13. Ibid., 11.

14. See Andronikof, *Des mystères sacramentels*, 94ff.

15. John Meyendorff, *Initiation à la théologie byzantine*, Editions du Cerf, Paris, 1975, 256.

emphasizes, children are only baptized in the understanding that they are living in a Christian surrounding. The baptism of children of non-Christian parents would not be considered valid by the Orthodox Church.[16]

Theological Understanding of Baptism Alexander Schmemann has pointed to the fact that baptism can only be understood if the close link between baptism and Easter is clear. The Easter liturgy is a baptismal liturgy, and the liturgical time of Lent has developed from the preparation for the celebration of baptism.[17] Baptism is dying and rising with Christ not only in a symbolic way, but in a real way—in the understanding that death is a spiritual reality as a life without God. Baptism is the sacrament of regeneration and re-creation, a personal Pascha (Easter) and a personal Pentecost. It is a "new birth," which also means that it is a free gift of God independent of any human choice.[18] Baptism is understood as a promise of greater and more perfect gifts; it is the model of the future resurrection.[19] As the passage into a new life, baptism is the integration into the people of God and finally an epiphany of the kingdom of God.

For the Orthodox tradition the trinitarian aspect of church life is very important. "The Eucharist ... represents the advent of the kingdom of the Father, Son and Holy Spirit, into which we have access through Trinitarian baptism ... Baptism, then, is both the gift of new life in the Spirit, the source of Trinitarian grace, and the entryway into the Church, where the sacrament of initiation is fulfilled."[20] Therefore baptism needs to be performed in the name of the Father and the Son and the Holy Spirit.

According to Orthodox *catechisms baptism is necessary for salvation, because in all phases of life—including the new-born—the human being needs to be regenerated and needs to begin a new life with Christ.[21] The Orthodox tradition emphasizes the "life in

---

16. See Schmemann, *Of Water and the Spirit*, 69.
17. Ibid., 8ff. and 16.
18. Meyendorff, *Initiation à la théologie byzantine*, 256, 266.
19. Ibid., 257. See also Pomazansky, *Orthodox Dogmatic Theology*, 269ff.
20. Schmemann, *Of Water and the Spirit*, 8.
21. Meyendorff, *Initiation à la théologie byzantine*, 256.

Christ"; this is the growth and proof in faith. Baptism is therefore the beginning of a process, the process of creating the image of Christ in the baptized person.

Baptism and Other Sacraments Consequently Orthodox Christians emphasize that baptism is part of Christian initiation, and belongs inseparably together with the two sacraments of chrismation and eucharist: "Together, these three constitute a unique and permanent foundation of new birth in the Spirit."[22] This understanding is based on writers of the early church, for example Symeon of Thessaloniki, who says: "Who does not receive the holy chrism is not perfectly baptized."[23]

The whole life of a Christian is understood as "an actual incorporation into Christ's death and resurrection," which is expressed in the fact that "the entire sacramental and liturgical life of the Church enables us to participate in his redemptive Pascha."[24] The role of the sacraments, including baptism, can therefore be described as follows: "The various stages of our human life are assumed under the direction of the Church by means of the sacraments, by which the light of the kingdom penetrates into the sphere of our human, earthly existence."[25] This shows the close connection between sacraments and the church. "The 'newness of life' which Baptism bestows is fulfilled only in the Church, or rather... the Church *is* that life, so radically different from the life of 'this world.'"[26] Therefore, "from the very beginning, baptism has been experienced as an event of the Church, one that concerns and involves the entire Eucharistic community."[27]

While in principle the baptismal rite in the Oriental Orthodox churches is similar to the Byzantine one described above, there are a few specific characteristics which distinguish the two traditions.

---

22. Bobrinskoy, "Baptism: Sacrament of the Kingdom," 7; see also Andronikof, *Des mystères sacramentels*, 92.

23. Symeon of Thessaloniki, Hom. 60, quoted by Meyendorff in *Initiation à la théologie byzantine*, 255.

24. Bobrinskoy, "Baptism: Sacrament of the Kingdom," 7.

25. Ibid.

26. See Schmemann, *Of Water and the Spirit*, 69.

27. Bobrinskoy, "Baptism: Sacrament of the Kingdom," 8-9.

Like the Eastern Orthodox churches, the Coptic Church practices a threefold *immersion, but only the third time is a full submersion.[28] Oil is poured three times into the baptismal water, and three anointings (during the exorcisms with oil, after the creed with "oil of joy," after the water rite with myron) are performed.[29] The child is vested with a white garment and wears a crown as well as a belt crossed around the waist which is taken off only on the eighth day after the baptism.[30] Boys are baptized 40 days after birth, girls 80 days after birth following the mosaic law of purity.

The Syrian Orthodox Church today even performs four anointings,[31] accompanying the inscription of the candidate (anointing of the forehead), after the completion of the catechumenal rites (anointing of the forehead), following the consecration of the water (anointing of the whole body) and following baptism (anointing of the sense organs); as Sebastian Brock has pointed out, this is a later development. Originally in the Syriac tradition there was only one pre-baptismal anointing; only in the fourth century was the post-baptismal anointing with myron introduced.[32] What is important is that anointing with oil and baptism are inseparably linked, and the gift of the Holy Spirit cannot be attributed to either one or the other in isolation.[33]

---

28. According to Friedrich Heyer, *Konfessionskunde*, De Gruyter, Berlin and New York, 1977, 230.

29. Clemens Leonhard, "Gestalt und Deutung der christlichen Initiation in den orientalischen Kirchen," in Christian Lange, Clemens Leonhard, and Ralph Olbrich, eds., *Die Taufe: Einführung in Geschichte und Praxis*, Wissenschaftliche Buchgesellschaft, Darmstadt, 2008, 125-142, with an overview 136ff.

30. Heyer, *Konfessionskunde*, 230.

31. Clemens Leonhard, "Gestalt und Deutung der christlichen Initiation," 136ff.; see also Sebastian Brock, *Holy Spirit in the Syrian Baptismal Tradition*, The Syrian Churches Series, Vol. 9, 2nd ed., ed. Jacob Vellian, Jyoti Book House, Kottayam, Kerala, India, 1998, 43ff.

32. Brock, *Holy Spirit in the Syrian Baptismal Tradition*, 218; Bobrinskoy also notes: "The Syriac tradition of the Church in Antioch, represented especially by St. John Chrysostom, knew of no such 'post-baptismal' unction even at the end of the fourth century ... The Syriac tradition underscores all the more the prior action of the Spirit, who sanctifies the baptismal waters and renders the candidate capable of renouncing Satanic powers and confessing Christ as Lord." Bobrinskoy, "Baptism: Sacrament of the Kingdom," 10.

33. See Brock, *Holy Spirit in the Syrian Baptismal Tradition*, 43.

In the Malankara Orthodox Syrian Church the child is partly immersed in the water of the font,[34] and in addition there is a crowning "to signify participation in the holy and royal priesthood of the new dispensation (1 Pet 2:5-9)."[35] Baptism is understood as "birth from above."[36]

In the Armenian Apostolic Church there is only one anointing, which is the chrismation after baptism. "While baptism gives spiritual birth to the catechumen who becomes the adopted child of God, the anointing with oil or chrism (confirmation) gives strength, courage, and the presence and grace of the Holy Spirit, enabling the baptized person to develop the virtues that have been promised to him or her."[37] The baptismal formula is: "N., the servant of God, coming from the state of catechumen to baptism, is now being baptized in the Name of the Father, and of the Son, and of the Holy Spirit. Redeemed by the Blood of Christ from the servitude of sin, he/she becomes an adopted child of the heavenly Father, a co-heir with Christ and a temple of the Holy Spirit."[38] Baptism is understood as "the ransom for captives, the remission of offense, the death of sin, and the generation of the soul" and "brings the baptized person into relationship with the once-for-all saving act of God in Christ."[39] Only a priest—no *deacon or lay person—can perform a baptism.[40]

Recognition of Baptism in Other Churches There is an ambiguity within Orthodoxy concerning baptism performed in other churches, manifest in the fact that the practice in cases of

---

34. Kondothra M. George, "Sacramental Theology in the Malankara Tradition," V. Международная Богословская Конференция Русской Православной Церкви, *Православное учение о церковних таинствах*, том III, Синодальная Библейско-богословская комиссия Москва, 2009, 573.

35. Jacob Kurien, "The Baptismal Liturgy of the Malankara Orthodox Syrian Church," in Thomas F. Best, ed., *Baptism Today*, 25.

36. Kurien, "The Baptismal Liturgy of the Malankara Orthodox," 26.

37. Mesrob Tashjian, "The Sacrament of Holy Baptism in the Armenian Apostolic Church," in Best, *Baptism Today*, 20.

38. Ibid., 19.

39. Ibid., 16 and 19.

40. See Friedrich Heyer, ed., *Die Kirche Armeniens*, Die Kirchen der Welt 18, Evangelisches Verlagswerk, Stuttgart, 1978, 108.

conversion of persons from other churches is not consistent. On the Oriental Orthodox side, not many theological reflections about this issue can be found, but the practice shows that the Coptic Church, for example, baptizes every person coming from another church to become a member of the Coptic Church. The Armenian Apostolic Church in principle follows the rule that all those converts who have not been baptized according to the *canons of the Armenian Apostolic Church are to be baptized. Those who have been baptized in accordance with the canons but have not been anointed will be received by chrismation, which is the usual practice with converts from Lutheran churches.[41] Those coming from another community who are baptized and anointed in the correct way are received by repentance and confession of the Orthodox faith; this is normally the case for converts from Eastern Orthodox and the Roman Catholic churches.

Within the Eastern Orthodox churches a variety of practices exists which also have changed in different places at different times.[42] Between the 11th century and the 15th century the Greek-speaking churches received converts by a special rite of anointing with myron,[43] and in some cases converts were even re-baptized—especially after the sacking of Constantinople by the Crusaders[44]—while Slavic churches celebrated the usual rite of the post-baptismal anointing (chrismation). Later, under the influence of Latin scho-

---

41. For this information I am grateful to the Rev. Dirardur Sardaryan, Göppingen, Germany.

42. See John H. Erickson, "The Problem of Sacramental 'Economy,'" in idem, ed., *The Challenge of Our Past: Studies in Orthodox Canon Law and Church History*, St. Vladimir's Seminary Press, Crestwood, NY, 1991, 115ff; see also idem, "Reception into the Orthodox Church," *Ecumenical Review* 54 (2002): 66.

43. Сергий Говорун, "Богословские аспекты и практика приема в Православие из инославия" (Sergiy [Cyrill] Hovorun, "The Theological and Practical Aspects of Admission of Non-Orthodox Christians into the Orthodox Church"), V. Международная Богославская Конференция Русской Православной Церкви, *Православное учение о церковних таинствах*, том I, Синодальная Библейско-богословская комиссия Москва, 2009, 350.

44. See George Dragas, "The Manner of Reception of Roman Catholic Converts into the Orthodox Church, with Special Reference to the Decisions of the Synods of 1484 (Constantinople), 1755 (Constantinople), and 1667 (Moscow)," paper presented at the Orthodox/Roman Catholic Dialogue (USA) in 1998, http://jbburnett.com/resources/dragas_baptism.pdf.

lasticism in Slavic Orthodoxy, converts from the Western church were re-baptized, because their baptism by aspersion was not considered valid.[45] This practice was abandoned in the Russian Orthodox Church in the 17th century, in order to be in conformity with the other Orthodox churches. Then, in Constantinople in the mid-18th century, Patriarch Cyril V introduced a directive that converts from the Armenian and Catholic Churches must be received by baptism. Since this directive was not accepted by all the Synod members, this initiative resulted finally in different practices in different parts of the Orthodox Church.[46] Concerning Protestants the practices varied as well. In 1644 Constantinople issued a decree whereby they should be re-baptized, while in 1872 the Council of Jerusalem decided that they should not be re-baptized. But in Russia, re-baptism of Protestants was continued until the 18th century.[47] To this day there are various practices, although the official position of Constantinople is that Lutherans and Reformed are not to be re-baptized.

ROMAN CATHOLIC CHURCH[48]

The Baptismal Rite According to the Rite of Christian Initiation of Adults (RCIA) from 1987,[49] which is now considered the normative rite, while infant baptism would be a special case, baptism is part of a "process of becoming a Christian, [which] parallels natural human development."[50] In the RCIA "there are four continuous periods: the precatechumenate, marked by the hearing of the first preaching of the Gospel; the catechumenate, set aside for a

---

45. See Hovorun, "Theological and Practical Aspects," 351, referring to the Council of Moscow in 1620, which sealed the practice of reception of Catholics through baptism.

46. For more details see Hovorun, "Theological and Practical Aspects."

47. Hovorun, "Theological and Practical Aspects," 351.

48. If not marked differently, my main source for this presentation of Roman Catholic practice and theology of baptism is James F. Puglisi, "Rite(s) of Baptism in the Catholic Church: A Theological-Pastoral Commentary," in Best, *Baptism Today*, 29-43.

49. Published on the internet by The Catholic Liturgical Library, http://www.catholicliturgy.com/index.cfm/FuseAction/DocumentContents /Index/2/SubIndex/40/DocumentIndex/539.

50. Puglisi, "Rite(s) of Baptism," 31.

complete *catechesis; the period of purification and enlightenment (Lenten preparation) for a more intense spiritual preparation; and the period of postbaptismal catechesis or *mystagogy marked by the new experience of sacraments and community."[51] The whole initiation process has a paschal character "since the initiation of Christians is the first sacramental sharing in the death and rising of Christ."[52] Therefore the most appropriate time for baptism is the Easter vigil, after the time of Lent as the time of preparation.

The precatechumenate "helps the individual examine the motive for requesting baptism." The catechumenate is marked by a "rite of acceptance into the order of catechumens." The third stage is the final preparation, which takes place at the beginning of Lent with an enrollment of the catechumens as candidates for baptism.[53] The following six-week period is a time of purification and enlightenment during which several rites are celebrated: *"scrutinies" or exorcisms, renouncing the glamour of this world and affirmation of faith (the catechumen is presented with the creed and the Lord's Prayer). On Holy Saturday, the catechumens "give back" the creed and the Lord's prayer by reciting them by heart. These rites are concluded by the *ephphetha rite, the "unstopping of the ears and mouth." "Two other rites may be included in this ritual: choosing a new baptismal name ... and anointing with the oil of catechumens."[54]

The baptismal rite proper begins with a greeting at the door of the church and a procession into the church. After the sign of the cross follows the proclamation of the word of God. An exorcism is said over the baptizand, in order to proclaim liberation from sin and the devil. Then the candidate is anointed, in order to be prepared for the fight against Satan, as in earlier times fighters were anointed for the contest. If anointing is not possible, there is a laying on of hands. Then the candidate renounces Satan and his works (*abrenuntiatio diaboli*) before he or she recites the Creed. Before the actual act of baptism the baptismal water is consecrated by calling

51. RCIA, I.7.
52. Ibid., I.8.
53. Puglisi, "Rite(s) of Baptism," 31ff.
54. Ibid., 32ff.

down the Holy Spirit. "Baptism is performed in the most expressive way by triple immersion in the baptismal water. However, from ancient times it has also been able to be conferred by pouring the water three times over the candidate's head."[55] The formula is "N., I baptize you in the name of the Father, and the Son, and the Holy Spirit." An anointing with holy chrism follows along with the clothing in a white garment as a sign of being clothed with Christ. The baptized person receives a baptismal candle as a sign that he or she is illumined and should be a light in the world. The ears and mouth of the baptized are touched to indicate the opening of the ears for Christ's teaching and the mouth for the praise of Christ.

"For adults the sacrament of confirmation is to follow immediately, completing baptism ... The rite is very simple, consisting of the imposition of hands and anointing with chrism."[56] In the case of children, the Roman Catholic tradition has two post-baptismal anointings, one immediately after the water baptism, and a second one at a later age, which is considered to be a sacrament on its own (confirmation).

Normally baptism is performed by a priest or a deacon. "In case of necessity, any person, even someone not baptized, can baptize, if he has the required intention,"[57] that is, the intention of the church, and if water is used and the trinitarian formula applied.

The Practice of Infant Baptism The baptismal rites in the Roman Catholic Church still show that they were originally meant for adults. The Second Vatican Council decided to adapt these rites to the situation of infants, arguing for infant baptism on account of original sin: "Born with a fallen human nature and tainted by original sin, children also have need of the new birth in Baptism to be freed from the power of darkness and brought into the realm of the freedom of the children of God, to which all men are called. The sheer gratuitousness of the grace of salvation is particularly manifest in infant Baptism. The Church and the parents would deny a

---

55. *Catechism of the Catholic Church* (CCC), 2nd ed., 1997, No. 1239ff., www.vatican.va/archive/ENG0015/engoois/_index.htm.

56. Puglisi, "Rite(s) of Baptism," 36.

57. CCC, No. 1256.

child the priceless grace of becoming a child of God were they not to confer Baptism shortly after birth."[58] Contemporary Catholic theologians make clear that infant baptism makes sense only if the parents are believers, and if the parish is taking responsibility for the baptized infants by making sure that baptism is embedded in a process of pastoral care including accompaniment of the parents, catechism while the children are growing, and other formation practices.[59] Infant baptism "means that one is baptized in the faith of the Church and it is the Church that embraces, with its faith, a child who cannot by himself or herself make a confession of faith."[60]

Theological Understanding of Baptism Baptism is one of the seven sacraments, and together with confirmation and ordination it bestows a *character indelibilis* upon the person.[61] It is "the gateway to life in the Spirit" and therefore also called "the basis of the whole Christian life."[62] Its first effect is the washing away of original sin,[63] and in this sense baptism is necessary for salvation. The *Catholic Catechism* says: "Baptism not only purifies from all sins, but also makes the *neophyte 'a new creature,'* an adopted son of God, who has become 'partaker of the divine nature,' member of Christ and co-heir with him, and a temple of the Holy Spirit."[64]

---

58. CCC, No. 1250; see also Puglisi, "Rite(s) of Baptism," 39. The rite for the baptism of children says: "To fulfill the true meaning of the sacrament, children must later be formed in the faith in which they have been baptized." (Rites of Baptism for Children, No. 3).

59. See Theodor Schneider, *Zeichen der Nähe Gottes: Grundriss der Sakramententheologie*, Matthias Grünewald, Mainz, 1992.

60. Puglisi, "Rite(s) of Baptism," 39.

61. According to CCC, No. 1121: "The three sacraments of Baptism, Confirmation, and Holy Orders confer, in addition to grace, a sacramental character or 'seal' by which the Christian shares in Christ's priesthood and is made a member of the Church according to different states and functions. This configuration to Christ and to the Church, brought about by the Spirit, is indelible, it remains for ever in the Christian as a positive disposition for grace, a promise and guarantee of divine protection, and as a vocation to divine worship and to the service of the Church. Therefore these sacraments can never be repeated." http://www.vatican.va/archive/ENG0015/__P31.HTM.

62. CCC, No. 1213.

63. Geldbach, *Taufe*, 32.

64. CCC, No. 1265.

In the newer Catholic theology baptism is understood in the first place as incorporation into the body of Christ.[65] According to the Second Vatican Council, it is at the same time participation in the priesthood of Christ. In this sense baptism is the precondition for participating in the mission of the church.[66] It is a gift in which the person is participating in a receptive way.

Catholic theology is interested in the question of the effects of baptism: "The two principal effects are purification from sins and new birth in the Holy Spirit."[67] This is explained more fully in the following way: "By Baptism all sins are forgiven, original sin and all personal sins, as well as all punishment for sin. In those who have been reborn nothing remains that would impede their entry into the Kingdom of God, neither Adam's sin, nor personal sin, nor the consequences of sin, the gravest of which is separation from God."[68] The *Catechism* also gives an explanation of why there are still sins happening after baptism: "Yet certain temporal consequences of sin remain in the baptized, such as suffering, illness, death, and such frailties inherent in life as weaknesses of character, and so on, as well as an inclination to sin that Tradition calls concupiscence, or metaphorically, the 'tinder for sin' (*fomes peccati*); since concupiscence 'is left for us to wrestle with, it cannot harm those who do not consent but manfully resist it by the grace of Jesus Christ.'"[69]

Baptism and Other Sacraments As in the Orthodox tradition, in the Catholic Church "Baptism, the Eucharist, and the sacrament of Confirmation together constitute the 'sacraments of Christian initiation', whose unity must be safeguarded."[70] Confirmation is "necessary for the completion of baptismal grace,"[71] but it is performed at a later age (often around the age of 12 or 13, and increasingly

---

65. See Karl Rahner, *Grundkurs des Glaubens*, Herder, Freiburg, 1976, 400, quoted in Geldbach, *Taufe*, 33.

66. Lumen Gentium 33, quoted in Geldbach, *Taufe*, 33.

67. CCC, No. 1262.

68. CCC, No. 1263.

69. CCC, No. 1264.

70. CCC, No. 1285.

71. Ibid.

later). Also, although baptism is closely linked with the eucharist, the Roman Catholic Church allows children to receive Holy Communion only when they have reached an age of understanding.

Recognition of Baptism in Other Churches In Roman Catholic teaching "baptism by immersion, or by pouring, together with the Trinitarian formula is, of itself, valid."[72] Any baptism performed in other churches following one of these practices is therefore valid.

REFORMATION CHURCHES
Lutheran Churches
The Baptismal Rite For the understanding and rite of baptism, the Lutheran Reformation undertook a revision of the medieval Latin rite as well as its translation into German. Martin Luther published two such revisions, *Taufbüchlein 1523*[73] and the revised *Taufbüchlein 1526.*[74] The second one—more influential during the later history—"removed many of the accompanying ceremonies (giving of salt, anointing) in order that the washing itself could stand out as the central act."[75]

The baptismal rite in the Lutheran churches can be described as follows. In the beginning is a short address, giving a theological explanation of baptism. Then the candidates are introduced. Often there is a renunciation of evil, in any case a profession of faith (normally the baptismal Apostles' Creed). The water rite is done with the triune formula: "N., I baptize you in the name of the Father, and of the Son, and of the Holy Spirit."[76] The laying on of hands

---

72. Pontifical Council for Promoting Christian Unity, *Directory for the Application of Principles and Norms on Ecumenism*, Vatican City, 1993, No. 95, 58.

73. "The Order of Baptism (1523)," in E. Theodore Bachmann and Helmut T. Lehmann, eds., Luther's Works (LW), American edition, Muhlenberg Press, 1960, vol. 53, 96-101.

74. "The Order of Baptism Newly Revised (1526)," *LW* 53, 107-109.

75. Jeffrey A. Truscott, "The Rite of Holy Baptism in the *Lutheran Book of Worship*," in Best, *Baptism Today*, 46.

76. In the USA, for example, the possibility of a passive formula is also provided.

with a prayer and a "seal of the Spirit" formula follows together with a sign of the cross on the forehead. Normally a prayer for the parents (originally only for the mother) follows and often nowadays a lighted candle is given to the *sponsors (godparents) or to the parents. Intercessions for the baptized are either offered within the baptismal rite or together with the general intercessory prayers of the congregation, as nowadays baptisms are often conducted in a normal Sunday service.

Practice of Infant Baptism Martin Luther inherited infant baptism from the Catholic Church, but he had to defend it against those called *Anabaptists ("re-baptizers") at the time. His argument for keeping infant baptism is a rather simple one: it has been proven through history that children received the Holy Spirit through baptism. Otherwise the church which practiced infant baptism for centuries would not have continued to exist.[77] From there Luther comes to the conclusion that children also have faith.[78] Children are being baptized in the hope that they will believe, but especially because of God's command. Therefore, in principle only children of baptized parents are baptized, as are those of unbaptized parents who desire baptism also for themselves.[79] One of the main dogmatic arguments in favor of infant baptism has been formulated by the 20th century Lutheran theologian Edmund Schlink: "Even though the infants have not rebelled against God by their own decision and are different from adult sinners in this respect, they cannot by their own decision rid themselves of the dominion of sin as they grow up."[80]

---

77. Martin Luther, *The Large Catechism*, part 4, translated by F. Bente and W.H.T. Dau, Published in: Triglot Concordia: The Symbolical Books of the Ev. Lutheran Church, Concordia Publishing House, St Louis, 1921) pp. 565-773, also: *Martin Luther's Large Catechism & Small Catechism*, NuVision Publications, Milton Keynes, 2007.

78. Martin Luther, Sermon on John 1:32-34 in E. Theodore Bachmann and Helmut T. Lehmann, eds., Luther's Works, American Edition, Muhlenberg Press, 1960, vol. 22, 174.

79. Edmund Schlink, *The Doctrine of Baptism*, Concordia Publishing House, Saint Louis and London, 1972, 130.

80. E. Schlink, *The Doctrine of Baptism*, 158.

Theological Understanding of Baptism Baptism is an "assignment" (*Übereignung*)[81] to Jesus Christ and thus assignment to Christ's death and resurrection. It gives new life and admonishes one to walk in this new life.

The reason for baptizing in general, for Luther, is first of all the command of God and therefore the institution of baptism by Jesus Christ.[82] For Martin Luther "baptism was a sacramental means of grace by which God delivered the person from sin, death, and the devil. Yet the efficacy of baptism resided not in the baptismal water itself, but in the fact that water was used by God's command and with his promise."[83] The Augsburg Confession stresses the necessity of baptism for salvation.[84] Edmund Schlink sees the necessity of baptism in two aspects: the necessity which results from the command of Jesus Christ is linked with the necessity of baptism for salvation. "The saving will of God is the inner basis of the command to receive salvation in Baptism ... We can, of course, speak of a necessity of Baptism for salvation only as we call to a reception of Baptism, but not if we establish theoretically that salvation is impossible without Baptism."[85]

Baptism is a pure gift. At the same time the external event of baptism remains incomplete if it is not grasped in faith.[86] A Christian has to learn throughout his or her whole life what baptism means and brings: baptism is the beginning of a life-long process. In a way, for Luther faith is a consequence of baptism. Luther distinguishes between the legitimacy (*Rechtmäßigkeit*) of baptism and the effect of baptism.[87] The legitimacy is not dependent on whether the baptizand believes or not. Therefore even

---

81. See ibid., 42-58.
82. See Geldbach, *Taufe*, 41.
83. Jeffrey A. Truscott, "The Rite of Holy Baptism," 45.
84. CA II. http://www.ccel.org/ccel/schaff/creeds3.iii.ii.html
85. Schlink, *The Doctrine of Baptism*, 107.
86. See Luther, *The Large Catechism*, Part 4. Translated by F. Bente and W.H.T. Dau, Published in: Triglot Concordia: *The Symbolical Books of the Ev. Lutheran Church*, Concordia Publishing House, St Louis, 1921) pp. 565-773
87. See Geldbach, *Taufe*, 46.

the baptism of a person who does not believe is a valid baptism,[88] because baptism is not dependent on the human person, but on God. But whether baptism has an effect is related to the faith of the person.

"Baptism in the name of Jesus Christ is at the same time Baptism by the Holy Spirit ... Through Baptism the Holy Spirit assigns the believer to Christ the Lord. He gives him a share in Christ's righteousness, holiness, life, and glory."[89] At the same time baptism is the reception into the church, incorporation into the people of God, the body of Christ.

Baptism and Other Sacraments Baptism is one of the two sacraments instituted by Jesus Christ, according to the Lutheran understanding of sacraments. As incorporation into the body of Christ, baptism leads to the eucharist and the eucharistic community is a community of the baptized.

Recognition of Baptism in Other Churches Baptism performed in other churches is recognized. Following the Augsburg Confession Lutheran theologians say: "A baptism administered according to the Gospel with water in the name of the triune God is a valid baptism."[90] Converts from other churches are received into the church in a normal Sunday service, sometimes with a laying on of hands.

Reformed Churches
The Baptismal Rite Within the family of Reformed Churches[91] there is a variety of baptismal practices existing today. A normal

---

88. See Luther, Sermon on John 1, LW 22: 174.

89. E. Schlink, *The Doctrine of Baptism*, 58 and 60.

90. Friederike Nüssel, "Baptism and Baptismal Order in the Life of the Protestant Church," in Michael Beintker, Viorel Ionita, and Jochen Kramm, eds., *Baptism in the Life of the Churches: Documents of an Orthodox-Protestant Dialogue in Europe*, Lembeck, Frankfurt am Main, 2011, 145ff.

91. The name "Reformed Churches" includes all those churches which are influenced in some way by the Swiss Reformation (Zwingli, Calvin and others) and nowadays brought together in the World Communion of Reformed Churches (WCRC).

baptismal service would begin with sentences of Scripture, always including the Great Commission from Matthew 28. In some— but not in all—Reformed churches the Apostles' Creed would be recited. Then follows the water rite with the baptismal formula "N., I baptize you in the name of the Father, and of the Son, and of the Holy Spirit." At the end there is an act of welcoming the person by the congregation. Some Reformed churches, under the influence of the ecumenical movement, have developed their baptismal rite to incorporate a renunciation of evil in the beginning, a thanksgiving over the water, and after the water rite a laying-on-of-hands on the head of the newly baptized with a brief prayer and a sign of the cross.[92] In some churches the candidate is then declared a member of the church of Christ.

Practice of Infant Baptism As an argument for maintaining infant baptism Reformed churches would go back to the Swiss reformer Ulrich Zwingli, who argued for use of a parallel between circumcision and baptism. As circumcision was the sign of the old covenant, so is baptism for the new covenant. "Christian children were God's children, just as the children of the old covenant were God's children … as the sign of the old covenant, circumcision, was given to Israelite children, so the sign of the new covenant, baptism, ought to be given to Christian children."[93] John Calvin used the same covenant theology as Zwingli in this matter.[94] In his *Institutes* he argues that infants "are baptized for future repentance and faith. Though these are not yet formed in them, yet the seed of both lies hid in them by the secret operation of the Spirit."[95]

---

92. For instance, the Presbyterian Church in the USA; see Martha Moore-Keish, "Baptism in the Presbyterian and Reformed Tradition" in Best, *Baptism Today*, 63-71.

93. John W. Riggs, *Baptism in the Reformed Tradition: An Historical and Practical Theology*, Westminster John Knox, Louisville and London, 2002, 24.

94. John Calvin, *Institutes of the Christian Religion*, translation by Henry Beveridge, Erdmans Publishing, Grand Rapids MI, 1989, book IV, chapter XVI, section 20, also at http://www.reformed.org/master/index.html?mainframe=/books/institutes/; cf. Riggs, *Baptism in the Reformed Tradition*, 65.

95. John Calvin, *Institutes* book IV, chapter XVI, section 20.

Theological Understanding of Baptism In principle the Reformed tradition followed Lutheran thinking, but due to specific historical developments in each tradition's context, there are different emphases. For Zwingli, for example, it was important to point out that the external rite as such cannot effect anything internally.[96] Baptism in the Spirit is therefore important. The crucial factor is confident faith, which is being infused by God's Spirit through the sermon. Baptism is an external "pledge sign" (*Pflichtzeichen*) which marks the person as a Christian and binds him or her in a committed way to Jesus Christ. Zwingli meant, however, not a pledge from the subjective standpoint of a person's faith. Instead, baptism is an objective sign of membership in the Christian community, a sign that finds fulfillment in God's blessings and promises.

For Calvin baptism in the first place makes a person a member of the church.[97] It has two aspects: the faith before God and the confession before human beings: Baptism was given us by God, "first, that it may be conducive to our faith in him; and, secondly, that it may serve the purpose of a confession among men."[98] Baptism confirms what has already happened, namely election by God. Baptism is a seal which confirms an inner event. But God's grace is not bound to the sacrament in such a way that one could receive it only through the sacrament, and not rather through the word of God in faith. In other words, baptism "reminds" and "makes sure" but it does not effect anything.[99] The water rite instituted by Jesus Christ aims at the promise of purification from sins. "This promise remained steadfast even though our faith might not grasp the promise God offered."[100]

Recognition of Baptism in Other Churches Concerning the recognition of baptism which is performed in other churches, the Reformed churches have the same position as the Lutheran churches.

---

96. See Geldbach, *Taufe*, 49.
97. See Geldbach, *Taufe*, 50; John Calvin, *Institutes* IV, 15, 1.
98. John Calvin, Institutes IV, 15,1.
99. See Geldbach, *Taufe*, 51ff.
100. Riggs, *Baptism in the Reformed Tradition*, 43.

ANGLICAN CHURCHES

The Baptismal Rite As Anglicanism came into existence in the
16th century within the Western tradition initially for non-theolog-
ical reasons,[101] its rite and understanding of baptism is not really
different from the Catholic and Reformation churches. The provinces of the Anglican Communion are free to order the baptismal
rites as they deem appropriate. For example, while the sign of the
cross has always been used by all Anglican churches, it is placed
differently within the rite, either before baptism or after the baptismal act. In some churches ancient accompanying rites have been
re-introduced, such as an optional post-baptismal clothing with a
white garment.[102] For those candidates who are old enough to confess their own faith, confirmation follows immediately, while for
infants it follows at a later age. Confirmation is performed by the
laying on of hands by the bishop. Anointing with oil is permitted as
an accompanying sign of confirmation.

Practice of Infant Baptism The practice of infant baptism, as
inherited from the Roman Catholic Church, has been continued
in the Anglican churches. Therefore, in the Articles of Religion
(known as the Thirty-nine Articles) accepted by the Protestant
Episcopal Church in the USA[103] (now called The Episcopal Church),
the baptism of infants is confirmed: "The Baptism of young Children is in any wise to be retained in the Church, as most agreeable
with the institution of Christ." However, since the end of the 20th

---

101. Though there were prior movements for reform in England, including
translations of the Bible into the vernacular, the immediate reason for the
English Reformation was a conflict between King Henry VIII of England with
Rome about the annulment of his marriage. This led to the rejection of the
pope and the recognition of the King as head of the Church of England by
Parliament. The Church of England was unified around common worship (more
so than common creed) and both worship and governance were the subject of
the Acts of Uniformity, most significantly that of Queen Elizabeth I in 1559.

102. See Paul F. Bradshaw, "Baptism in the Anglican Communion," in Best,
Baptism Today, 57ff.

103. Articles of Religion, known as the Thirty-nine Articles, from 1563:
these are the defining historical statements of Anglican doctrine. http://
anglicansonline.org/basics/thirty-nine_articles.html.

century, different efforts have been made in order to end what is called "indiscriminate baptism," so that only children of practicing Anglicans who take seriously the task of Christian education may be baptized.[104]

Theological Understanding of Baptism The traditional understanding of baptism is expressed in the 27th article of the Thirty-nine Articles: "Baptism is not only a sign of profession, and mark of difference, whereby Christian men are discerned from others that be not christened, but it is also a sign of Regeneration or New-Birth, whereby, as by an instrument, they that receive Baptism rightly are grafted into the Church; the promises of the forgiveness of sin, and of our adoption to be the sons of God by the Holy Ghost, are visibly signed and sealed, Faith is confirmed, and Grace increased by virtue of prayer unto God."[105] All human beings are born in sin; therefore rebirth from water and Spirit are necessary.

Anglicans distinguish the role of the Holy Spirit in baptism and in confirmation. In water baptism the Holy Spirit works as Spirit of life and rebirth, while in confirmation it is the Spirit of power and movement. Both are necessary for initiation into Christian faith and the life in the church.[106]

Baptism and Other Sacraments Baptism and eucharist are called "sacraments of the Gospel," distinguished from the "commonly called sacraments."[107] Confirmation, performed at a later age (in the case of infants) is an affirmation of baptism and has to be conducted by the bishop.

Recognition of Baptism in Other Churches Baptism performed in other churches is recognized, if it is done with water and the use

---

104. See Colin Buchanan, *Infant Baptism and the Gospel: The Church of England's Dilemma*, Darton, Longman & Todd, London, 1993, 103ff.

105. Articles of Religion (Thirty-nine Articles), 27, at http://anglicansonline. org/basics/thirty-nine_articles.html.

106. See Geldbach, *Taufe*, 55.

107. See Thirty-nine Articles, 25.

of the trinitarian formula. In case this is not clear, a conditional baptism is advised.[108]

METHODIST CHURCHES

The Baptismal Rite Methodism came into existence through the efforts of the Anglican priest John Wesley—under the influence of pietism—to reform the Church of England in the 18th century. The rite of baptism is, therefore, based on an abridged version of the Anglican *Book of Common Prayer* prepared by Wesley himself. "He did not claim any particular mode as necessary for the efficacy of the sacraments, but he insisted upon application of the water in the name of the Father, Son, and Holy Ghost."[109]

Practice of Infant Baptism As John Wesley defended infant baptism,[110] the Methodists practice both infant baptism and adult baptism. For infant baptism it is a precondition that the child later on be instructed in the Christian faith and that the parents express their firm intention to raise the child in this faith.

Theological Understanding of Baptism Baptism is a sharing in Christ's death and resurrection.[111] During their history Methodists have put more emphasis on the profession of personal assurance, and have not had a strong understanding of baptismal regeneration. On the other hand "baptism as a sign of adoption and an act of initiation was accentuated ... In effect, the sacramental action of divine grace took second place to human decision." [112] The contemporary Methodist liturgical scholar Karen Westerfield Tucker states that there is a certain disagreement within Methodism on "what

---

108. See *Book of Common Prayer*, 313, at http://www.bcponline.org/.

109. Karen B. Westerfield Tucker, "The Initiatory Rites of the United Methodist Church," in Best, *Baptism Today,* 100.

110. Bryan D. Spinks, *Reformation and Modern Rituals and Theologies of Baptism: From Luther to Contemporary Practice*, Ashgate, Aldershot, UK and Burlington, VT, 2006, 108.

111. See Geoffrey Wainwright, *Worship with One Accord: Where Liturgy and Ecumenism Embrace,* Oxford University Press, New York and Oxford, 1997, 106.

112. Karen B. Westerfield Tucker, "The Initiatory Rites of the United Methodist Church," 101.

baptism actually 'does,' and how baptism stands in relation to the fullness of Christian life."[113] This is confirmed by Gayle Felton,[114] who states that there was an ambiguity in Wesley's teaching and that Wesley's successors did not feel bound by this teaching.[115]

Wesley was of the opinion that baptism is not just rebirth because he feared that this idea led to a passive attitude.[116] For him it was important to call for repentance and sanctification, even "Christian perfection," as a consequence of baptism.

Baptism, for Wesley, is also "the initiatory sacrament"[117] which admits a person to the church. But, as Erich Geldbach has pointed out, baptism in the Methodist churches tends to be understood as reception into the catechumenate, while the reception into membership is another act,[118] related to confirmation. In recent liturgical work within the United Methodist Church the close link between baptism and confirmation has been made clearer and stronger.[119]

Recognition of Baptism in Other Churches Methodists have never (re-)baptized converts.

OLD CATHOLIC CHURCH

Although some beginnings can be traced back to the 18th century, the Old Catholic Church as such came into existence in the 19th century out of the inner-Catholic opposition against the development of the papacy. The doctrine of the infallibility of the pope, pronounced at the First Vatican Council in 1870, and the idea of the immaculate conception of Mary, from 1854, were the main issues which led to the foundation of the Union of Utrecht in 1889 as a federation of eight national churches in Europe and North America.

---

113. Ibid.

114. Gayle Carlton Felton, *The Gift of Water: The Practice and Theology of Baptism among Methodists in America*, Abingdon Press, Nashville, 1992, 48.

115. Spinks, *Reformation and Modern Rituals*, 107.

116. Geldbach,*Taufe*, 58.

117. John Wesley, "Treatise on Baptism," *Works*, I.1 (Jackson Edition, vol. 10), 188, quoted in Wainwright, *Worship with One Accord*, 116.

118. Geldbach, *Taufe*, 58ff.

119. See Tucker, "The Initiatory Rites of the United Methodist Church," 105ff.

The Baptismal Rite In keeping with its historical background, the Old Catholic Church did not change the baptismal liturgy inherited from the Roman Catholic Church. Baptism is with water with the formula "N., I baptize you in the name of the Father and of the Son and of the Holy Spirit."[120] Normally baptism is conducted by an ordained person; in emergency cases everyone can baptize.[121]

As a consequence of their ecumenical engagement Old Catholics recently developed new baptismal orders which understand baptism as part of a process of initiation and therefore foresee a catechumenate.[122] Baptism, therefore, is also usually practiced in connection with the eucharist.

Practice of Infant Baptism Infant baptism is the predominant practice.

Theological Understanding of Baptism Old Catholic theology understands itself as Catholic theology, and therefore in succession of the teaching of the early church. Consequently the theological understanding of baptism is in line with Roman Catholic theology.

Recognition of Baptism in Other Churches For Old Catholic theology, baptism plays an important role for the search for unity among Christians.[123] The recognition of baptism conducted within other churches is not questioned.

---

120. In Germany the passive formula "N., you are baptized..." is offered as an alternative.

121. In such a case the baptism should be confirmed later in a worship service in the congregation.

122. See Angela Berlis, "Heute leben aus der Taufe: Theologische Reflexionen in praktischer Perspektive," *Ökumenische Rundschau* 53 (2004): 282-297.

123. Werner Küppers, "Altkatholizismus," in *Theologische Realenzyklopädie* 2, 342.

Churches Practicing Believers' Baptism
(*Credobaptist Churches)

The history of baptism started with the baptism of adults, but it was rather early that infant baptism became the dominant practice. Therefore, while in the course of history minority groups appeared which refused infant baptism, it was not until the 16th century that this became a distinctive feature for a church.

This section will present an overview of those churches which baptize only persons who can speak and express their faith for themselves. For the sake of short wording they are called "credo-baptist churches," although the confession of faith (creed or credo) is not the distinctive factor as such in comparison with paedobaptist churches, which also claim that confessing the faith belongs intrinsically to baptism.

MENNONITE CHURCHES

The Baptismal Rite The Mennonites are the descendants of the Anabaptist movement in the 16th century. They have no fixed rite for baptism, but there are manuals to help preserve the basic purpose of the rite.[124] The overall common pattern is that there is a period of instruction and preparation for baptism. The rite itself is introduced with an explanation of the nature and purpose of baptism. The candidates are asked a number of questions concerning Christian faith. Before or after the water rite there is a prayer asking for the Holy Spirit's activity in the life of the believers. The candidates kneel for baptism while water is poured over the candidate's head. The baptismal formula is "I baptize you in the name of the Father, and of the Son, and of the Holy Spirit." After this the right hand of fellowship is extended to the newly baptized.

---

124. Rebecca Slough, "Baptismal Practice among North American Mennonites," in Best, *Baptism Today*, 92. This article is also the main source for my presentation of the Mennonite tradition.

Theological Understanding of Baptism "A benchmark in an Anabaptist-Mennonite understanding of baptism and church membership"[125] is the Schleitheim Confession of 1527. It says:

> *Baptism shall be given to all those who have learned repentance and amendment of life, and who believe truly that their sins are taken away by Christ, and to all those who walk in the resurrection of Jesus Christ, and wish to be buried with Him in death, so that they may be resurrected with Him and to all those who with this significance request [baptism] of us and demand it for themselves. This excludes all infant baptism, the highest and chief abomination of the Pope. In this you have the foundation and testimony of the apostles. Matt. 28, Mark 16, Acts 2, 8, 16, 19. This we wish to hold simply, yet firmly and with assurance.*[126]

This pattern is repeated in the writings of other 16th century Anabaptists, emphasizing "the priority of preaching/teaching, followed by a response of faith, inner regeneration, a commitment to discipleship, and baptism and a public confession of faith."[127]

Baptism is directly linked to entry into the Christian church. There is an emphasis on baptism "as a visible testimony to faith and as a sign of obedience," [128] which indicates a rejection of the understanding of baptism as a sacrament and a means of grace. Most 16th century Anabaptists focused on the sequence of teaching, faith response, and baptism. But within this common understanding at least two different tendencies can be distinguished: Balthasar Hubmaier[129] represents a "moderate spiritualism" by emphasizing baptism as the "pledge of a good conscience before God,"[130]

---

125. Marlin E. Miller, "The Mennonites," in Merle D. Strege, ed., *Baptism and Church: A Believers' Church Vision*, Sagamore Books, Grand Rapids, MI, 1986, 16.

126. http://www.anabaptists.org/history/schleith.html. See also Miller, "The Mennonites," 16.

127. Miller, "The Mennonites," 17.

128. Ibid., 18.

129. Balthasar Hubmaier, one of the first Anabaptists in Southern Germany, was burned at the stake in Vienna in 1528.

130. Miller, "The Mennonites," 19.

referring to 1 Pet 3:20ff. Menno Simons[131] is a representative of a "subjective" tendency, emphasizing baptism as a personal "covenant of a good conscience with God."[132] He describes baptism as a sign of obedience which proceeds from faith, and he emphasizes that regeneration comes by faith in God's Word rather than by receiving the sacrament. Thus he reiterates that baptism follows regeneration rather than effecting it.[133] In comparison with the Schleitheim Confession, Simons focuses more on the individual believer than on the community. Other Anabaptists held the more "objective" view that baptism is an outer sign of the new birth which already happened before.

Recognition of Baptism in Other Churches In case of conversion, baptism by immersion is usually required.[134] In some churches in North America nowadays in such cases baptism is not always required.[135]

BAPTIST CHURCHES

The Baptist churches find their origins in the Puritan movement in England in the beginning of the 17th century, when a group of people gathered around John Smyth, who denied his Anglican ordination and wrote a new confession of faith. Under the influence of Swiss and Dutch Anabaptists, they discovered believers' baptism and the importance of immersion.

---

131. Menno Simons, from whom the Mennonites take their name, lived 1496-1561 in Frisia and became the leader of the Anabaptists in that region.

132. Menno Simons, *Foundation of Christian Doctrine*, 1539, in *Complete Writings of Menno Simons*, ed. J. C. Wenger, Herald, Scottsdale, PA, 1974, 103ff., quoted by Miller in "The Mennonites," 20ff.

133. Menno Simons, *Christian Baptism, 1539* in *Complete Writings of Menno Simons*, ed. J. C. Wenger, Herald, Scottsdale, PA, 1974, 227ff.

134. See for example the decision of the Mennonite Brethren General Conference in 1963: http://www.directionjournal.org/article/?509.

135. Tom Sinclair-Faulkner, "A Church Historian's Response," in Ross Thomas Bender and Alan P. F. Sell, eds., *Baptism, Peace, and the State in the Reformed and Mennonite Traditions,* Calgary Institute for the Humanities, Waterloo, ON, 1991, 223.

The Baptismal Rite As Paul Fiddes points out, there is "no accepted liturgy for baptism among Baptist churches worldwide ... However, there is a generally recognizable pattern."[136] This overall shape of baptism today is: (1) ministry of the word; (2) the act of baptism; (3) laying on of hands; (4) reception into membership; (5) participation in the Lord's supper. Baptism is done by immersion[137] in the name of the triune God.

Theological Understanding of Baptism The Baptist churches, although from a different historical background, follow the same idea as the Mennonites, namely that only "believers" can be baptized, that is, persons who can profess their own faith. Therefore, the baptism of infants was and in many places still is rejected as unlawful.[138] "Baptists are very diverse in their understanding of the meaning of baptism."[139] As Paul Fiddes shows, there are two understandings within the Baptist tradition, one following a more "sacramental" understanding of baptism as a rite through which God is transforming the believer, and a second understanding, which puts the emphasis on baptism as a "witness to what the grace of God *has* already achieved in the experience of those baptized."[140] Baptists who would emphasize the second understanding would rather use the term "ordinance" instead of "sacrament" to describe baptism, in order to stress baptism as a command of Christ, that is, ordained by him. In early Baptist writings the two terms though were used

---

136. Paul Fiddes, "The Baptism of Believers," in Best, *Baptism Today*, 73. This article is my main source for the presentation of baptismal theology and practice in Baptist churches.

137. Exceptionally, in case of physical disability, pouring of water is permissible.

138. Geldbach, *Taufe*, 64. See also H. Leon McBeth, *A Sourcebook for Baptist Heritage*, Broadman Press, Nashville, 1990, 27.

139. Faith and Unity Executive Committee of the Baptist Union of Great Britain and The Council for Christian Unity of the Church of England, *Pushing at the Boundaries of Unity: Anglicans and Baptists in Conversation*, Church House Publications, London, 2005, 32.

140. Fiddes, "The Baptism of Believers," 76; see also J. Mark Beach, "Original Sin, Infant Salvation, and the Baptism of Infants," *Mid-American Journal of Theology* 12 (2001): 64.

interchangeably.[141] However, there is agreement among Baptists that baptism is an act of obedience to God following the command of the risen Christ.

The theological meaning of baptism is, according to James Garrett, "the sign of the believer's identification with the death, burial, and resurrection of Jesus; the outward sign of an inner cleansing or of the remission of sins; the sign of the eschatological resurrection of believers; the sign of the believer's entry into the body of Christ; a testimony both to believers and to nonbelievers; and an act of obedience to Jesus Christ."[142] Thus most Baptist churches understand baptism as entrance into the membership of a local church.[143] However, S. Mark Heim, another Baptist scholar, notes: "The act of baptism does not itself alone make the recipient a member of the congregation that baptizes: A separate act of reception is required."[144] Usually baptism is not seen as being necessary for salvation.[145]

Recognition of Baptism in Other Churches With the exception of a few Baptist churches that are involved in ecumenical discussions, for example in England, most Baptist congregations baptize converts who come from other confessional traditions.

THE CHURCH OF THE BRETHREN
The Baptismal Rite The Church of the Brethren is a third denomination within the family of the "believers' baptism" (credobaptist) churches. The origin of this church is within radical pietism, and it belongs to the so-called "*non-credal churches." An official statement about baptism can be found in the *Church of the Brethren*

---

141. Fiddes, "The Baptism of Believers," 76.
142. James Leo Garrett, *Systematic Theology: Biblical, Historical, and Evangelical*, vol. 2, Eerdmans, Grand Rapids, MI, 1995, 529.
143. Fiddes, "The Baptism of Believers," 77.
144. S. Mark Heim, "Baptismal Recognition and the Baptist Churches," in Michael Root and Risto Saarinen, eds., *Baptism and the Unity of the Church*, Eerdmans, Grand Rapids MI and WCC Publications, Cambridge and Geneva, 1998, 155.
145. S. Mark Heim, "Baptismal Recognition," 151.

Manual of Organization and Polity,[146] which makes clear that baptism is practiced by threefold immersion in the name of the triune God and is connected with a confession of faith. Following baptism there is a laying on of hands as "a powerful symbol to point to the truth that the Spirit comes to us through the lives of others in the body of Christ."[147]

Theological Understanding of Baptism Baptism is for the forgiveness of sins. Justification and rebirth into a new life in following Christ are closely linked in the Brethren's understanding of baptism. But private celebrations of baptism are rejected: baptism needs the community of the faithful. Water baptism does not save. Salvation comes by faith alone. Baptism is an act of obedience, because faith—if it is a saving faith—produces works of love and obedience. "From Acts 2:38 Brethren have associated baptism with repentance and the forgiveness of sins ... The candidate is baptized for the forgiving of sins, the entire formula being, 'Upon the confession of faith which you have made before God and these witnesses you are baptized for the remission of sins in the name of the Father, and of the Son and of the Holy Spirit.'"[148] The second promise, however, moves the baptized to a call to discipleship. "Baptism signifies a conversion experience which involves both justification and regeneration. Which is emphasized more has varied according to ... historical shifts."[149] But one does not fully receive the Holy Spirit apart from a relationship with the community of faith.

Recognition of Baptism in Other Churches Nowadays most congregations receive members from other churches with a reaffirmation and no longer require baptism, if the candidate has been baptized in his or her previous church.

---

146. Church of the Brethren, *Manual of Organization and Polity,* Church of the Brethren General Board, Elgin, IL, 1979, D-3.

147. Dale Brown, "The Brethren," in Merle D. Strege, ed., *Baptism and Church: A Believers' Church Vision*, Sagamore Books, Grand Rapids, MI, 1986, 33. This article is my main source for the presentation on the Disciples of Christ.

148. Ibid., 32.

149. Ibid., 33.

DISCIPLES OF CHRIST

The Baptismal Rite The beginning of the Disciples of Christ goes back to 1809, when Thomas Campbell, a Scottish immigrant in the US from the Presbyterian Church, wanted to seek unity by reforming the church according to the model of the early church as found in the New Testament. In consequence the Disciples of Christ practice the baptism of adults by immersion.

The most common liturgical pattern used by Disciples consists of two parts. The Confession of Faith is the focus in the first part.

> *Following the sermon, the pastor invites persons to come to the front of the church during the singing of a hymn, in order to confess their faith in Christ in preparation for baptism or to transfer membership to this congregation. The persons who respond to the invitation are asked to affirm the Christian faith, usually in words adapted from Peter's confession in Matthew 16:16: "Do you believe that Jesus is the Christ, the son of the living God?" After the candidate's response, the pastor offers a brief commendation or blessing...*
>
> *The baptism ordinarily takes place the following Sunday in the church ... While the pastor and baptismal candidates clothe themselves ... for the baptism, another leader of worship reads Scripture texts about baptism and the congregation sings a hymn. The pastor enters the baptistery, followed by a candidate. While reciting the baptismal formula, the pastor leans the candidate backward into the water until he or she is fully immersed, and then brings the person back to an upright position. Later in the service ... the newly baptized are welcomed into membership in the congregation.[150]*

Theological Understanding of Baptism "In baptism we are passive in everything but in giving our consent. We are buried and raised by another. Hence no view of baptism can be called a good work."[151]

---

150. Keith Watkins, "Baptismal Understanding and Practice in the Christian Church (Disciples of Christ)," in Best, *Baptism Today*, 110.

151. Howard E. Short, "The Christian Church (Disciples of Christ)," in Strege, *Baptism and Church*, 75.

The Disciples understand baptism as a step in the process of salvation—baptism for the forgiveness of sins—while the Baptists normally think that baptism is a visible and symbolic sign of the forgiveness of sins, which has already taken place.[152]

Recognition of Baptism in Other Churches Nowadays, as a result of the involvement in the ecumenical movement, the Disciples of Christ are not baptizing converts who have been baptized in another churcs, except for a few congregations which require adult baptism.

PENTECOSTAL CHURCHES

The Baptismal Rite The Pentecostal churches are a new type of church, one which came into being at the end of the 19th and beginning of the 20th century. In general there is no single over-all organization, which means that each local congregation has more autonomy than in most traditional churches.[153] Therefore there is a lot of variety within the Pentecostal movement, as Pentecostals prefer to call it. In addition Pentecostals avoid written liturgy. Nevertheless there are common emphases, traits and values which characterize Pentecostal spirituality and liturgical life. Daniel Albrecht describes phenomenologically the basic outline of the baptismal rite in the Pentecostal movement as a "dramatized liturgy of testimony"[154] with a twofold structure. The two parts are described as movements, namely "Into the Waters" and "Out of the Waters."[155] The first part contains the candidate's testimony (often just a response to the question whether he or she accepts Jesus as personal savior), a pastoral address and prayer, and the immersion in water. Before the immersion the pastor states, in a form not completely standardized but resembling the following, "Upon your profession of faith in Jesus Christ as your personal Saviour

---

152. See Geldbach, *Taufe*, 70.

153. Within larger Pentecostal denominations, such as the Assemblies of God, there is, of course, a certain common understanding of baptism.

154. Daniel Albrecht, "Witness in the Waters: Baptism and Pentecostal Spirituality," in Best, *Baptism Today*, 151.

155. See ibid., 149.

... I now baptize you in the name of the Father and Son and Holy Spirit."[156] The second part of the baptismal rite is the raising up out of the water, followed (though not always) by signs of the Spirit,[157] the response of the congregation by singing, shouts of joy, raising of hands and applause, exit from the waters and entrance into the waiting congregation.

However, as Cecil M. Robeck and Jerry L. Sandidge point out,[158] there is variety in the practice of baptism among Pentecostals and immersion is not its only form. The Trinitarian formula is also not used unanimously.[159] A minority of Pentecostals, the "Oneness Pentecostals," baptize "in the name of Jesus" in accord with Acts 2:38 and oppose the trinitarian formula with the understanding that "father," "son" and "holy spirit" are not names but titles of the one God who appears in three modes.

Theological Understanding of Baptism "Water baptism is seen as a public testimony of identification with Christ, his universal Church, and a local assembly of believers."[160] It is considered to be death, burial and resurrection with Jesus Christ.

What is new and especially different from the traditional churches is what Pentecostals call "Baptism in the Holy Spirit" or "Anointing in the Holy Spirit." In most Pentecostal churches a distinction is made between the gift of the Holy Spirit at the time of a person's rebirth and the baptism in water. In other words, in the moment of rebirth the Spirit effects the divine life in the reborn person and leads him or her to baptism in the Spirit. Speaking in tongues, for example, is seen as a beginning sign of the baptism in the Holy Spirit. Other such signs include prophecies, visions, healings and miracles. Normally a person undergoes water baptism after the experience of rebirth, at the time when he or she is able

---

156. Ibid., 154.

157. Speaking in tongues or other manifestations of the Holy Spirit.

158. Cecil M. Robeck, Jr. and Jerry L. Sandidge, "The Ecclesiology of *Koinonia* and Baptism: A Pentecostal Perspective," *Journal of Ecumenical Studies* 27 (1990): 509.

159. Ibid., 514ff.

160. Albrecht, "Witness in the Waters," 148.

to confess his or her faith and before baptism in the Spirit.[161] Baptism with water is the ecclesial rite, which is normally celebrated in the context of the congregation, while the baptism in the Holy Spirit is a personal experience. Baptism is "viewed more as a step of obedience that gives witness to the grace of God than a sacrament through which grace flows."[162] Conversion is much more important. Thus baptism with water is not at the centre of Pentecostal spirituality, although it is in many Pentecostal churches a precondition for participation in the Lord's supper.

While most Pentecostals distinguish between water baptism and Spirit baptism, Oneness Pentecostals see an intimate relationship between conversion, water baptism and Spirit baptism. Therefore for them baptism plays a more central role in salvation[163] and can even be understood as a sacrament.

Some marginal Pentecostal groups practice re-baptism for people who have 'lapsed' and are coming back to the church.[164]

Most Pentecostals oppose calling water baptism a sacrament. They speak rather of an "ordinance."[165]

Recognition of Baptism in Other Churches From these various different positions within the Pentecostal movement, there follows a variety of positions towards infant baptism. "As it stands, some Pentecostals are unwilling to accept as valid the baptisms performed within certain other denominations, including those performed by other Pentecostals."[166] But a majority would recognize a believer's baptism performed in another church, except Oneness Pentecostals. [167]

---

161. There are, however, a few Pentecostal churches which practice infant baptism. See Albrecht, "Witness in the Waters," 158.

162. Ibid.

163. See Robeck and Sandidge, "The Ecclesiology of *Koinonia* and Baptism," 517.

164. See Geldbach, *Taufe*, 77.

165. See Koo Dong Yun, "Water Baptism and Spirit Baptism: Pentecostals and Lutherans in Dialogue," *Dialog: A Journal of Theology* 43 (2004): 346; see also Robeck and Sandidge, "The Ecclesiology of *Koinonia* and Baptism," 520-524.

166. Robeck and Sandidge, "The Ecclesiology of *Koinonia* and Baptism," 532.

167. I am grateful to Jean-Daniel Plüss for this information.

AFRICAN INDEPENDENT CHURCHES
(AFRICAN INSTITUTED CHURCHES/AIC)

Another type of church, influenced to a great extent by Pentecostal ideas, is the broad group known as "African Instituted Churches."[168] These churches are not a single entity and are, therefore, very different in their practices.[169] James Amanze, a theologian from Botswana, summarizes their view of baptism in the following way: "By and large they practice believer's baptism after confession in Jesus Christ as a personal Saviour. Infant baptism is rejected as unscriptural. Baptism is by immersion in a river, dam or pool in the name of the Trinity. Baptism by sprinkling of water on the forehead is declared null and void and a second baptism is required by immersion. Baptism by the Holy Spirit and by fire is emphasized."[170]

For example the baptismal rite of the Christ Holy Church International[171] is described in the following way. A normal service, in which the sermon explains the significance, need and value of baptism, precedes the baptism. Then the congregation travels to the closest river.

> *At the riverside, the officiating minister blesses the river and asks God to rid it of all evil forces and dangerous elements, thus making it holy and fitting for the sacrament. Two booths are provided for men and women to change their clothing. The officiating minister is the first to change; he wears a white T-shirt and shorts, as this color is understood to symbolize purity. Men precede women in the river, as was done in the order of creation. The person to*

---

168. Also known as African Independent Churches, African Initiated Churches, African Indigenous Churches, and other names always abbreviated as AIC. See Thomas Oduro, "Water Baptism in African Independent Churches: The Paradigm of Christ Holy Church International," in Best, *Baptism Today*, 181.

169. See John Pobee, "Baptismal Recognition and African Instituted Churches," in Root and Saarinen, *Baptism and the Unity of the Church*, 168.

170. James N. Amanze, *A History of the Ecumenical Movement in Africa*, Pula Press, Gaborone, Botswana, 1999, 116.

171. An African Instituted Church founded in 1947 in Nigeria. See http://gntcs.org/Christ_Holy_%20Church.html.

*be baptized is made to sit in the river—a posture ... that makes
the convert relaxed. The sitting posture enables the officiating
minister to control the body of the convert,[172] whatever their rela-
tive sizes may be. The officiating minister then asks the convert:
"Do you believe in Jesus Christ? Do you believe that Jesus is your
Savior? Have you rejected Satan and all his works?" After the
one to be baptized has answered all questions in the affirmative,
the minister asks the person "What is your name?" The minister
repeats the name and says, "because of your confession of faith I
baptize you in the name of the Father, Son and Holy Spirit." The
candidate is then immersed once, while the pastor mentions the
name of the triune God ... All newly baptized persons go back to
the worship center, the officiating minister immediately teaches
them about the baptism of the Holy Spirit. After this the pastor
lays his hands on one or two persons, and other persons are then
asked to lay their hands on others. The pastor prays for the infill-
ing of the Holy Spirit and in the course of the prayer some begin
to speak in tongues, while others begin to shake their bodies, a
gesture indicating possession by the Holy Spirit.[173]*

The word "sacrament" is hardly used in African Independent
Churches, but these churches believe that baptism was instituted
by God, thus making it obligatory for all Christians and requiring
careful preparation. Baptism symbolizes the death and resurrection of Jesus Christ. This brings newness of life and integrates the
baptized person into a new family. The preparation is done by confession of sins and by prescribed lessons. A few days before baptism
the candidates have to fast and pray.[174]

Some African Independent Churches, such as the Kimbanguists[175] in the Congo and the African Holy Ghost Christian

---

172. Although many African Independent Churches have ordained women,
some of them prohibit women from baptizing, because once they are immersed
many candidates behave as if they were possessed and it is difficult to control
them. See Albrecht, "Witness in the Waters," 185.

173. Albrecht, "Witness in the Waters," 188ff.

174. Cf. Oduro, "Water Baptism in African Independent Churches," 184.

175. The official name is The Church of Jesus Christ on Earth through the
Prophet Simon Kimbangu. This church emerged through a revival movement

Church in Kenya, do not practice baptism with water.[176] Water baptism is related to the baptism of John the Baptist, who was the last to practice it. Christian baptism is the baptism with the Holy Spirit, because with Jesus the era of the Holy Spirit began. Baptism is practiced by laying on of hands and prayer.[177] It is at the same time the reception into the Christian congregation. [178]

Another well-known African Instituted church is the Church of the Lord (Aladura) Worldwide,[179] which practices water baptism but as adult baptism, because "only an adult can make a confession or profession of faith in the Lord Jesus Christ."[180]

The "Article of Faith of The Church of the Lord (Aladura) Worldwide" says:

We believe...

- *In the Baptism of the Holy Spirit, received subsequent to the new birth with the speaking of other tongues, as the Holy Spirit gives utterance through grace, as the initial physical sign and evidence. And it is the same Holy Spirit of God that is filling the hearts of those who diligently seek Him today.*

- *In the water baptism by immersion for the believers only, which is a direct commandment of our Lord, in the name of the Father, and of the Son, and of the Holy Spirit. We believe in baptism by immersion after confession of sins and accepting*

---

initiated in 1921 by Simon Kimbangu, a Baptist mission catechist in the Congo region. The church was formally recognized in 1959 by the state.

176. See Allan H. Anderson, *African Reformation: African Initiated Christianity in the 20th Century*, Africa World Press, Trenton, NJ, 2001, 129 and 159.

177. Diangienda Kuntima, *L'histoire du Kimbanguisme*, Editions Kimbanguistes, Kinshasa 1984, 266-269.

178. See Geldbach, *Taufe*, 82-85; see also Diangienda Kuntima, *L'histoire du Kimbanguisme*.

179. Founded in 1930 by Dr. Josiah Olunowo Ositelu in Nigeria.

180. Rufus Okikiolaolu Olubiyi Ositelu, *African Instituted Churches: Diversities, Growth, Gifts, Spirituality and Ecumenical Understanding of African Initiated Churches*, Lit-Verlag, Hamburg, 2002,192, quoted in Benjamin Simon, *Afrikanische Kirchen in Deutschland*, Lembeck, Frankfurt am Main 2003, 180.

> *Jesus Christ as Lord, Saviour, Redeemer and King. We believe*
> *in adult baptism and infant dedication.*[181]

The candidate is clothed in white and is immersed three times in a river or lake after having confessed his or her sins. This baptism is at the same time reception into the community of the church.

John Pobee gives some more examples of African Independent Churches and points out that baptism in their understanding is:

> *a rite which symbolizes the believer's identification with Jesus*
> *Christ in his death and resurrection … water baptism is a rite of*
> *entering into the church, a family, a community. The rite is not*
> *only symbolism; in the African holistic understanding of reality,*
> *the rite represents the integration of the symbol and reality of the*
> *baptism. In the same spirit, baptism is a symbol of renewed life*
> *and the means of effecting the renewal.*[182]

Recognition of Baptism in Other Churches In the view of the Kimbanguists there is nothing wrong with water baptism, but it cannot be binding for a church. Therefore baptism in other churches is recognized. As John Pobee shows, many African Instituted Churches would recognize the baptism in other churches "as long as it is in the threefold name."[183] Others state that the AIC baptize "even if those who join them have been previously baptized,"[184] for which Oduro gives the concrete example of the Christ Holy Church International.[185] In summary, the practices in these churches seem to differ quite substantially from one another.

---

181. Found in Ositelu, *African Instituted Churches*, 203ff.
182. Pobee, "Baptismal Recognition and African Instituted Churches," 179.
183. Pobee, "Baptismal Recognition and African Instituted Churches," 181.
184. C.G. Oosthuizen, *Baptism in the Context of the African Indigenous/Independent Churches (A.I.C.),* University of Zululand, Kwadlangezwa, South Africa, 1985, 18.
185. See Oduro, "Water Baptism in African Independent Churches," 187.

SUMMARY

In summary we can say that all the churches share the theological understanding of baptism as death and resurrection with Christ, as beginning of a new life, but also as entering into the community of believers. Practices, though, differ, especially concerning the question at what age a person can be baptized. These different positions are rooted in theological differences at a deeper level, related to the question of whether baptism is a sacrament, and thus carries grace, or whether it is an act of obedience and thus rather a testimony to Christian faith.

Consequences for the Mutual Recognition of Baptism

Mutual recognition of baptism is usually tested in cases of conversions: is a person who was baptized in a certain church (re-)baptized in another church in which he or she wants to become a member?

Looking at the ecumenical ecclesial landscape as a whole in this regard, there are in a theological view mainly two lines of division concerning the issue of baptism. The most obvious line is the separation between churches which baptize infants and those churches which baptize only persons who can confess their faith. The latter, therefore, often baptize a person who has been baptized as a child and now wants to become a member of their church. In the eyes of paedobaptist churches this looks like re-baptism—which it is not in the understanding of credobaptist churches, for whom baptism is, per definition, baptism only if the candidate him- or herself professes his or her faith. Therefore, such (re-)baptism is, in fact, an expression of the fact that the first baptism of such a convert is not recognized. Paedobaptist churches, on the other hand, usually recognize baptism performed in credobaptist churches. This leads to a certain imbalance in the mutual relationship of the two groups: one side does not recognize the baptism of the other, while the second recognizes the baptism of the first.

Within both of these groups of churches—paedobaptist and credobaptist churches—there are other lines of separation. Within the group of churches which baptize infants, lack of clarity among

Orthodox churches about the recognition of baptism performed in other churches is based on ecclesiological divergences. Within the group of churches which reject infant baptism, some Pentecostal and African Independent churches do not recognize baptism of believers performed in other churches, even in some cases if it was performed in churches of the same type. This is also related to ecclesiological questions.

Thus, the ecumenical situation in regard to the mutual recognition of baptism is more complex than it might appear at first glance. What is presented here is the overall situation as it can be discerned today. It has to be noted though that in the past other stances existed: even among paedobaptist churches, recognition of baptism was not always self-evident, and re-baptism of Orthodox by Catholics (for example) happened. Nowadays it has to be noted that there is a certain asymmetry when it comes to mutual recognition of baptism: churches which baptize infants (except Orthodox) have, in general, no difficulty in recognizing baptism performed in churches which baptize only believers. Recognition the other way around is only possible in limited cases. A similar asymmetry occurs when we look into the controversy between Orthodox and non-Orthodox. The Roman Catholic Church and the Reformation churches especially seem to have the least problems in recognizing baptism performed in other churches.

CHAPTER 2
BAPTISM IN HISTORICAL PERSPECTIVE

THE ECUMENICAL SITUATION IN THE VARIOUS CHURCHES concerning baptism and its mutual recognition is the result of a long history. Many of the divergences can only be understood against the background of this history. This chapter offers an insight into the most important developments of the rite and the understanding of baptism.

Baptism in the New Testament

Although the New Testament is somewhat contradictory about whether Jesus himself baptized people or not,[1] it is manifest that from the beginning the Christian communities practiced baptism.[2] Central for this practice is the command of Jesus after his resurrection in Mt 28:18-20. It is also clear that Jesus himself was baptized by John the Baptist and that he clearly took up John's central ideas.[3] "Although the New Testament never asserts that the baptism

---

1. See Jn 3:22ff and Jn 4:1ff.; more in George R. Beasley-Murray, *Baptism in the New Testament*, Macmillan, London, 1962, 67-72.
2. See Ralph G. Wilburn, "The One Baptism and the Many Baptisms," *Mid-Stream* 3 (1964): 74.
3. See Lk 7:24-28 ff.

of Jesus was the foundation of Christian baptism or a prototype for it ... the declaration of Jesus' Sonship and the coming of the Holy Spirit on him at this time provide a parallel to the promises attached in a lesser sense to Christian baptism."[4] Christian baptism is therefore grounded in Jesus' own baptism, which was the baptism of John, and is based on Christ's command to baptize all nations. The German Lutheran theologian Edmund Schlink comes to the conclusion: "Thus we have the paradoxical situation that the command of the Risen One, which eludes historical grasp, is the most reliable historical explanation for the origin of Christian Baptism."[5]

When we consider the main source texts on baptism in the New Testament,[6] five categories of texts can be distinguished. In the following I will give an overview of what can be drawn from these texts.

THE STORY OF JESUS' BAPTISM

This story is found in Mk 1: 9-11;Mt 3:13-17;Lk 3:21ff.; and Jn 1:29-34.

Since Jesus' baptism by John the Baptist is considered the precedent for Christian baptism,[7] the reports about it need to be examined.

---

4. Everett Ferguson, *Baptism in the Early Church: History, Theology and Liturgy in the First Five Centuries*, Eerdmans, Grand Rapids, MI, 2009, 100.

5. Edmund Schlink, *The Doctrine of Baptism*, Concordia Publishing, Saint Louis and London, 1972, 30.

6. I am considering here only texts which explicitly mention the term "baptism." There are many other texts in the New Testament which have a more or less clear reference to baptism as well as texts which have been interpreted throughout Christian history as related to baptism. More extensive analyses of such texts can be found in other works and exegetical commentaries. In addition to Beasley-Murray, *Baptism in the New Testament* and Ferguson, *Baptism in the Early Church*, see Kenan B. Osborne, *The Christian Sacraments of Initiation: Baptism, Confirmation, Eucharist*, Paulist Press, New York and Mahwah, NJ, 1987 and Maxwell E. Johnson, *The Rites of Christian Initiation: Their Evolution and Interpretation*, Liturgical Press, Collegeville, MN, 2007.

7. See James D. G. Dunn, "Baptism and the Unity of the Church in the New Testament," in Michael Root and Risto Saarinen, eds., *Baptism and the Unity of the Church*, Eerdmans, Grand Rapids, MI and WCC Publications, Geneva, 1988.

The fact that Jesus was baptized is mentioned in all four gospels. It is also presumed in Acts 1:22 and mentioned in other sources from the same period, for example, the Gospel According to the Hebrews.

Reading and comparing the four gospel texts on Jesus' baptism it becomes clear that their common goal is to point to Jesus' identity. The important event here is not so much the immersion into the water or the meaning of this baptism as repentance, but the coming down of the Holy Spirit and the voice saying: "You are my Son, the Beloved." In other words, John's baptism receives here a new emphasis, the fact of being accepted by God.[8]

In all four gospels John the Baptist announces the coming "baptism in the Holy Spirit." In John's gospel it is not even mentioned that Jesus was dipped in water, which highlights even more the focus on the Holy Spirit in the event. Here John the Baptist calls Jesus the one "who takes away the sin of the world" (1:29). Thus the story of Jesus' baptism gives two further indications about Christian baptism: it involves the bestowal of the Holy Spirit and the removal of sin.

THE COMMANDMENT OF JESUS

This commandment is found in Mt 28:18-20 and Mk 16:15ff.

Mt 28:18-20: The historicity of these verses is, in general, doubted by New Testament scholars, but the undoubted fact that Jesus' disciples practiced water baptism is likely to be based on "some authorization by Jesus himself."[9]

What can be drawn from this text is the close relation between baptism and teaching, as well as baptism performed with the trinitarian formula. Here baptism is clearly meant for "all nations" and therefore has a universal meaning. At the same time, the text relates baptism to a certain lifestyle, to living as a disciple of Jesus Christ.

Mk 16: 15ff.: This passage interprets baptism as a condition for salvation and points out the connection of baptism with faith.

---

8. See also Ferguson, *Baptism in the Early Church*, 101.
9. Ibid., 133.

BAPTISM STORIES IN THE FIRST CHRISTIAN COMMUNITIES

These stories are found in Acts 1:5ff.; Acts 2: 38ff.; Acts 8:12-17 and 8:36-38; Acts 9:17-19; Acts 10:44-48; Acts 16:15 and 16:29-34; Acts 18:7ff.; and Acts 19:1-7.

In the accounts of baptisms in Acts, no theological interpretation is given to baptism. What becomes clear is that baptism occurs either with individuals or with groups of people after some form of teaching, and that it is done with water. Baptism is associated with repentance, the remission of sins and the bestowal of the Holy Spirit. It is related to faith in Jesus Christ. It was done by immersion.

THEOLOGICAL EXPLANATIONS OF THE MEANING OF BAPTISM

Theological explanations of the meaning of baptism are found in Rom 6:1ff.; Gal 3:26ff.; Col 2:12ff.; 1 Cor 6:11; 1 Cor 12:13; Eph 1:30 and 4:30; 1 Cor 1:11-17; Eph 4:5; 1 Jn 2:20, 27; and 1 Pet 3:20ff.

From this material the following can be said about baptism:

- Baptism is dying and rising with Christ.

- Baptism results in a new life/new allegiance.

- Baptism means being dressed with Christ, thus belonging to Christ.

- Baptism is liberation from sin/brings forgiveness of sin.

- There is only one baptism.

- Baptism brings salvation.

- Baptism unites into one body.

- Baptism is connected with faith.

- Baptism is not self-baptism.

- Baptism is connected with justification and with sanctification.

OTHER TEXTS

References to baptism are also found in the following texts: Lk 12:50; Mk 10:38ff.; 1 Cor 15:29; and others.

Lk 12:50 and Mk 10:38ff. use the term "baptism" in a metaphorical sense for Jesus' death. These verses are therefore not speaking directly about baptism, but they build a connection to the later understanding of *martyrdom as baptism. In a similar way, 1 Cor 10:1ff. talks about a baptism "into Moses," a figurative use of the term in order to express the effect of the events reported in Genesis. 1 Cor 15:29 mentions a baptism "on behalf of the dead"; as Ferguson notes, this verse cannot be clearly explained.[10]

From the New Testament sources we do not know much about the baptismal rite as such. According to Acts, baptism was administered "in the name of Jesus Christ" or "in the name of the Lord Jesus" (Acts 2:38; 8:16; 10:48; 19:5). From other New Testament sources we know that Jesus was confessed as Christ and Lord (Rom 10:9; Eph 5:26; 1 Pet 3:18ff).

Baptism in the Early Church

What we know about baptism in the early church comes from a variety of sources. There are liturgical texts, church orders, treatises, letters and sermons as well as stories or so-called "Acts."[11] Paintings, icons and baptisteries are also sources on which we can draw.

In the following narrative I will focus on written texts. In the first part I will look into the development of the baptismal rite and baptismal theology. The second part is dedicated to some theological issues which resulted from differences in baptismal practices and which played a role in later developments.

---

10. Ibid., 155.

11. "Acts" are a genre of literature in the early church such as the "Acts of the Apostles" in the New Testament but also others, which are not part of the Bible (for example Acts of Thomas).

BAPTISMAL RITE AND THEOLOGY

As there were liturgical and theological centers in the early church which differed slightly from each other in their thinking (for example Syria with the city of Antioch, the cities of Rome and Milan, Northern Africa and others), I will group the sources (except for the two oldest ones) along these regional lines and look into the main features which can be distinguished. The presentation is by no means exhaustive,[12] but tries to give an insight into some of the main sources about baptismal practices and theologies in the early church.

The *Didache*

One of the oldest texts outside the New Testament is the *Didache* (or *Teaching of the Lord through the Twelve Apostles to the Nations*),[13] which is dated toward the end of the 1st century[14] and was probably drafted in Egypt or Syria.[15] It is the earliest surviving text which gives an explicit explanation of the baptismal rite. The section on baptism says:

> *Concerning baptism, baptize in this way: after speaking all these words, baptize into the name of the Father, of the Son, and of the Holy Spirit in living water. If you do not have living water, baptize in other water; if you are not able in cold water, in warm. If you do not have either, pour water on the head three times into the name of the Father, Son, and Holy Spirit. Before the baptism, the one baptizing, the one being baptized, and others if they are able are to observe a preliminary fast. Command the one being baptized to fast beforehand for one or two days.[16]*

---

12. For a more detailed and complete presentation on the early church see Ferguson, *Baptism in the Early Church*.

13. The *Didache* was discovered in 1873 in the library of the Monastery of the Holy Tomb in Constantinople in a manuscript from the 11th century.

14. There is currently some discussion and controversy about the date of the *Didache*. See Ferguson, *Baptism in the Early Church*, 201.

15. André Tuilier, "Didache," in Gerhard Krause et al., *Theologische Realenzyklopädie* Vol. 8, de Gruyter, Berlin, 1981, 735.

16. Did. 7, in *Didache (Apostellehre), Barnabasbrief, Zweiter Klemensbrief, Schrift an Diognet*, ed. by Klaus Wengst, Wissenschaftliche Buchgesellschaft, Darmstadt, 1984, 66-91, 70. English translation taken from Ferguson, *Baptism in the Early Church*, 202. Also quoted in Osborne, *The Christian Sacraments of Initiation*, 63.

This text shows that:

• Baptism was done in the name of the triune God.

• Baptism was done by immersion.

• Baptism was normally done in running water, that is, a stream, river or a lake, but pouring water over the candidate was also permissible.

There was a time of preparation before baptism; this was characterized by fasting not only by the candidate, but also by the baptizer and others.

From Did. 9, 5 it becomes clear that baptism was the precondition for receiving the eucharist.[17]

This text refers obviously to the baptism of adults and does not give any evidence whether children were baptized in the historical context in which the text was written. The *Didache* does not explain the meaning of baptism in any detail. But the common fasting by the candidate along with other persons hints at the understanding of baptism as entrance into the communion of believers.

The Epistle of Barnabas

A text which was written probably a bit later than the *Didache*[18] and thought to have originated in either Asia Minor, Syria or Alexandria,[19] the Epistle of Barnabas gives little information about

---

17. "No one is to eat or drink of your eucharist except those who have been baptized into the name of the Lord"; see Ferguson, *Baptism in the Early Church*, 203.

18. The Epistle of Barnabas is dated around 130 to 132; see Christian Lange, "Gestalt und Deutung der christlichen Initiation in der Alten Kirche," in Christian Lange, Clemens Leonhard, and Ralph Olbrich, eds., *Die Taufe: Einführung in Geschichte und Praxis*, Wissenschaftliche Buchgesellschaft, Darmstadt, 2008, 6.

19. See Everett Ferguson, "Christian and Jewish Baptism according to the Epistle of Barnabas," in Stanley E. Porter and Anthony A. Cross, eds., *Dimensions of Baptism: Biblical and Theological Studies*, Journal for the Study of the New Testament Supplement no. 234, Sheffield Academic Press / T&T Clark, London and New York, 2002, 207-223.

the administration of baptism but does explain the meaning of baptism:

> *Let us inquire if the Lord was careful to give a revelation in advance concerning the water and the cross. It was written concerning the water with regard to Israel how they will not receive the baptism that brings forgiveness of sins but will establish (another) for themselves ... perceive how he defines the water and the cross together. For he says this: "Blessed" (Ps 1:1) are those who with hope in the cross went down into the water, because he speaks of the reward "in its season" (Ps. 1:3); at that time he says, "I will reward." For the present, what he says, "The leaves will not fall off" (Ps. 1:3), means this: Every word that proceeds out of your mouth in faith and love will be for conversion and hope to many. And again another prophet says, "The land of Jacob was praised above every land." This means, he glorifies the vessel of his Spirit. Next, what does he say? "A river was flowing along on the right, and beautiful trees come up out of it. Whoever eats of the trees will live forever" (based on Ez. 47:1-12). He means this: That we go down unto the water full of sins and uncleanness, and we come up bearing as fruit in our heart reverence and having hope in Jesus in our spirit. And "whoever eats from these will live forever" (Ez. 47:9; Gen 3:22) means this: Whoever, he says, hears these when they speak and believes will live forever.[20]*

Here Christian baptism is described as conveying forgiveness of sins. This is confirmed in the description of baptismal immersion. The effect of baptism is reverence and hope in Jesus, which refers to a certain lifestyle in which the word is being spread to others. The final goal of baptism is to "live forever."

---

20. Epistle of Barnabas, 11.1-11 in *Didache (Apostellehre), Barnabasbrief, Zweiter Klemensbrief, Schrift an Diognet*, ed. by Klaus Wengst, Wissenschaftliche Buchgesellschaft, Darmstadt, 1984, 138-202, 169ff. English translation taken from n Ferguson, *Baptism in the Early Church*, 210ff.

Sources from Rome

The Shepherd of Hermas The Shepherd of Hermas is a text from around the first half of the 2nd century in Rome.[21] According to Ferguson it "contains the greatest number of references to baptism (but not the word itself) among the Apostolic Fathers: it also presents the strongest statements concerning the necessity of baptism for salvation in Early Christian literature."[22]

> *"The tower that you see being built is myself, the church" ... I asked her, "Why, Lady, was the tower being built on the waters?" She said ... "It is because your life was saved and will be saved through water. The tower has been founded by the spoken word of his almighty and glorious Name and is supported by the invisible power of the Master..." Do you wish to know who are the other stones which fall near the waters and are not able to be rolled into the water? These are those who heard the word and wanted to be baptized into the name of the Lord, but when they remember the purity of the truth they change their minds and return again to their evil desires.[23]*

The reference is obviously to baptism, which brings salvation. It is understood as entry into the church, because those not baptized "fall near the waters." Also, baptism implies a pure life, "the purity of the truth," which not everyone seems to be able to follow. This is developed further in another part of the text:

> *I said, "Sir, I heard from some teachers that there is no other repentance except that one when we went down into the water and received the forgiveness of our former sins." He said to me, "You heard correctly, for it is so. The one who has received the forgiveness of sins ought no longer to continue in sin but to live in purity."[24]*

---

21. See Ferguson, *Baptism in the Early Church*, 214.
22. Ibid., 215.
23. Translation taken from ibid., 215.
24. Quoted in ibid., 216.

Consequently baptism was a single and unrepeatable event. This raised the question of what happens if someone falls into sin after baptism, an issue which became a problem later on.

In another passage the necessity of baptism for salvation is stated even more strongly:

> I said, "Why, Sir, did the stones come up from the depth and were placed in the structure of the tower, after having borne these spirits?" "It was necessary," he said, "for them to come up through water in order that they might be made alive. They were not able otherwise to enter into the kingdom of God unless they put away the mortality of their former life. Therefore, even these who have fallen asleep [died] received the seal of the Son of God and entered into the kingdom of God. For," he said, "before a person bears the name of the Son of God he is dead, but whenever one receives the seal, that person puts away mortality and receives life. The seal then is the water. They went down into the water dead and they came up alive. The seal itself, then, was preached to them also, and they made use of it in order that they might enter into the kingdom of God."[25]

Thus baptism is the entry into the kingdom of God. Baptism here is also called a "seal," which emphasizes a person's belonging. Thirdly, baptism means birth or becoming alive.

Justin of Rome (Justin Martyr) From the second half of the second century we have a representative text from Justin of Rome (also known as Justin Martyr), a philosopher and teacher who converted to Christianity and suffered *martyrdom. In his *First Apology*, written for the Emperor Antoninus Pius, he gives the fullest account of the baptismal practice we have from that time:

> We shall explain in what way we dedicated ourselves to God and were made new through Christ ... As many as are persuaded and believe that the things said and taught by us are true and promise

---

25. Ibid., 217.

to be able to live accordingly are taught while fasting to pray and ask God for the forgiveness of past sins, while we pray and fast together with them. Then they are led by us to where is water, and in the manner of the regeneration by which we ourselves were regenerated they are regenerated. For at that time they are washed in the water in the name of God the Master and Father of all, and of our Saviour Jesus Christ, and of the Holy Spirit. For Christ also said, "Unless you are regenerated you cannot enter into the king-dom of heaven.".…

And we have learned from the apostles the reason for this practice. Since at our first birth we have been born without our knowledge or choice from the moist seed at the union of our par-ents with each other and have existed in bad habits and evil con-duct, in order that we might not remain children of ignorance and necessity but become children of choice and knowledge and might obtain the forgiveness of sins committed in the past, there is called in the water upon the one who chooses to be regenerated and who repents of sins the name of God the Master and Father of all. The one leading the person being washed to the bath speaks only this name … And this washing is called illumination, because they who learn these things are illuminated in their understandings. And in the name of Jesus Christ, who was crucified under Pontius Pilate, and in the name of the Holy Ghost, who through the proph-ets foretold all things about Jesus, he who is illuminated is washed.

After we thus wash the person who has been persuaded and who has given consent, we lead this one to where those called brothers and sisters have gathered together to make fervent prayers in common on behalf of themselves and of the one who has been illuminated and of all others everywhere. We pray that hav-ing learned the truth we may be accounted worthy and through our deeds be found good citizens and guardians of what is com-manded in order that we may be saved with eternal salvation.[26]

---

26. Justin Martyr, *First Apology*, chapters 61 and 65. In *Ante-Nicene Fathers*, Vol. 1. Edited by Alexander Roberts, James Donaldson, and A. Cleveland Coxe, Christian Literature Publishing Co., Buffalo, NY, 1885. Quote taken from Ferguson, *Baptism in the Early Church*, 237ff.; partly also taken from Osborne, *The Christian Sacraments of Initiation*, 63ff.

This text confirms the use of the trinitarian formula, as well as fasting and prayer by the candidate(s) together with companions for preparation. Repentance and the remission of sins are emphasized. Baptism as forgiveness of sins is rebirth and regeneration; it is by one's own choice, with an explicit reference to John 3. But Justin is also the first author in whom we find the term "illumination" as a technical term for baptism, something which already seemed usual for him.

A consequence of baptism is a life which is judged worthy, meaning that the baptized person is found "a good citizen and guardian of what is commanded." Interestingly, here salvation is not related so much to baptism itself as to the good deeds performed by the baptized person.

We find here also a connection between baptism and the eucharist which follows baptism[27] and which is only for baptized persons.[28] Thus baptism is also entry into the community of the church.

In another text, Justin develops the idea of baptism as spiritual circumcision.[29]

---

27. "But we, after we have thus washed him who has been convinced and has assented to our teaching, bring him to the place where those who are called brethren are assembled, in order that we may offer hearty prayers in common for ourselves and for the baptized [illuminated] person, and for all others in every place ... Having ended the prayers, we salute one another with a kiss. There is then brought to the president of the brethren bread and a cup of wine mixed with water; and he taking them, gives praise and glory to the Father of the universe, through the name of the Son and of the Holy Ghost, and offers thanks at considerable length for our being counted worthy to receive these things at His hands ... And when the president has given thanks, and all the people have expressed their assent, those who are called by us deacons give to each of those present to partake of the bread and wine mixed with water over which the thanksgiving was pronounced, and to those who are absent they carry away a portion." Justin Martyr, First Apology, Chapter 65. http://www.earlychristianwritings.com/text/justinmartyr-firstapology.html.

28. "This food is called by us eucharist, of which no one is allowed to partake except the one who believes the things taught by us to be true, was washed in the bath for forgiveness of sins and regeneration, and who lives in the manner Christ taught." Justin Martyr, *First Apology*, Chapter 66.1, in Ferguson, *Baptism in the Early Church*, 242.

29. Justin Martyr, *Dialogue with Trypho*; in *Iustini Martyris Dialogus cum Tryphone*, ed. Miroslav Marcovich, Walter de Gruyter, Berlin, 1997. English

The **Apostolic Tradition** Probably a much later, but important, source is the *Apostolic Tradition*, a church manual attributed to the *presbyter Hippolytus in Rome (ca. 170-235). Recent research, however, has proven that it is not from the second century.[30] It remains unclear where and when it was written, but it certainly already existed in the fourth century. It seems to contain material from different sources and from different regions and times[31] and it had a strong influence on the development of the baptismal rite, especially in the West. The part of the text related to baptism reads:

> *15 Those who are newly brought forward to hear the Word shall first be brough before the teachers at the house, before all the people enter. Then they will be questioned concerning the reason that they have come forward to the faith. Those who bring them will bear witness concerning them as to whether they are able to hear. They shall be questioned concerning their life and occupation, marriage status, and whether they are slave or free.*
> *If they are the slaves of any of the faithful, and if their masters permit them, they may hear the Word. If their masters do not bear witness that they are good, let them be rejected.*
>   *If their masters are pagans, teach them to please their masters, so that there will be no blasphemy.*
>   *If a man has a wife, or a woman has a husband, let them be taught to be content, the husband with his wife, and the wife with her husband. If there is a man who does not live with a woman, let him be taught not to fornicate, but to either take a wife according to the law, or to remain as is.*
>   *If there is someone who has a demon, such a one shall not hear the Word of the teacher until purified.*
>   *16 They will inquire concerning the works and occupations of those who are brought forward for instruction. If someone is a pimp who supports prostitutes, he shall cease or shall be rejected. If someone is a sculptor or a painter, let them be taught not to*

translation taken from Ferguson, *Baptism in the Early Church*, 243.
   30. Lange, "Gestalt und Deutung," 7; see Ferguson, *Baptism in the Early Church*, 325.
   31. See Ferguson, *Baptism in the Early Church*, 327.

make idols. Either let them cease or let them be rejected. If some-
one is an actor or does shows in the theater, either he shall cease or
he shall be rejected. If someone teaches children [worldly knowl-
edge], it is good that he cease. But if he has no [other] trade, let
him be permitted. A charioteer, likewise, or one who takes part
in the games, or one who goes to the games, he shall cease or he
shall be rejected. If someone is a gladiator, or one who teaches
those among the gladiators how to fight, or a hunter who is in the
wild beast shows in the arena, or a public official who is concerned
with gladiator shows, either he shall cease, or he shall be rejected.
If someone is a priest of idols, or an attendant of idols, he shall
cease or he shall be rejected. A military man in authority must not
execute men. If he is ordered, he must not carry it out. Nor must
he take military oath. If he refuses, he shall be rejected. If someone
is a military governor,[32] or the ruler of a city who wears the purple,
he shall cease or he shall be rejected. The catechumen or faithful
who wants to become a soldier is to be rejected, for he has despised
God. The prostitute, the wanton man, the one who castrates him-
self, or one who does that which may not be mentioned, are to be
rejected, for they are impure. A magus shall not even be brought
forward for consideration. An enchanter, or astrologer, or diviner,
or interpreter of dreams, or a charlatan,[33] or one who makes amu-
lets, either they shall cease or they shall be rejected. If someone's
concubine is a slave, as long as she has raised her children and has
clung only to him, let her hear. Otherwise, she shall be rejected.
The man who has a concubine must cease and take a wife accord-
ing to the law. If he will not, he shall be rejected.

17 Catechumens will hear the word for three years. Yet if
someone is earnest[34] and perseveres well in the matter, it is not the
time that is judged, but the conduct.

18 When the teacher finishes his instruction, the catechu-
mens will pray by themselves, separate from the faithful … After
the catechumens have finished praying, they do not give the kiss of

---

32. Literally "has the authority of swords."
33. Literally "one who stirs up the people."
34. Or "eager."

peace, for their kiss is not yet pure. But the faithful shall greet one another with a kiss, men with men, and women with women. Men must not greet women with a kiss...

19 After the prayer, the teacher shall lay hands upon the cat-echumens, pray, and dismiss them...

If any catechumens are apprehended because of the Name of the Lord, let them not be double-hearted because of martyrdom. If they may suffer violence and be executed with their sins not removed, they will be justified, for they have received baptism in their own blood.

20 When they are chosen who are to receive baptism, let their lives be examined, whether they have lived honorably while cat-echumens, whether they honored the widows, whether they visited the sick, and whether they have done every good work. If those who bring them forward bear witness for them that they have done so, then let them hear the gospel.

From the time at which they are set apart, place hands upon them daily so that they are exorcised. When the day approaches on which they are to be baptized, let the bishop exorcise each one of them, so that he will be certain whether each has been purified. If there are any who are not purified, they shall be set apart...

Let those who are to be baptized be instructed that they bathe and wash on the fifth day of the week. If a woman is in the manner of women, let her be set apart and receive baptism another day.

Those who are to receive baptism shall fast on the Preparation of the Sabbath.[35] On the Sabbath, those who are to receive baptism shall all gather together in one place chosen according to the will of the bishop. They shall be commanded to pray and kneel. Then, laying his hand on them, he will exorcise every foreign spirit, so that they flee from them and never return to them. When he has finished exorcising them, he shall breathe on their faces and seal their foreheads, ears and noses. Then he shall raise them up.

They shall all keep vigil all night, reading and instructing them...

---

35. I.e. on Friday.

21 At the hour in which the cock crows, they shall first pray over the water. When they come to the water, the water shall be pure and flowing, that is, the water of a spring or a flowing body of water. Then they shall take off all their clothes. The children shall be baptized first. All of the children who can answer for themselves, let them answer. If there are any children who cannot answer for themselves, let their parents answer for them, or someone else from their family. After this, the men will be baptized. Finally, the women, after they have unbound their hair, and removed their jewelry. No one shall take any foreign object with themselves down into the water.

*At the time determined for baptism, the bishop shall give thanks over some oil, which he puts in a vessel. It is called the Oil of Thanksgiving. He shall take some more oil and exorcise it. It is called the Oil of Exorcism. A *deacon shall hold the Oil of Exorcism and stand on the left. Another deacon shall hold the Oil of Thanksgiving and stand on the right.*

When the elder takes hold of each of them who are to receive baptism, he shall tell each of them to renounce, saying, "I renounce you Satan, all your service,[36] and all your works." After he has said this, he shall anoint each with the Oil of Exorcism, saying, "Let every evil spirit depart from you." Then, after these things, the bishop passes each of them on nude to the elder who stands at the water. They shall stand in the water naked. A deacon, likewise, will go down with them into the water. When each of them to be baptized has gone down into the water, the one baptizing shall lay hands on each of them, asking, "Do you believe in God the Father Almighty?" And the one being baptized shall answer, "I believe." He shall then baptize each of them once, laying his hand upon each of their heads. Then he shall ask, "Do you believe in Jesus Christ, the Son of God, who was born of the Holy Spirit and the Virgin Mary, who was crucified under Pontius Pilate, and died, and rose on the third day living from the dead, and ascended into heaven, and sat down at the right hand of the Father, the one coming to judge the living and the dead?"

---

36. Some sources read "servants."

When each has answered, "I believe," he shall baptize a second time. Then he shall ask, "Do you believe in the Holy Spirit and the Holy Church and the resurrection of the flesh?" Then each being baptized shall answer, "I believe." And thus let him baptize the third time.

Afterward, when they have come up out of the water, they shall be anointed by the elder with the Oil of Thanksgiving, saying, "I anoint you with holy oil in the name of Jesus Christ." Then, drying themselves, they shall dress and afterwards gather in the church.

The bishop will then lay his hand upon them, invoking, saying, "Lord God, you who have made these worthy of the removal of sins through the bath of regeneration, make them worthy to be filled with your Holy Spirit, grant to them your grace, that they might serve you according to your will, for to you is the glory, Father and Son with the Holy Spirit, in the Holy Church, now and throughout the ages of the ages. Amen.

After this he pours the oil into his hand, and laying his hand on each of their heads, says, "I anoint you with holy oil in God the Father Almighty, and Christ Jesus, and the Holy Spirit."

Then, after sealing each of them on the forehead, he shall give them the kiss of peace and say, "The Lord be with you." And the one who has been baptized shall say, "And with your spirit." So shall he do to each one.

From then on they will pray together will all the people. Prior to this they may not pray with the faithful until they have completed all. After they pray, let them give the kiss of peace.

Then the deacons shall immediately bring the oblation. The bishop shall bless the bread, which is the symbol of the Body of Christ; and the bowl of mixed wine,[37] *which is the symbol of the Blood which has been shed for all who believe in him.*[38]

---

37. Wine mixed with water.

38. Translation by Kevin B. Edgecomb, California, based on the work of Bernard Botte (*La Tradition Apostolique*, Sources Chrétiennes, 11 bis, Editions du Cerf, Paris, 1984) and of Gregory Dix (*The Treatise on the Apostolic Tradition of St. Hippolytus of Rome, Bishop and Martyr,* Alban Press, London, 1992). A

From this text it is clear that the period for preparation before baptism as well as the baptismal liturgy itself had been developed in an intensive way:

- There is a three-year preparation time, the catechumenate.

- Not everyone is received into catechumenate; a number of professions are considered inappropriate for Christians. There is an examination of the lifestyle of the candidates.

- During the time of the catechumenate the candidates have a separate place in the church.

- Martyrdom is considered to be a valid baptism.

- Candidates have *sponsors who testify about their good behaviour.

- Shortly before the baptism there is daily exorcism as well as a special exorcism by the bishop.

- The preparation time includes fasting (on Friday and Saturday).

- Before baptism the candidates spend a night in vigil.

- Before baptism a prayer over the water is said.

- Baptismal water should be flowing water, if possible.

- The candidate is naked when immersed.[39]

- This is the first testimony that children are being baptized, even at an age where they cannot speak for themselves.

- Two sorts of oil are in use: the "oil of exorcism" and the "oil of thanksgiving."

- The oil of exorcism is used in an anointing before baptism, after the candidate has renounced Satan.

---

simplified version for ease of reading can be found here: http://www.bombaxo.com/hippolytus.html.

39. It is unclear whether this meant total nakedness or light clothing. See Ferguson, *Baptism in the Early Church*, 330.

- The candidate is immersed three times while affirming his or her faith in the Father, the Son and the Holy Spirit. It should be noted that there is no familiar formula mentioned such as "I baptize you in the name of ..."

- After the baptism the candidate is anointed with the oil of thanksgiving.

- After this, there is another anointing with oil on the forehead by the bishop.

- After the baptism follows the kiss of peace and, immediately the eucharist.

There is a striking emphasis on purity to be found in this text: purity and a particular lifestyle are the precondition for baptism. Baptism itself is a regeneration. From the prayer of the priest after the immersion, it seems as if baptism is understood as a precondition for receiving the Holy Spirit.

Pope Innocent I The Letter of Pope Innocent I to Bishop Decentius of Gubbio[40] (416) is one of the first evidences for the practice of a laying on of hands by the bishop and a *postbaptismal anointing as part of the Roman rite. These rites are closely associated with the bishop, so that, if no bishop is present they have to be performed later when it is possible for a bishop to be present.[41]

Sources from Africa

A rich collection of sources for the baptismal rite of the third century comes from Africa. For example, from Tertullian's (ca. 150-230) *De Baptismo* we know that in case of emergency a layman—but not a laywoman—can baptize. Before baptism the candidates fast, have a night vigil and confess all their sins. Every kind of water can be

---

40. English translation in Edward Charles Whitaker, *Documents of the Baptismal Liturgy*, SPCK, London, 1960, 229ff.

41. Cf. Hans-Jürgen Feulner, "The Sacraments of Baptism and Holy Chrism in the Western Tradition prior to the VIIIth Century," in V. Международная Богославская Конференция Русской Православной Церкви, *Православное учение о церковних таинствах*, том I, Синодальная Библейско-богословская комиссия Москва, 2009, 270.

used, but God must be invoked so that the Holy Spirit comes. Twice the candidate has to renounce Satan, the second time immediately before baptism. Baptism is done with triple immersion. The body is marked with the sign of the cross. After baptism the head of the candidate is anointed with oil. Thereafter the bishop lays his hands on the candidate while invoking the Holy Spirit. After this the candidates are received in the community and receive milk and honey.[42]

Tertullian explicitly separates the gift of the Holy Spirit from baptism: "Not that the Holy Spirit is given to us in the water, but that in the water we are made clean by the action of the angel and made ready for the Holy Spirit."[43] The gift of the Holy Spirit is connected with the laying on of hands after the post-baptismal anointing: "Next [after the unction] follows the imposition of the hand in benediction, inviting and welcoming the Holy Spirit."[44]

For Tertullian, baptism primarily signifies the forgiveness of sins.[45] Tertullian also understands baptism as regeneration and new birth. It is entry into the church and it is necessary for salvation.[46]

A similar rite can be found in the works of Cyprian of Carthage (bishop ca. 248-258).[47] For him the water act is a new birth, while the laying on of hands is related to the gift of the Holy Spirit.[48]

Augustine, bishop of Hippo (354-430), follows the African tradition of understanding the anointing as gift of the Holy Spirit. But on the question of the relationship between the sacrament and the giver of the sacrament, he follows the Roman line. According to Augustine, baptism:

---

42. Tertullian, *De Baptismo*; in B. Luselli, Q. Septimi Florentis Tertulliani De Baptismo, Turin ²1968. cf. Edward J. Yarnold, "Taufe III: Alte Kirche," in *Theologische Realenzyklopädie* Vol. 32, 2001, 678ff.

43. Tertullian, *De Baptismo* 6.1; English translation taken from Ferguson, *Baptism in the Early Church*, 344.

44. Tertullian, *De Baptismo* 8.1; English translation taken from Ferguson, *Baptism in the Early Church*, 344.

45. Ferguson, *Baptism in the Early Church*, 346.

46. "It is prescribed that without baptism no person can obtain salvation"; Tertullian, *De Baptismo* 12.1, quoted in Ferguson, *Baptism in the Early Church*, 349.

47. Yarnold, "Taufe III: Alte Kirche," 679.

48. Cyprian of Carthage, Ep.74; see Ferguson, *Baptism in the Early Church*, 354.

- Liberates from the power of the devil.
- Effects reconciliation with God by purifying the person from guilt.
- Infuses *caritas into the baptized person.
- Incorporates the person into the body of Christ.[49]

Sources from Milan

The most important witness for the baptismal ceremony in Milan is Ambrose, bishop of Milan (beginning in 374). His treatises *On the Sacraments* and *On the Mysteries* were written around 390.

According to Ambrose, catechumens enrolled for baptism at Epiphany and were signed with the cross. During the subsequent time of preparation they received instructions. "On Saturdays *scrutinies or exorcisms were held to determine the fitness of the candidates for baptism."[50] The ritual of baptism began in the Saturday night before Easter at the door of the baptistery with the ceremony of *ephphetha*, the "opening of the ears," in which the bishop touched the ears and nose of the candidate. This is understood as a reference to Mk 7:38. "Then the candidate entered the baptistery, where a deacon and presbyter anointed his body as an athlete being prepared to wrestle."[51] After this followed the candidates' renunciation of the devil. The renunciation is described as a promise and a contract. The bishop consecrated the water, after which the candidate descended into the pool together with the bishop, presbyter and deacon. The baptism itself was a triple immersion with a triple interrogatory confession.[52] After the baptized came out of the font, the bishop anointed his or her head with myron. "This anointing is associated with eternal life, and enrichment of human facilities by grace, and the priestly and royal anointing of the Old Testament but notably not with the giving of the Holy Spirit."[53]

---

49. See Ralph G. Wilburn, "The One Baptism and the Many Baptisms," *Mid-Stream* 3 (1964): 92.

50. Ferguson, *Baptism in the Early Church*, 636.

51. Ibid.

52. Ibid., 638.

53. Ibid., 639.

A distinctive element, one not known in other baptismal orders, was a footwashing understood as removing hereditary sins; the baptism itself remitted a person's own sins.[54] The newly baptized, after being clothed in white garments, received the "spiritual seal," which was distinct from the post-baptismal unction and "seems to have been accompanied by making the sign of the cross (on the forehead)."[55] The ritual was followed by a celebration of the eucharist.

Ambrose frequently explained baptism in terms of the death, burial and resurrection of Christ.[56] The baptistery was understood as a tomb, and the coming up from the water was associated with resurrection.

Sources from Antioch and Other Parts of Syria

In Antioch there were two different branches of baptismal practice, namely a Syrian-speaking rite and a Greek-speaking rite. Typical for the early Syrian rite is the dominance of an anointing before the water rite (pre-baptismal anointing), mainly of the head, which is connected to the gift of the Holy Spirit.[57] This understanding of baptism recalls Old Testament models of royal unction and prophetic unction; on the other hand, it is understood as new birth, with reference to the Gospel of John. Therefore the baptistery is compared with the uterus. In this rite baptism is the entrance into the church, parallel to circumcision as entry into the synagogue.[58]

Ephrem the Syrian The classic writer of the Syrian-speaking community is Ephrem the Syrian (ca. 306-373), a deacon first in Nisibis, later in Edessa. In Ephrem's *Hymns on Virginity* (7.2, 5-10) the baptismal ceremony is described as follows: before baptism, which

---

54. Ibid.

55. Ibid., 640.

56. Ibid., 643.

57. See Harald Buchinger, "Baptism and Chrismation in the Syrian Tradition of the third to fourth century", in V. Международная Богословская Конференция Русской Православной Церкви, *Православное учение о церковних таинствах*, том I, Синодальная Библейско-богословская комиссия Москва, 2009, 223.

58. See Lange, "Gestalt und Deutung," 10ff.

was done in the paschal season, there was a period of fasting. At the beginning of the baptismal ceremony the waters are sanctified,[59] which means that Christ and the Spirit are present in the water. There was also the custom of placing a cross in the water. The anointing precedes the baptism which is done by immersion[60] and with pronouncement of the triune formula. As Ferguson states, there is no trace of a post-baptismal anointing.[61]

Ephrem understands baptism mainly in two ways: as the forgiveness of sins and as the gift of the Holy Spirit. The latter is especially linked to the pre-baptismal unction. Ephrem understands the water of baptism as a womb, and therefore baptism as a birth.[62]

John Chrysostom The Greek-speaking authors of the Antiochian tradition also emphasize the anointing as the point which makes a human being a Christian. This is the case in the baptismal catecheses of John Chrysostom (ca. 349-412), a presbyter from Antioch who became bishop of Constantinople in 397. According to him baptisms were performed in the Easter vigil, with the preparation coinciding with Lent. Some days before, the candidates had to confirm their faith by reciting the Creed in front of the bishop. In connection with this they renounced Satan and pledged to follow Christ. Chrysostom interprets this as a contract.[63] Thereafter the priest anointed the forehead of the candidate in the form of a cross. This was understood as a sealing of the candidate, but also as empowerment: the anointed is sometimes understood as "a combatant chosen for the spiritual arena."[64] In the Easter vigil the candidates were anointed over the whole body[65] before they were

---

59. See Ferguson, *Baptism in the Early Church*, 507.

60. Ephrem, *Hymns on Virginity*, 7.8., in Ephrem the Syrian: Hymns, translated by Kathleen E. McVey, Paulis Press, Mahwah NJ, 1989, 261-473.

61. Ferguson, *Baptism in the Early Church*, 506.

62. See ibid., 509 and 517

63. See ibid., 536 and 539.

64. Quoted in ibid., 540. See also Thomas M. Finn, *The Liturgy of Baptism in the Baptismal Instructions of St. John Chrysostom,* Catholic University of America Press, Washington, 1967, 137.

65. As Thomas M. Finn points out, these two anointings were originally one act. For Chrysostom the two acts are separated by an interval of time. Finn, *The*

immersed by the bishop or priest. After this they were greeted by the community and the Eucharist ended the rite.[66] The only post-baptismal act expressly described is the kiss.[67] The conferring of the Holy Spirit happens in the baptismal action itself. "Thus, although Chrysostom agreed with earlier practice in Syria of pre-baptismal anointing, he differed in attributing the coming of the Holy Spirit not to an anointing but to the water bath itself."[68]

Theodore of Mopsuestia Another author from this tradition is Theodore, bishop of Mopsuestia in Cilicia (bishop from ca. 390-426). According to Sebastian Brock, Theodore is the first in the Syrian tradition to lay great stress on baptism as an image of the death and resurrection of Christ.[69] Theodore says: "[Paul] clearly taught here that we are baptized so that we might imitate in ourselves the death and the resurrection of our Lord, and that we might receive from our remembrance of the happening that took place the confirmation of our hope in future things."[70] There is a clear eschatological emphasis.[71] Theodore mentions that the trinitarian formula is used, not a confession made in response to an interrogation as we have seen earlier. Theodore does not know a post-baptismal anointing with oil, but rather a signing on the forehead after the immersion,[72] accompanied by the trinitarian formula and related to the gift of

Liturgy of Baptism, 119ff.

66. John Chrysostom, Baptismal Instructions 2.27. in *St. John Chrysostom, Baptismal Instructions*, translated and annotated by Paul W. Harkins, Newman Press, New York, 1963, 53.

67. Ibid.

68. Ferguson, *Baptism in the Early Church*, 559; see also ibid., 543.

69. Sebastian Paul Brock, "The Transition to a Post-Baptismal Anointing in the Antiochene Rite," in Bryan D. Spinks, ed., *The Sacrifice of Praise: Studies on the Themes of Thanksgiving and Redemption in the Central Prayers of the Eucharistic and Baptismal Liturgies,* In Honour of Arthur Hubert Couratin, Edizioni Liturgiche, Rome, 1979, 221ff. with reference to Theodore of Mopsuestia, *Catechetical Homilies* 12, 7.

70. Theodore of Mopsuestia, *Cat. Hom.* 12, 20, quoted in Ferguson, *Baptism in the Early Church,* 528.

71. For further quotations to confirm this, see Ferguson, *Baptism in the Early Church*, 531.

72. According to Buchinger, "Baptism and Chrismation," 5, it is unclear whether oil was used.

the Holy Spirit.[73] The pre-baptismal anointing on the other hand, in contrast to the earlier texts, is a sign of the immortality which is to be received in baptism.[74]

In his "Instruction to Candidates for Baptism," Theodore of Mopsuestia writes, in Sermon 3:

> *When you go to be enrolled in the hope of acquiring the abode and citizenship of heaven, you have, in the ceremony of exorcism, a kind of law-suit with the Demon, and by a divine verdict you receive your freedom from his servitude. And thus you recite the words of the profession of faith and of prayer, and through them you make an engagement and a promise to God, before the priests, that you will remain in the love of the divine nature ... and that you will live in this world to the best of your ability in a way that is consonant with the life and citizenship of heaven ... After you have been taken away from the servitude of the Tyrant by means of the words of exorcism, and have made solemn engagements to God along with the recitation of the Creed, you draw nigh unto the sacrament itself; you must learn how this is done.*
>
> *You stand barefoot on sackcloth while your outer garment is taken off from you, and your hands are stretched towards God in the posture of one who prays...*
>
> *First you genuflect while the rest of your body is erect, and in the posture of one who prays you stretch your arms towards God...*
>
> *When you have, therefore, made your promises and engagements, the priest draws near to you, wearing, not his ordinary garments ... but clad in a robe of clean and radiant linen, the joyful appearance of which denotes the joy of the world to which you will move in the future, and the shining ... And he signs you on your forehead with the holy Chrism and says "So-and-so is signed in the Name of the Father and of the Son and of the Holy Spirit."... The sign with which you are signed means that you have been stamped as a lamb of Christ and as a soldier of the heavenly King ... After you have been singled out and stamped as a soldier of*

---

73. Ferguson, *Baptism in the Early Church*, 526.
74. Ibid., 525.

Christ the Lord, you receive the remaining part of the sacrament and are invested with the complete armour of the Spirit, and with the sacrament you receive participation in the heavenly benefits.[75]

In Sermon 4 of the same "Instruction," Theodore writes:

You draw, therefore, nigh unto the holy baptism, and before everything you take off your garment ... After you have taken off your garment, you are rightly anointed all over your body with the holy Chrism: a mark and a sign that you will be receiving the covering of immortality, which through baptism you are about to put on ... After these things have happened to you ... you descend into the water, which has been consecrated by the benediction of the priest, as you are not baptized only with ordinary water, but with water of the second birth, which cannot become so except through the coming of the Holy Spirit on it. For this it is necessary that the priest should have beforehand made use of clear words, according to the rite of the priestly service, and asked God that the grace of the Holy Spirit might come on the water and impart to it the power of conceiving that awe-inspiring child and becoming a womb to the sacramental birth ... The priest stands up and approaches his hand, which he places on your head and says: "so-and-so is baptized in the Name of the father and of the Son and of the Holy Spirit" [follows threefold immersion] ... After you have received the grace of baptism and worn a white garment that shines, the priest draws nigh unto you and signs you on your forehead ... When Jesus came out of the water he received the grace of the Holy Spirit who descended like a dove and lighted on him, and this is the reason why he is said to have been anointed.[76]

Theodore understands baptism as giving "second birth, renewal, immortality, incorruptibility, impassibility, immutability, deliverance from death and servitude and all evils, happiness

---

75. Theodore of Mopsuestia, *Catechetical Homilies*, Part 2, Sermon 3, translation in Whitaker, *Documents of the Baptismal Liturgy*, 40ff.

76. Theodore of Mopsuestia, *Catechetical Homilies*, Part 2, Sermon 4, translation in Whitaker, *Documents of the Baptismal Liturgy*, 40ff.

of freedom, and participation in the ineffable good things which we are expecting."[77] He has a strong emphasis on the trinitarian aspect of baptism, and therefore his rite has an *epiclesis in order for the grace of the Holy Spirit to come upon the water.[78] The idea of becoming a soldier is new.

The **Apostolic Constitutions** A change seems to have occurred in the Syriac tradition by the end of the 4th or beginning of the 5th century. The *Apostolic Constitutions*, a collection of church orders from the Syrian region from between 375 and 400, show three *pre-baptismal anointings and, unlike the earlier Syriac sources, an anointing after the candidate's immersion in the water.[79] The pre-baptismal anointing is understood as a "participation in the Holy Spirit."[80] The post-baptismal anointing is understood as sealing or "seal of the covenants." The water is a symbol of death. "This baptism therefore is given into the death of Jesus; the water is instead of the burial, and the oil instead of the Holy Ghost: the seal instead of the cross; the chrism is the confirmation of the confession ... the descent into the water the dying together with Christ; the ascent out of the water the rising again with him."[81]

The baptistery is no longer understood as a womb, as with Ephrem and Theodore, but as a tomb. This means that the understanding of baptism is no longer determined by the Gospel of John and Jesus' talk with Nicodemus (Jn 3), but rather is inspired by Paul and the letter to the Romans, where baptism is explained as dying and rising with Christ (Rom 6). In the *Apostolic Constitutions* we also find the language of illumination related to baptism.[82]

---

77. Theodore of Mopsuestia, *Catechetical Homilies* 14, 62, quoted in Ferguson, *Baptism in the Early Church*, 527.

78. Ibid.

79. Ferguson, *Baptism in the Early Church*, 567.

80. *Apostolic Constitutions* VII 22.2-3, quoted in Ferguson, *Baptism in the Early Church,* 570.

81. *Apostolic Constitutions* III, 17, translation in Whitaker, *Documents of the Baptismal Liturgy*, 28.

82. See Ferguson, *Baptism in the Early Church*, 572.

Sources from Jerusalem

Cyril of Jerusalem From Jerusalem we have the first full testimony for the developed baptismal ceremony in the 4th century. Cyril, bishop of Jerusalem (ca. 313-386), wrote several texts which give information about the ceremonies and their meaning. Especially interesting are the *Mystagogical Catecheses*. These are lectures which were held during the weeks after baptism in order to explain the rite to the *neophytes. The baptismal rite was under the **dis-ciplina arcani* (discipline of the secret) and therefore had not been explained before.

In his first *Mystagogical Catechesis*, Cyril writes:

> *2. First you entered the antechamber of the baptistery and faced towards the west. On the command to stretch out your hand, you renounced Satan as though he were there in person... 4. You were told, however, to address him as personally present, and with arm outstretched to say: "I renounce you, Satan." Allow me to explain the reason for your facing west, for you should know it. Because the west is the region of visible darkness; that is the significance of your looking steadily towards the west while you renounce that gloomy Prince of night... 5. Then in a second phrase you are taught to say, "and all your works." All sin is "the work of Satan"; and sin too, you must renounce, since he who has escaped from a tyrant has also cast off the tyrant's livery... 6. Next you say, "and all his pomp." The pomp of the Devil is the craze for the theatre, the horse races in the circus, the wild-beast hunts and all such vanity... 8. After this you say, "and all your service." The service of the Devil is prayer in the temple of idols, the honoring of lifeless images, the lighting of lamps or the burning of incense by springs or streams... 9. When you renounce Satan, trampling underfoot every covenant with him then you annul that ancient "league with Hell," and God's paradise opens before you... 11. That was what was done in the outer chamber.[83]*

---

83. Cyril of Jerusalem, *Mystagogical Catechesis* I, in *Cyrill von Jerusalem. Mystagogical Catecheses. Mystagogische Katechesen*, Georg Röwekamp, ed., Herder, Freiburg-Basel-Wien, 1992, English translation taken from Osborne, *The Christian Sacraments of Initiation*, 73ff.

The second *Mystagogical Catechesis* states:

> *2. Immediately, then, upon entering [the inner chamber], you removed your tunics. This was a figure of the "stripping off of the old man with his deeds." Having stripped, you were naked, in this also imitating Christ, who was naked on the cross... 3. Then, when stripped, you were anointed with exorcised olive oil from the topmost hairs of your head to the soles of your feet, and became partakers of the good olive tree, Jesus Christ. Cuttings from the wild olive tree, you were grafted into the good olive tree and became partakers of the fatness of the true olive tree... 4. After this you were conducted to the sacred pool of divine Baptism, as Christ passed from the cross to the sepulcher ... You were asked, one by one, whether you believed in the name of the Father and of the Son and of the Holy Spirit; you made that saving confession, and then you dipped thrice under the water and thrice rose up again, therein mystically signifying Christ's three days' burial.[84]*

In the third *Mystagogical Catechesis*, Cyril continues:

> *1. Similarly for you, after you had ascended from the sacred streams, there was an anointing with chrism, the antitype of that with which Christ was anointed, that is, of the Holy Spirit... 4. You were anointed first upon the forehead to rid you of the shame which the first human transgressor bore about with him everywhere... Then upon the ears, to receive ears, quick to hear the divine mysteries... Then upon the nostrils, that scenting the divine oil, you may say: "We are the incense offered by Christ to God, in the case of those who are on the way to salvation." Then on the breast, that "putting on the breastplate of justice you may be able to withstand the wile of the Devil." ... 5. Once privileged to receive the holy Chrism, you are called Christians and have a name that bespeaks your new birth. Before admission to Baptism you were not strictly entitled to this name but were like people on the way towards being Christians.[85]*

---

84. Ibid.
85. Ibid.

From another writing of Cyril, the *Catecheses*, we know that the candidates registered at the beginning of Lent for the final period of preparation for baptism. During this time they regularly had exorcisms and lessons. They also received the creed, which they had to memorize and, later, recite before the bishop.[86] While before they were called "catechumens" they now became *photizomenoi*, that is, "those being illuminated" or "those being enlightened." Thus the whole catechumenate is a time of transition, a process of gradual illumination.[87] Cyril also stresses the need for repentance and confession of sins during this time.

The *Mystagogical Catecheses* of Cyril describe the ceremony of baptism itself. According to these, the candidate renounces Satan in the direction of the West, then confesses Christ in the Eastern direction. There is an anointing of the whole body before the baptism, which signifies the embodiment into Christ as the true olive tree. A threefold immersion follows. After baptism the candidate is anointed with chrism on the forehead, ears, nose and breast, which is related to receiving the gift of the Holy Spirit.

"Cyril consistently relates the experience of his hearers to that of Christ."[88] Baptism thus becomes a dramatic event, in which the candidate experiences the death and resurrection of Jesus Christ. At the same time the baptism of Jesus by John becomes the model for Christian baptism. Consequently the new post-baptismal anointing—and not the pre-baptismal anointing—was understood as the conferring of the Holy Spirit. This is a difference in understanding compared with earlier Syrian texts[89] but is in line with Western sources.[90] The pre-baptismal anointing received the meaning of empowerment against hostile powers.

---

86. Yarnold, "Taufe III," 680; Ferguson, *Baptism in the Early Church*, 475. Baptized Christians were instructed to be careful not to recite the creed in front of the catechumens (Cyril, *Cat.* 5.12), which highlights the *disciplina arcani*.

87. See Ferguson, *Baptism in the Early Church*, 474.

88. Ibid., 481.

89. See above under "Sources from Antioch and Other Parts of Syria."

90. See Ferguson, *Baptism in the Early Church*, 480; cf. also Lange, "Gestalt und Deutung," 16.

Sources from Egypt

Clement of Alexandria One of the best known figures of the early church in Egypt is Clement of Alexandria, a presbyter at the end of the second century (+ after 215). He is "the earliest datable Christian writer to propose the baptism of Christ as the model for Christian baptism."[91] In his work *The Tutor* (*Paidagogos*) Clement writes:

> *This is what happens with us, whose model the Lord made himself. When we are baptized, we are enlightened; being enlightened, we become adopted sons; becoming adopted sons, we are made perfect; and becoming perfect, we are made divine ... This ceremony is often called "free gift" (Rom 5:2,15, 7:24), "enlightenment" (Heb 6:4; 10:32), "perfection" (Jas 1:7; Heb 7:11), and "cleansing" (Tit 3:5; Eph 5:26)—"cleansing", because through it we are completely purified of our sins; "free gift," because by it punishments due to our sins are remitted; "enlightenment," since by it we behold the wonderful holy light of salvation, that is, it enables us to see God clearly, finally, we call it "perfection" as needing nothing further, for what more does he need who possesses the knowledge of God? ... Moreover, release from evil is only the beginning of salvation...*
>
> *In the same way, those who are baptized are cleansed of the sins which like a mist overcloud their divine spirit and then acquire a spiritual sight which is clear and unimpeded and lightsome, the sort of sight which alone enables us to behold divinity, with the help of the Holy Spirit who is poured forth from heaven upon us ... Perfection lies ahead, in the resurrection of the faithful, but it consists in obtaining the promise which has already been given to us.[92]*

In Clement's view Jesus' own baptism is the model for Christian baptism.[93] The meaning of baptism is cleansing from sins. It is, therefore, related to illumination and enlightenment, leading to

---

91. Thomas M. Finn, *Early Christian Baptism and the Catechumenate: Italy, North Africa, and Egypt,* Liturgical Press, Collegeville, MN, 1992, 185.

92. Clement of Alexandria, *The Tutor (Paidagogos)*, Book I, 6:26-28 and Book 3, 12:10, quoted in Finn, *Early Christian Baptism,* 186-188.

93. See also Johnson, *The Rites of Christian Initiation,* 66.

perfection. Ferguson, referring to another important text, points out that "the terminology of regeneration is Clement's favorite imagery for baptism."[94]

Origen Another author from Alexandria around the same time was Origen, the head of a catechetical school; in 233 he went to Caesarea and became a presbyter. Origen did not write a work specifically on baptism, but in his numerous books there are many references to baptism. He interpreted events in the Old Testament as shadows or "types" for what happened in the New Testament. In this way, for example, Israel's crossing of the Red Sea is understood as an image of baptism.[95] Origen understands baptism as "a symbol of the purification of the soul, which is washed clean from all filth of evil, and is in itself the beginning and source of divine gifts to the one who surrenders to the divine power at the invocation of the worshipful Trinity."[96] He is one of the first authors to combine the traditional emphasis on Jesus' baptism with the theology of Paul's letter to the Romans, chapter 6.[97] Origen distinguishes the water from the work of the Spirit, but does not separate them.[98] In fact he identifies "a baptism of water and Spirit, and fire, and to some even of blood."[99]

In the passages in which Origen is talking about the baptismal liturgy or its liturgical elements, he speaks of a close connection between the water bath and an anointing: "All of us may be baptized in those visible waters and in a visible anointing, in accordance with the form handed down to the churches."[100] The gift of the Holy Spirit is not connected with the anointing, but with the laying on of hands.[101] The baptismal act is followed by the eucharist,

---

94. Ferguson, *Baptism in the Early Church,* 310.

95. More in ibid., 401-405.

96. Origen, *Commentary on John* 6:33, translation in Ferguson, *Baptism in the Early Church*, 407.

97. Johnson, *The Rites of Christian Initiation*, 73.

98. Ferguson, *Baptism in the Early Church*, 407.

99. Origen, *Commentary on John* 6:43, Translation in Ferguson, *Baptism in the Early Church*, 408.

100. Origen, Commentary on Romans 5.8.3, in Ferguson, *Baptism in the Early Church*, 426.

101. Ferguson, *Baptism in the Early Church*, 427.

which seems to be understood with an emphasis on the image of the wedding feast of Mt 22:12, or as the "eating of Christ."[102] Thus the communion with Christ is more in the foreground than entering into the community of believers.

Serapion of Thmuis From a collection of prayers[103] by Serapion, Bishop of Thmuis (339-363), it seems that in Egypt a variety of practices existed for the anointing.[104] There is an anointing before the water rite and Serapion also knows a post-baptismal anointing, associated with the gift of the Holy Spirit. Some other Egyptian sources have only an anointing *before* baptism.

The Coptic Baptismal Rite The Coptic baptismal rite, which has its origin before 451, has the following features.[105]

There is a catechumenate as a time of preparation for baptism. The baptism itself begins with a consecration of the water, while the priest breathes three times upon the water in the form of a cross. The rite has two pre-baptismal anointings. The first one with the "oil of catechesis" on the forehead of the candidate, the breast, hands and the back is followed by an exorcism and an elaborate threefold renunciation of Satan. Then comes the second anointing with "oil of gladness" on the breast, the arms, the front of the heart and the back, and the middle of the hands with the sign of the cross. A laying on of hands follows. Oil is poured into the font with several prayers for exorcism and sanctification of the water. Then the candidate is immersed three times, and after each immersion the priest breathes in his or her face saying "I baptize thee, N., in the Name of the Father [1st immersion], and of the Son [2nd immersion], and of the Holy Spirit. Amen [3rd immersion]." There is a post-baptismal anointing with chrism on the forehead and eyes, nostrils and mouth, ears, both sides of the hands, breast, knees, the instep of the feet, back, arms and the front of the heart. A final

---

102. See ibid., 429.
103. Texts in English in Whitaker, *Documents of the Baptismal Liturgy*, 74-76 and in Finn, *Early Christian Baptism*, 212-216.
104. Ferguson, *Baptism in the Early Church*, 464.
105. According to ibid., 695-699.

laying on of hands with a blessing concludes with a breathing on the face of the baptized with the words "receive the Holy Spirit." The baptized are clothed with white garments and receive crowns and girdles around their waist; they then receive holy communion.

The understanding of baptism as shown in these liturgical texts combines regeneration, the forgiveness of sins and the gift of the Holy Spirit.

Sources from Armenia

Gregory the Illuminator A source from the fifth century is *The Teaching of Saint Gregory*, attributed to Gregory the Illuminator, who brought Christianity to Armenia. It is a *catechism dated after 430-440.[106] Baptism in this text is related to creation:

> *And because He made the first earth emerge from the waters by his command, and by water were fattened all plants and reptiles and wild animals and beasts and birds, and by the freshness of the waters they sprang from the earth; in the same way by baptism He made verdant the womb of generation of the waters, purifying by the waters and renewing the old deteriorated earthly matter, which sin had weakened and enfeebled and deprived of the grace of the Spirit. Then the invisible Spirit opened again the womb of visible water, preparing the newly born fledglings for the regeneration of the font, to clothe all with robes of light who would be born once more.[107]*

This catechism puts an emphasis on Jesus' baptism as the model for Christian baptism. The idea is that Christ, through his own baptism, sanctified the waters so that they now give life to those who follow Christ's example. Christ's purity casts out impurity. For the person to be baptized is "to imitate the divine image of salvation."[108] Baptism brings illumination, saving, washing, deliverance from

---

106. Ferguson, *Baptism in the Early Church*, 709.
107. Quoted in ibid.
108. Ibid., 710.

bondage, the seal of Christ, the indwelling of the Spirit, adoption and access to the eucharist.

Agathangelos From the *Life of Gregory the Illuminator* in the *History of the Armenians* of Agathangelos, an author from the 5th century, we know about a sign of the cross with myron on the forehead, as well as the pouring of myron and olive oil into the water followed by immersion in a river. After this rite the baptized were clothed with a white garment and received holy communion. There was obviously no post-baptismal anointing.[109]

Summary

The sources from the early church present some variety in the baptismal rite and the understanding of baptism. Differences existed, especially in the earliest times, between the Syriac (and Armenian) tradition and the Western liturgies in the use or absence of a post-baptismal anointing. As Dominic Serra has pointed out,[110] this is related to different emphases: in the West the pre-baptismal anointing is related to exorcism, while the post-baptismal one has a consecratory meaning. In the early Syrian tradition the pre-baptismal anointing is a consecratory one[111] and has a greater significance than the water bath. The exorcistic preparation enters into the Syrian rite only later. This means that "the earliest rites stress that Christian initiation consists in an identification with the 'Anointed One' by means of an outpouring of the messianic spirit."[112] Paschal imagery and the motif of dying and raising with Christ, which we know from Paul's letters, become dominant only at a time when Easter became the preferred date for baptism, in the 4th century.

---

109. Yarnold, "Taufe III," 684.

110. Dominic E. Serra, "Syrian Prebaptismal Anointing and Western Postbaptismal Chrismation", *Worship,* 79 (2005): 328-341; see also Johnson, *The Rites of Christian Initiation.*

111. See Gabriele Winkler, "The Original Meaning of the Prebaptismal Anointing and Its Implications," in Maxwell E. Johnson, *Living Water, Sealing Spirit : Readings on Christian Initiation*, Liturgical Press, Collegeville, MN, 1995, 58-91.

112. Serra, "Syrian Prebaptismal Anointing," 335, referring to Gabriele Winkler.

There is also some variety in the total number of anointings. In some regions or cities (for example, in Rome) three anointings were practiced. One, before baptism, was for the whole body as an empowerment for the fight against the devil. (In the practice in Southern Gaul [present-day France] this anointing is explained as similar to the anointing of wrestlers, which is meant to make it more difficult for one enemy to grasp the other.) The two other anointings were after baptism: a pouring of myron on the head of the candidate, signifying the priestly and royal anointing of Christ; and, finally an anointing as seal for receiving the gift of the Spirit.[113] In Milan and in Gaul there was, in addition, a washing of the candidates' feet after baptism.

What is especially to be noted is that there is a difference in the interpretation given to the conferring of the Holy Spirit. It seems that in earlier liturgies, the gift of the Holy Spirit is related to the post-baptismal anointing (if it exists) but that in some cases it is related to a laying on of hands; in some later texts, the gift of the Holy Spirit is connected with the water bath itself.

Another difference is in the baptismal formula: in some regions the immersion into the water was performed together with a creed, given in response to a threefold interrogation, obviously without the baptismal formula. Where the formula was used it was known in two forms: the first person active formula "I baptize" was used in the Coptic and Latin rites, while the Greek and Syrian rites used the passive form: "N. is baptized."

As Serra showed, all the rites describe a journey of the baptizand from a preparation to a turning point which leads the person into the messianic reign of Christ. The difference is in the liturgical location of the turning point: either in an anointing or in the water bath.[114]

---

113. Yarnold, "Taufe III," 681.
114. Serra, "Syrian Prebaptismal Anointing," 339.

SPECIFIC ISSUES
Infant Baptism in the Early Church

Tertullian is one of the oldest sources from which we know that infant baptism was certainly practiced by the end of the 2nd century.[115] He prefers not to baptize small children:

> *According to the circumstances and nature, and also age, of each person, the delay of baptism is more suitable, especially in the case of small children. What is the necessity, if there is no such necessity, for the sponsors as well to be brought into danger, since they may fail to keep their promises by reason of death or be deceived by an evil disposition which grows up in the child? The Lord indeed says "do not forbid them to come to me." Let them "come" then while they are growing up, while they are learning, while they are instructed why they are coming. Let them become Christians when they are able to know Christ.[116]*

From Origen we come to know some of the reasons for the baptism of small children: "Was a newborn child able to sin? And yet it has a sin for which sacrifices are commanded to be offered, and from which it is denied that anyone is pure, even if his life should be one day long. It has to be believed, therefore, that concerning this David also said what we quoted above, 'in sins my mother conceived me' (Ps. 51:5). According to the historical narrative no sin of his mother is revealed." Origen continues by stating that to baptize infants is "a tradition from the apostles."[117] Cyprian of Carthage allowed for baptism immediately after birth.[118]

In the 4th century, however, we find a complete lack of evidence for infant baptism in the church fathers, except for emergency baptism.[119] But the decisions of the Synod of Elvira (Spain) in the

---

115. See also Joachim Jeremias, *Infant Baptism in the First Four Centuries*, SCM Press, London, 1960, 55 and 70ff.

116. Tertullian, *De Baptismo* 18, quoted in Ferguson, *Baptism in the Early Church*, 364.

117. Origen, *Commentary on Romans* 5:9.11, quoted in translation in Ferguson, *Baptism in the Early Church*, 368; see also Johnson, *The Rites of Christian Initiation*, 74.

118. Ferguson, *Baptism in the Early Church*, 370.

119. Jeremias, *Infant Baptism in the First Four Centuries*, 91.

period 306-312 prove that children were still baptized. The situation changes after 365, when many literary sources for the baptism of infants are known.

At the same time, in the 3rd and 4th century, there was a tendency to postpone baptism.[120] The best-known example for this phenomenon is the emperor Constantine the Great, who was baptized immediately before his death, although he had been converted to Christian faith much earlier. Many Christians believed that if a baptized person were to commit sins, the unique gift of baptism would be forfeited and salvation would be lost. There is evidence of this in the fact that Basil the Great tried to persuade people who were not yet baptized yet were trained in Christianity to apply for the catechumenate.[121] Gregory Nazianzen also criticizes those who delay baptism and argues that it is better "to be sanctified unconsciously" than to leave this life unbaptized.[122]

Kevin Roy states that these contradictory testimonies can only be explained as stemming from two divergent baptismal practices existing side by side:[123] "On the one hand, anxiety that baptismal grace might be lost by post-baptismal sin led to its prolonged delay. On the other hand, anxiety that sudden premature death would result in the eternal loss of an unbaptized child led to the baptism of infants as soon after birth as possible."[124] It seems that both ideas are based on the same understanding of the effect of baptism for salvation, but that one focuses more on the effect of baptism on past sins while the other focuses on the danger of future sins. Both practices developed gradually and their appearance cannot be clearly dated. Tertullian, for example, cautioned against both tendencies.[125]

---

120. Tertullian, for example in *De Poenitentia* 6.3-24, opposed this tendency.

121. Basil the Great, Hom. 13, *Exhortatoria ad sanctum baptisma*; see Jeremias, *Infant Baptism in the First Four Centuries*, 89.

122. Gregory Nazianzen, Oration 20, "On the Holy Baptism," 28; see Konstantin Scouteris, "Baptism and Original Sin", in V. Международная Богословская Конференция Русской Православной Церкви, *Православное учение о церковних таинствах*, том I, Синодальная Библейско-богословская комиссия Москва, 2009, 336.

123. Kevin Roy, *Baptism, Reconciliation and Unity*, Paternoster Press, Carlisle, UK, 1997, 56.

124. Ibid., 56.

125. Ibid., 57.

After the 4th century infant baptism prevailed and became the norm. Augustine, for example, is a strong defender of infant baptism. He writes to the Pelagians[126] "that they would have reason to fear that men would spit in their faces and women would throw their sandals at their heads if they dared to say of infants 'let them not be baptized.'"[127]

The reasons for the origin of infant baptism are not very clear. Different explanations have been advanced by scholars, such as the solidarity of the family in ancient societies[128] or the acceptance of a doctrine of original sin.[129] Based on inscriptions, Ferguson sees a strong influence of John 3:5 in the 2nd century as "requiring the necessity of baptism for entrance into heaven. When a child of Christian parents became seriously ill, there was the natural human concern about the welfare of the child's soul."[130] With a high infant mortality rate, this kind of emergency baptism was a visible, existential reality and led eventually to infant baptism as the normal practice. Roy also credits the development of Christianity as the state religion, with the effect that forgiveness of sins committed after baptism came to be seen as possible.[131] The Council of Carthage in 417 declared it anathema to say that newborn children should not be baptized.

The Baptism of Heretics in the Early Church

In the middle of the 3rd century a conflict occurred between Rome and Carthage over the question whether *heretics[132]—i.e. persons who followed a teaching which had been discerned by the synodical

---

126. Augustine, *Contra Iulianum Pelagianum* III, 5.11. in "Contra Iulianum libri VI" (P.L., XLIV, 640 sqq.), engl.:The Works of Saint Augustine: A Translation for the 21st Century, ed. J. E. Rotelle, New City Press, New York, 1990-, Vol. I.

127. See Jeremias, *Infant Baptism in the First Four Centuries*, 97.

128. Ibid., 19-58.

129. Kurt Aland, *Did the Early Church Baptize Infants?* Westminster Press, Philadelphia, 1963, 100-111.

130. Ferguson, *Baptism in the Early Church*, 378ff.

131. Roy, *Baptism, Reconciliation and Unity*, 58.

132. The specific case was that of the so-called Novatians, followers of a rival bishop to the bishop of Rome named Novatian.

decision to be unacceptable - needed to be baptized upon converting to the officially recognized faith. Cyprian of Carthage stands in opposition to bishop Stephen of Rome, who is of the opinion that a baptism in the name of the triune God is valid independently of the person of the baptizer. This is because it is God who causes the effect of a sacrament. If someone who has been baptized by a heretic wants to enter the church, according to Stephen, all that is required is a laying on of hands.[133] Cyprian, on the other hand, thinks that the Holy Spirit is at work only within the church; therefore there is no valid baptism outside of the one church.[134] The slogan *extra ecclesiam nulla salus*—outside of the church, there is no salvation— is attributed to him.

The Roman position somehow prevailed in the West and was confirmed at the Council of Arles (314), but the Council of Nicea (325) confirmed Cyprian's position, at least in relation to a group known as the Paulianists.[135]

In the 4th century a similar conflict occurred around an opposition group known as the Donatists.[136] The Donatists held a rigorist view of the church as a community of perfect saints in which there was no room for sinners. They excluded especially people who, during the persecutions of Christians, had denied their faith and later wanted to come back to the church. The Donatists declared that sacraments conducted by a priest who had denied his Christian faith during the persecution were null and void and thus re-baptized followers of such priests. Augustine, on the contrary, understood the effect of the sacrament as independent from the dignity of the priest because in the sacrament it is Christ himself who is the actor. The priest is only an instrument or a mediator; the power of the divine word is greater than the human action.[137]

---

133. Quoted by Cyprian of Carthage in Ep. 74,1,2.

134. Cyprian of Carthage, Ep. 69,7,2 and Ep. 69,11,2-3.

135. Council of Nicea, Canon 19. Paulinianists were followers of Paul of Samosata, bishop of Antioch (260-268), excommunicated because of his adoptionist teaching that Jesus was a normal human being.

136. So called because they were followers of Donatus of Carthage (315-355).

137. Augustine, Tractates on the Gospel of John 80,3. See http://www.new advent.org/fathers/1701.htm

Baptism in the Middle Ages

The Council of Chalcedon in 451 brought an end to a first important phase of Christian history. It witnessed the first serious schism between the church in the Roman Empire (with Rome and Constantinople as centers) and the "Oriental" churches, which did not accept the decisions of Chalcedon about the nature of Christ. The Oriental churches developed their own liturgies, for example the Coptic, Syriac and Armenian liturgies.

The church in the Roman Empire, however, had its own divisions: the East, with Constantinople (Byzantium) as its center and the West, with Rome as its center, had different histories and developed differences in their liturgical life. In the West the Roman papacy established its power, which led to the Roman rite becoming the prevailing model while the churches under Byzantine influence developed their own rite.

BAPTISM IN THE BYZANTINE MIDDLE AGES

By the year 600 at the latest, infant baptism had become the normal feature in the East, which meant that the catechumenate could not be practiced as before. Nevertheless the process of initiation was retained. According to Stefanos Alexopoulos[138] three developments characterize the change which took place: (1) the sacrament of initiation slowly disappeared from public worship; (2) there was an adaptation, and an addition, of prayers for children; and (3) all rites and cultic actions which were connected to catecheses were collected into rites which were performed before baptism. These pre-baptismal rites contained three different prayers: on the first day, on the eighth day, and on the fortieth day after birth. Except for the first, these prayers were originally related to adults and came to be used for children who were consequently treated as adults. In the 12th and 13th century a few more prayers were added, focusing more on the purification of the mother after birth.

---

138. Stefanos Alexopoulos, "Gestalt und Deutung der christlichen Initiation im mittelalterlichen Byzanz," in Lange et al., *Die Taufe: Einführung in Geschichte und Praxis*, 49-66.

For adult candidates the catechumenate began, according to the Codex Barberini gr.336,[139] with a series of rites (taking off the outer garments and shoes, threefold breathing on the candidate, turning to the East, unction of forehead, mouth and breast with the sign of the cross). However, the catechumenate was no longer practiced as it had been in the early church. Candidates were only asked to know the creed by heart.[140]

During the time of preparation a series of exorcisms was performed.

The last steps on the way to baptism were the rites of renunciation of Satan and the acceptance of Christ on Good Friday (as was the case in liturgies in Constantinople). The candidates had to turn to the West and to renounce Satan and spit on him.[141] They then turned to the East in order to accept Christ. After the sign of peace the candidates took off clothes and shoes. The bishop then laid his hands on them.

In this rite, the baptism proper begins, after various prayers, with the blessing of the baptismal water, which ends with the greeting of peace. Then the oil for the pre-baptismal anointing is blessed and poured into the water three times. The candidates are anointed by the priest on the forehead, breast and back with the sign of the cross. Then the deacon anoints the body of the candidate. Baptism follows with threefold immersion.

After this the candidates are anointed with chrism (forehead, nostrils, mouth and ears), which is understood as the seal of the gift of the Holy Spirit.[142]

---

139. The Codex Barberini gr.336, dated to the second half of the 8th century, is the oldest manuscript containing the Byzantine Euchologion, i.e. the liturgical book which presents the eucharistic prayers, the presidential prayers of the liturgy of the hours, the rites of the sacraments and a large collection of blessings and prayers for various situations and necessities.

140. Alexopoulos, "Gestalt und Deutung der christlichen Initiation im mittelalterlichen Byzanz," 51.

141. The spitting is a later custom, appearing for the first time in a manuscript of the 13th century.

142. Alexopoulos, "Gestalt und Deutung der christlichen Initiation im mittelalterlichen Byzanz," 56.

The Byzantine rite also has two additional post-baptismal rituals, *ablution and *tonsure. The ablution takes place eight days after baptism, the tonsure at the candidate's first haircut following baptism.

Some manuscripts also mention a post-baptismal crowning and the removal of the crown a week later.

In the 13th and 14th century at the latest, we know that these rites were celebrated with mothers and their children.

For the understanding of baptism in the Byzantine Middle Ages, two commentaries are of major importance, those of Nicolas Cabasilas (ca. 1319-1397) and Symeon of Thessaloniki (+1429).

In book 1 of his *Life in Christ*, Cabasilas writes:

> *In the sacred Mysteries, then, we depict His burial and we proclaim His death. By them we are begotten and formed and wondrously united to the Saviour, for they are the means by which, as Paul says, "in Him we live, and move, and have our being. (Acts 17:28)." Baptism confers being and in short, existence according to Christ. It receives us when we are dead and corrupted and first leads us into life. The anointing with chrism perfects him, who has received [new] birth by infusing into him the energy that befits such a life. The holy Eucharist preserves and continues this life and health, since the Bread of Life enables us to preserve that which has been acquired and to continue in life. It is therefore by this Bread that we live and by the chrism that we are moved, once we have received being from the baptismal washing.*[143]

Baptism, chrismation and eucharist are clearly distinguished, but belong together. In Book II this close connection is confirmed and further explained. Baptism is participation in the dying and rising of Christ; anointing is participation in the royal and divine chrism; the eucharist is participation in the body and the blood of Christ. Baptism is a birth, the chrism gives energy and movement and the eucharist is true food and drink. Baptism reconciles the

---

143. Nicholas Cabasilas, *The Life in Christ*, Book I.6, St. Vladimir's Seminary Press, Crestwood, 1974, 49ff.

human being with God, chrismation prepares him or her to receive the gifts which follow baptism, especially the eucharist. Baptism is a washing which is at the same time birth and beginning of the life in Christ.[144] Chrismation is clearly related to the conferring of the Holy Spirit.[145]

Symeon of Thessaloniki, in his work *On the Sacraments*, supports the traditional unity of baptism, chrismation and eucharist. In contrast to Nicholas Cabasilas, he emphasizes more the Pauline understanding of baptism as imitating Jesus' death and resurrection.[146]

BAPTISM IN THE MIDDLE AGES IN THE WEST

In the West in the early Middle Ages the baptism of infants also became more and more common. This led to the disappearance of the traditional catechumenate. The phase of direct preparation for baptism became characterized by the scrutinies. Originally the bishop examined the effect of those exorcisms in the celebration of mass during Lent, but with the prevalence of infant baptism this sense of examination was more and more lost:[147] the long period of the catechumenate disappeared and exorcisms appeared instead of instruction.[148] Stephan Wahle also observes a ritualization in which it was more important that the rite be performed in its traditional form than that it be understood by the people.[149]

For the Roman liturgy in the early Middle Ages (7th century), the main sources are especially the Gelasian Sacramentary (*Sacramentarium Gelasianum*) and the *Ordo Romanus XI*.[150] These became

---

144. See ibid., Book III.3.

145. Ibid., Book III.4.

146. Alexopoulos, "Gestalt und Deutung der christlichen Initiation im mittelalterlichen Byzanz," 61.

147. Stephan Wahle, "Gestaltung und Deutung der christlichen Initiation im mittelalterlichen lateinischen Westen," in Lange et al., *Die Taufe: Einführung in Geschichte und Praxis*, 30.

148. J. D. C. Fisher, *Christian Initiation: Baptism in the Medieval West; A Study in the Disintegration of the Primitive Rite of Initiation*, SPCK, London, 1965, 7ff.

149. Wahle, "Gestaltung und Deutung der christlichen Initiation im mittelalterlichen lateinischen Westen," 32.

150. English texts in Whitaker, *Documents of the Baptismal Liturgy*, 156-193.

normative in the West. Baptism, according to these sources, is still ideally conducted in the Easter Vigil or at Pentecost. [151]

From the Gelasian Sacramentary it can be seen that the rite was conducted for an infant as it was for an adult, but that in the rite for an infant, an *acolyte places his hand upon the head of the infant, answers the questions of the priest, and recites the creed,[152] "thus representing the best that can be done to create the appearance that the candidate is personally confessing his faith."[153]

The baptismal rite itself starts with a blessing of the font, ending with an epiclesis:[154] "May the power of thy Holy Spirit descend into all the water of this font and make the whole substance of this water fruitful with regenerating power." In the *Ordo Romanus* chrism is poured into the water. What follows is a creed in answers to three questions, after which the candidates are "dipped" three times into the water. Immediately after baptism there follows an anointing of the head with chrism by the presbyter, signifying the gift of eternal salvation.[155] Then comes a vesting in white robes and an invocation of the sevenfold grace of the Holy Spirit. The bishop prays by laying his hands on the head of the baptized and makes the sign of the cross on the forehead. The rite concludes with the eucharist.

From a letter of the bishops in the Carolingian Empire in 812 we have proof that in practice—and in opposition to the liturgical sources—baptism, post-baptismal chrismation by the priest and first eucharist were kept together, but that the laying on of hands and the sign of the cross on the forehead with chrism by the bishop were separate and happened at a later time.[156] This was an effect of the practice of infant baptism: it reflected the understanding that while the conferring of the Holy Spirit was reserved to the bishop,[157] the bishop was not able to be present at the baptism of

---

151. Fisher, *Christian Initiation*, 2ff.

152. See Whitaker, *Documents of the Baptismal Liturgy*, 165.

153. Fisher, *Christian Initiation*, 9ff.

154. Ibid., 12-16.

155. See ibid., 17ff.

156. See Wahle, "Gestaltung und Deutung der christlichen Initiation im mittelalterlichen lateinischen Westen," 34.

157. Cf. Pope Innocent I, Ep. 25, 3 in *PL* 20, 554. Innocent allows, though, that in the absence of a bishop a presbyter may confers this chrismation, though

every newborn infant. This was the beginning of the development which led in the Roman Catholic Church to the separation between baptism, chrismation and eucharist. In the East the whole rite of baptism, chrismation and eucharist was kept together, conducted by a presbyter,[158] while the link with the bishop was ensured by the blessing of the chrism by the bishop.

In the High Middle Ages the doctrine of baptism in the West was further developed through scholasticism, with the baptism of infants being justified through the idea of the vicarious faith of the church.[159]

Thomas Aquinas especially developed the teaching on baptism in his *Summa Theologiae*, where he writes:

> *In the sacrament of Baptism, three things may be considered: namely, that which is "sacrament only"; that which is "reality and sacrament"; and that which is "reality only." That which is sacrament only, is something visible and outward; the sign, namely, of the inward effect: for such is the very nature of a sacrament. And this outward something that can be perceived by the sense is both the water itself and its use, which is the washing. Hence some have thought that the water itself is the sacrament...*
>
> *But this is not true. For since the sacraments of the New Law effect a certain sanctification, there the sacrament is completed where the sanctification is completed. Now, the sanctification is not completed in water; but a certain sanctifying instrumental virtue, not permanent but transient, passes from the water, in which it is, into man who is the subject of true sanctification. Consequently the sacrament is not completed in the very water, but in applying the water to man, i.e. in the washing. Hence the Master (iv, 3) says that "Baptism is the outward washing of the body done together with the prescribed form of words."*
>
> *The Baptismal character is both reality and sacrament: because it is something real signified by the outward washing; and*

---

only with oil which was consecrated by a bishop.

158. Yarnold, "Taufe III," 690.

159. See Wilburn, "The One Baptism and the Many Baptisms," 93.

a sacramental sign of the inward justification: and this last is the reality only, in this sacrament—namely, the reality signified and not signifying...

That which is both sacrament and reality—i.e. the character—and that which is reality only—i.e. the inward justification—remain: the character remains and is indelible, as stated above (Question 63, Article 5); the justification remains, but can be lost.

Consequently Damascene defined Baptism, not as to that which is done outwardly, and is the sacrament only; but as to that which is inward. Hence he sets down two things as pertaining to the character—namely, "seal" and "safeguarding"; inasmuch as the character which is called a seal, so far as itself is concerned, safeguards the soul in good. He also sets down two things as pertaining to the ultimate reality of the sacrament—namely, "regeneration" which refers to the fact that man by being baptized begins the new life of righteousness; and "enlightenment," which refers especially to faith, by which man receives spiritual life, according to Habakkuk 2 (Hebrews 10:38; cf. Habakkuk 2:4): "But (My) just man liveth by faith"; and Baptism is a sort of protestation of faith; whence it is called the "Sacrament of Faith."...

When the words are added, the element becomes a sacrament, not in the element itself, but in man, to whom the element is applied, by being used in washing him. Indeed, this is signified by those very words which are added to the element, when we say: "I baptize thee," etc.

By Divine institution water is the proper matter of Baptism; and with reason. First, by reason of the very nature of Baptism, which is a regeneration unto spiritual life. And this answers to the nature of water in a special degree; wherefore seeds, from which all living things, viz. plants and animals are generated, are moist and akin to water...

Secondly, in regard to the effects of Baptism, to which the properties of water correspond. For by reason of its moistness it cleanses; and hence it fittingly signifies and causes the cleansing from sins. By reason of its coolness it tempers superfluous heat: wherefore it fittingly mitigates the concupiscence of the fomes. By reason of its transparency, it is susceptive of light; hence its adaptability to Baptism as the "sacrament of Faith."

Thirdly, because it is suitable for the signification of the mysteries of Christ, by which we are justified. For, as Chrysostom says (Hom. xxv in Joan.) on John 3:5, "Unless a man be born again," etc., "When we dip our heads under the water as in a kind of tomb our old man is buried, and being submerged is hidden below, and thence he rises again renewed."

Fourthly, because by being so universal and abundant, it is a matter suitable to our need of this sacrament: for it can easily be obtained everywhere...

Fire enlightens actively. But he who is baptized does not become an enlightener, but is enlightened by faith, which "cometh by hearing" (Romans 10:17). Consequently water is more suitable, than fire, for Baptism.

But when we find it said: "He shall baptize you in the Holy Ghost and fire," we may understand fire, as Jerome says (In Matth. ii), to mean the Holy Ghost, Who appeared above the disciples under the form of fiery tongues (Acts 2:3). Or we may understand it to mean tribulation, as Chrysostom says (Hom. iii in Matth.): because tribulation washes away sin, and tempers concupiscence. Or again, as Hilary says (Super Matth. ii) that "when we have been baptized in the Holy Ghost," we still have to be "perfected by the fire of the judgment."...

Wine and oil are not so commonly used for washing, as water. Neither do they wash so efficiently: for whatever is washed with them, contracts a certain smell therefrom; which is not the case if water be used. Moreover, they are not so universal or so abundant as water...

Water flowed from Christ's side to wash us; blood, to redeem us. Wherefore blood belongs to the sacrament of the Eucharist, while water belongs to the sacrament of Baptism. Yet this latter sacrament derives its cleansing virtue from the power of Christ's blood...

Christ's power flowed into all waters, by reason of, not connection of place, but likeness of species...

The blessing of the water is not essential to Baptism, but belongs to a certain solemnity, whereby the devotion of the faithful is aroused, and the cunning of the devil hindered from impeding the baptismal effect...

Action is attributed to an instrument as to the immediate agent; but to the principal agent inasmuch as the instrument acts in virtue thereof. Consequently it is fitting that in the baptismal form the minister should be mentioned as performing the act of baptizing, in the words, "I baptize thee"; indeed, our Lord attributed to the ministers the act of baptizing, when He said: "Baptizing them," etc. But the principal cause is indicated as conferring the sacrament by His own power, in the words, "in the name of the Father, and of the Son, and of the Holy Ghost": for Christ does not baptize without the Father and the Holy Ghost...

In the sacrament of Baptism water is put to the use of a washing of the body, whereby to signify the inward washing away of sins. Now washing may be done with water not only by immersion, but also by sprinkling or pouring. And, therefore, although it is safer to baptize by immersion, because this is the more ordinary fashion, yet Baptism can be conferred by sprinkling or also by pouring, according to Ezekiel 36:25: "I will pour upon you clean water" ... And this especially in cases of urgency: either because there is a great number to be baptized ... or through there being but a small supply of water, or through feebleness of the minister, who cannot hold up the candidate for Baptism; or through feebleness of the candidate, whose life might be endangered by immersion. We must therefore conclude that immersion is not necessary for Baptism...

What is accidental to a thing does not diversify its essence. Now bodily washing with water is essential to Baptism: wherefore Baptism is called a "laver," according to Ephesians 5:26: "Cleansing it by the laver of water in the word of life." But that the washing be done this or that way, is accidental to Baptism. And consequently such diversity does not destroy the oneness of Baptism...

Christ's burial is more clearly represented by immersion: wherefore this manner of baptizing is more frequently in use and more commendable. Yet in the other ways of baptizing it is represented after a fashion, albeit not so clearly; for no matter how the washing is done, the body of a man, or some part thereof, is put under water, just as Christ's body was put under the earth...

The principal part of the body, especially in relation to the exterior members, is the head, wherein all the senses, both interior and exterior, flourish. And therefore, if the whole body cannot be covered with water, because of the scarcity of water, or because of some other reason, it is necessary to pour water over the head, in which the principle of animal life is made manifest.

And although original sin is transmitted through the members that serve for procreation, yet those members are not to be sprinkled in preference to the head, because by Baptism the transmission of original sin to the offspring by the act of procreation is not deleted, but the soul is freed from the stain and debt of sin which it has contracted. Consequently that part of the body should be washed in preference, in which the works of the soul are made manifest...

Baptism cannot be reiterated.

First, because Baptism is a spiritual regeneration; inasmuch as a man dies to the old life, and begins to lead the new life. Whence it is written (John 3:5): "Unless a man be born again of water and the Holy Ghost, He cannot see [Vulgate: 'enter into'] the kingdom of God." Now one man can be begotten but once. Wherefore Baptism cannot be reiterated, just as neither can carnal generation. Hence Augustine says on John 3:4: "'Can he enter a second time into his mother's womb and be born again': So thou," says he, "must understand the birth of the Spirit, as Nicodemus understood the birth of the flesh ... As there is no return to the womb, so neither is there to Baptism."

Secondly, because "we are baptized in Christ's death," by which we die unto sin and rise again unto "newness of life" (cf. Romans 6:3-4). Now "Christ died" but "once" (Romans 6:10). Wherefore neither should Baptism be reiterated. For this reason (Hebrews 6:6) is it said against some who wished to be baptized again: "Crucifying again to themselves the Son of God"; on which the gloss observes: "Christ's one death hallowed the one Baptism."

Thirdly, because Baptism imprints a character, which is indelible, and is conferred with a certain consecration. Wherefore, just as other consecrations are not reiterated in the Church, so neither is Baptism. This is the view expressed by Augustine, who says (Contra Epist. Parmen. ii) that "the military character is not renewed": and that "the sacrament of Christ is not less enduring than this bodily mark, since we see that not even apostates are deprived of Baptism, since when they repent and return they are not baptized anew."

Fourthly, because Baptism is conferred principally as a remedy against original sin. Wherefore, just as original sin is not renewed, so neither is Baptism reiterated, for as it is written (Romans 5:18), "as by the offense of one, unto all men to condemnation, so also by the justice of one, unto all men to justification of life."...

The use of water in Baptism is part of the substance of the sacrament; but the use of oil or chrism is part of the solemnity. For the candidate is first of all anointed with Holy oil on the breast and between the shoulders, as "one who wrestles for God," to use Ambrose's expression (De Sacram. i): thus are prize-fighters wont to besmear themselves with oil. Or, as Innocent III says in a decretal on the Holy Unction: "The candidate is anointed on the breast, in order to receive the gift of the Holy Ghost, to cast off error and ignorance, and to acknowledge the true faith, since 'the just man liveth by faith'; while he is anointed between the shoulders, that he may be clothed with the grace of the Holy Ghost, lay aside indifference and sloth, and become active in good works; so that the sacrament of faith may purify the thoughts of his heart, and strengthen his shoulders for the burden of labor." But after Baptism, as Rabanus says (De Sacram. iii), "he is forthwith anointed on the head by the priest with Holy Chrism, who proceeds at once to offer up a prayer that the neophyte may have a share in Christ's kingdom, and be called a Christian after Christ." Or, as Ambrose says (De Sacram. iii), his head is anointed, because "the senses of a wise man are in his head" (Ecclesiastes 2:14): to wit, that he may "be ready to satisfy everyone that asketh" him to give "a reason of his faith" (cf. 1 Peter 3:15; Innocent III, Decretal on Holy Unction)...

This white garment is given, not as though it were unlawful for the neophyte to use others: but as a sign of the glorious resurrection, unto which men are born again by Baptism; and in order to designate the purity of life, to which he will be bound after being baptized, according to Romans 6:4: "That we may walk in newness of life.".....

Although those things that belong to the solemnity of a sacrament are not essential to it, yet are they not superfluous, since they pertain to the sacrament's wellbeing, as stated above.[160]

Aquinas distinguishes two effects of baptism: the washing away of sin and the release from punishment. In baptism, the salvation, which has been achieved in Christ, is *realiter* (in reality) given to be owned by the sinner. The water is the material of the sacrament, but it contains a *sanctificationis virtus instrumentalis (instrumental power of sanctification)*.[161]

In the High Middle Ages there also appeared groups which either rejected baptism completely (in Aquitaine and Orleans in the 11th century) or which rejected infant baptism (Henry of Lausanne, 12th century).[162] In the mid-12th century occurred the large "heretical" movements of the Cathars and Waldensians, which were—in part—wrongly suspected of being against infant baptism.[163] John Wycliff and Jan Hus were radically opposed to the exorcisms in the baptismal liturgy, mainly using the argument that they are not biblical.

Summary

While Western theology had a strong interest in the *relationship* between sign (*signum*) and thing (*res*)[164] the East emphasized the *identity* between the two. Commonly in the East and the West

---

160. Thomas Aquinas, *Summa Theologica* III, q. 66.

161. Ibid.

162. See Wilburn, "The One Baptism and the Many Baptisms," 88.

163. Jörg Ulrich, "Taufe IV: Mittelalter," *Theologische Realenzyklopädie* 32, 699.

164. See Thomas Aquinas.

Baptism is understood as the first mystery which gives access to the other mysteries. The aspects of rebirth and illumination are emphasized. Baptism makes it possible for the human being to live a life according to God's will. What happens in baptism is not to be grasped by human reasoning.

Baptism in the Time of Reformation

The Reformation in the 16th century deeply changed the ecclesial landscape in the West. Part of this new picture was a changed understanding of baptism.

For Martin Luther, and also for John Calvin, baptism is based on God's promise (*promissio*), on the visible sign which God gave, and on God's institution of the sacramental practice. These three factors become the criteria for the understanding of sacrament. The act of baptism, in the eyes of Luther, has no value without faith; consequently he stresses the aspect of a lifelong process which begins with baptism. While the sacrament of baptism is an outward purification, a purification also takes place inwardly.

At the same time the forerunners of the Radical Reformation developed a critical relationship to baptism. For example Andreas Bodenstein, called Karlstadt (ca. 1480-1541), emphasized baptism in the Spirit as being more important than water baptism. Consequently he rejected infant baptism.

Ulrich Zwingli was, in a way, also critical of the traditional understanding of baptism. For him the sacrament is only a sign, not a means of grace. Baptism becomes a sign of commitment to belonging to the Christian community. But for Zwingli this does not lead to a rejection of infant baptism; rather he retained the practice of infant baptism, as did the other reformers.[165] Philipp Melanchthon, who became influential in formulating the basic theology of the reformation, also underlines the necessity of infant baptism for salvation.

The understanding of baptism as an act exclusively for persons who can confess their faith became prevalent in the *Anabaptist

---

165. See Chapter One, above.

movement. This movement had multiple origins, on the one hand in the Reformation in Zürich, and on the other hand through influences of the so-called *enthusiasts[166] and others. The Anabaptists, reading holy scripture, discovered that in the New Testament most persons first believed in the gospel which they heard and then were baptized upon request. Consequently they questioned whether an infant in its inner being could respond to the movement of the Holy Spirit. "They were most concerned that believers correctly understood the implications of baptism for a life of discipleship."[167] Finally, they did not count baptism as a sacrament, but as an action commanded by Christ. "It is a particular event within a larger process in which a person hears the gospel preached and taught, confesses, repents, is forgiven, is regenerated, requests baptism, is incorporated into the church, and remains a disciple."[168] In 1527, in a meeting in Schleitheim, the Anabaptists clearly rejected infant baptism. Balthasar Hubmaier, a former Catholic professor of theology, formulated the new faith: water baptism is just an external sign for confession of faith, with which the believer integrates himself into the community of the reborn. With baptism a person submits him- or herself to the discipline of the congregation. For Hubmaier the order within this process was word–listening–faith–baptism–works. He rejects the idea that one person could confess faith on behalf of another.

A slightly different understanding of baptism is represented by Hans Hut, who understands water baptism as the agreement of a human being to receive the inner baptism which consists in suffering.

After the fall of the self-proclaimed "kingdom of God" in Münster (1535), the spiritual and apocalyptic understanding of baptism

---

166. In German "Schwärmer": people who base their opinions on visions and other super-natural phenomena and act with a certain fanatism.

167. Rebecca Slough, "Baptismal Practice among North American Mennonites," in Thomas F. Best, ed., *Baptism Today: Understanding, Practice, Ecumenical Implications*, Faith & Order Paper No. 207, WCC Publications, Geneva and Liturgical Press, Collegeville, MN, 2008, 89.

168. Ibid., 89ff.

disappeared among the Anabaptists, but the idea of Spirit baptism and the rejection of infant baptism remained.

In the Roman Catholic Church during the same era, the Council of Trent (1545-1563) was decisive in bringing reforms. It did not, however, bring a new doctrine of baptism but rather confirmed the Roman Catholic Church's distance from the Reformation as well as from the Anabaptist understanding of baptism. This means that it retained infant baptism and the sacramental character of baptism. Against the reformers, Trent rejects the notion that sins which were committed after baptism would be forgiven purely through remembrance and faith in that baptism which had already been received. Rather, Trent insisted on the sacrament of repentance. Baptism takes away original sin; it is a means to convey the grace of God.

Developments after the Reformation until Today

The development of baptism and baptismal theology has been manifold since the Reformation. The following presentation will only give a rough overview of the most important developments in Western Christianity,[169] especially in the perspective of their ecumenical relevance. A more systematic discussion will follow in Chapter Four.

For the time after the Reformation Bryan D. Spinks[170] identifies five different forms of the baptismal order for the Western churches, depending on different theological understandings of baptism:

a. The Roman baptismal rite of 1614, which prescribed an order for infant baptism and an order for adult baptism. The old exorcisms were kept; the order prescribed baptism by immersion, which, however, disappeared in practice. Confirmation, which was considered a separate sacrament, was to be given

---

169. As in the East, after the schism of the 11th century, no new ideas concerning the understanding and practice of baptism were discussed, this section focuses on discussions in Western Christianity.

170. Bryan D. Spinks, "Taufe VI: Neuzeit," *Theologische Realenzyklopädie* 32, 710-719.

by the bishop immediately after baptism, but in practice this was very seldom the case.

b. In the Lutheran orders for baptism based on Luther's order of baptism from 1526, some old parts of the ritual were removed, such as the blessing of the water and especially the anointings. The center of the event was the promise of baptism and the baptismal act, that is, the trinitarian formula and the water baptism. Luther himself promoted baptism by immersion, but this was very seldom practiced. He also retained the exorcisms.

c. The Reformed tradition also removed the anointing and the exorcisms. Instead of baptismal *sponsors, a commitment by the parents is included in the ritual. In prayers and formulas there is a reference to the Old Testament concept of covenant.

d. Under the influence of Thomas Cranmer, the Church of England, and later the Anglican Communion, removed the exorcisms and the anointings, but kept the baptismal sponsors and did not take over the covenant theology. Cranmer defended infant baptism by referring to Mk 10:13-16. Confirmation, as given by the bishop, is kept with a prayer for empowerment (instead of a prayer for the gift of the Spirit) and remains in close connection with formation in faith. Confirmation was initially a precondition for receiving communion.

e. The fifth sort of baptismal order was developed within the communities of the Anabaptists. Hubmaier defined baptism as a threefold act: the first part is the illumination of the new convert through the word, which is initiated by the Spirit; the second part is the water baptism as public testimony of faith; and the third part is the blood baptism, which means the killing of the flesh until the end of life. The baptismal order contains an invocation of the Holy Spirit, the confession of faith, and immersion, as well as an exhortation to leading a Christian life. Other Anabaptist groups did not produce a written order of baptism.

During the latter part of the 17th century the theology of baptism was further developed and discussed. During the period of Lutheran Orthodoxy, a whole series of arguments for the necessity of infant baptism was found: the general necessity of salvation, the commandment of Christ, the general promise of salvation in Acts 2:38ff., the closeness of children to the kingdom of God (Mk 10:14) as well as the tradition of the early church. The exorcisms were understood more and more as *adiaphora*, not necessary for the faith, and finally disappeared.

In the 18th century, during the time of pietism and rationalism, the person's "inner experience" became more important. John Wesley, for example, removed the idea of rebirth in relation to baptism: rebirth cannot happen through the external act of baptism. In Lutheran liturgical formulas in Germany and Scandinavia, the influence of pietism is also visible.

In the 19th century, various movements initiated a new discovery of the sacraments. For example, the baptismal rite of the English-speaking Reformed churches was renewed in a way that combined a Catholic liturgy with Protestant spirituality and an emphasized eschatology. In Denmark the exorcisms were rediscovered (see, for instance, the Danish theologian Grundtvig). On the other hand, theologians such as Friedrich Schleiermacher were critical of infant baptism and saw the danger of a magical understanding of the sacraments.

In the 20th century the discussion about baptism was nurtured by the Reformed theologian Karl Barth's hesitation about infant baptism.[171] For Barth, "the ritual act is not itself the cause of regeneration; it only points back to what was already achieved by Jesus Christ."[172] Baptism, therefore, is "an active obedient response" which needs the human person as an active partner. Therefore infant baptism is only "half baptism" and is complete only after

---

171. See Bryan D. Spinks, *Reformation and Modern Rituals and Theologies of Baptism: From Luther to Contemporary Practices,* Ashgate Publishing, Aldershot, UK and Burlington, VT, 2006, 137-142.

172. Ibid., 138.

the profession of faith, which follows instruction.[173] This led to a defense of infant baptism by a number of other theologians, such as Oscar Cullmann and Joachim Jeremias.

Barth went even further and rejected the term "sacrament" for baptism.[174] He also strictly distinguished water baptism from baptism with the Holy Spirit, which is hoped to occur. Other Reformed and Lutheran theologians kept the terminology of "sacrament."

Another point of discussion in several churches and church families was the meaning and role of confirmation. In the second half of the 20th century many Protestant churches, under the influence of the ecumenical movement, changed their attitude towards confirmation and opened the eucharist to baptized children even before their confirmation.

In the Roman Catholic Church the Second Vatican Council changed, among other things, the fact that confirmation is no longer reserved for the bishop. In the Rite of Christian Initiation of Adults, the baptizing priest may confirm the newly baptized. For centuries now in the Roman Catholic Church, confirmation has no longer been a precondition for receiving the eucharist. Confirmation is still seen as a sacrament, but there is a tension in the understanding of its effect. This discussion has also taken place within the Anglican Communion. While the Anglican scholar Gregory Dix understood baptism as forgiveness of sins and confirmation as the conferring of the gifts of the Holy Spirit, others understood the water rite as a complete integration into the church and confirmation as a profession of faith by those who have been baptized as infants.[175]

In many 20th century baptismal orders of paedobaptist churches, the accent is no longer on the removal of original sin through baptism (Augustine), but more on integration into the body of Christ (Cyprian). The Roman Catholic Church has developed an order for

---

173. Karl Barth, *The Teaching of the Church regarding Baptism*, trans. Earnest Payne, SCM Press, London, 1948, 47.

174. Karl Barth, *Church Dogmatics IV*, 4, "The Doctrine of Reconciliation," ed. G. W. Bromiley and T. F. Torrance, T&T Clark International, London and New York, 1969.

175. See Spinks, "Taufe VI" .

initiation which emphasizes the understanding of baptism as part of a longer process. This has also influenced Anglican and Lutheran churches and their baptismal orders.

Within the Baptist churches in the 20th century, especially in Britain, Bryan Spinks states that there is "a tendency to find new emphasis in the divine action in the ritual of baptism, though without abandoning the emphasis on personal faith."[176] Therefore some Baptists nowadays consider infant baptism as valid in cases where it is part of an ongoing process of growth in faith.

With the growth of churches in the global South and through their independent development, several specific issues related to their various cultural contexts have emerged. Rituals, symbols and gestures originating in the respective cultural traditions have been developed as part of the baptismal rite, especially in African churches.[177] This has led, especially in the Lutheran World Federation and in the Roman Catholic Church, to a discussion about the inculturation of baptism.[178]

Another discussion, initiated by the feminist movement in the 20th century, takes up the question of the baptismal formula and tries to find possibilities for inclusive language.[179]

---

176. Spinks, *Reformation and Modern Rituals*, 158.

177. Some examples can be found in F. Kabasele Lumbala, "Black African and Baptismal Rites," in Thomas F. Best and Dagmar Heller, eds., *Becoming a Christian: The Ecumenical Implications of Our Common Baptism*, WCC Publications, Geneva, 1999, 36-40.

178. See Best and Heller, *Becoming a Christian*; S. Anita Stauffer, ed., *Baptism, Rites of Passage, and Culture*, Lutheran World Federation, Geneva, 1998; and F. Kabasele Lumbala, *Celebrating Jesus Christ in Africa: Liturgy and Inculturation*, Orbis, Maryknoll, NY, 1998.

179. See Ruth Duck, *Gender and the Name of God: The Trinitarian Baptismal Formula*, Pilgrim Press, Cleveland, 1991, discussed in Spinks, *Reformation and Reformation and Modern Rituals*, 158ff.

CHAPTER 3
Baptism in Ecumenical Discussion

Ecumenical discussions take place in different settings and on different levels: multilateral dialogues as well as bilateral dialogues are conducted on the international level and on regional, national and local levels.

This chapter will give an overview of the multilateral and bilateral discussions on baptism on the international level only. It will explore which issues related to baptism have been raised, and which solutions for common agreements have been proposed.

Baptism in Multilateral Discussions

FAITH AND ORDER BACKGROUND

The multilateral discussion on baptism on the international level started early in the 20th century with the work done by the Faith and Order movement, which became, with the foundation of the World Council of Churches (WCC) in 1948, the Commission on Faith and Order of the WCC. It has to be noted that this Commission is the most representative ecumenical international body because its by-laws provide the possibility for non-member churches of the WCC to send official delegates. This is the case at present for some Pentecostal and Evangelical churches, the Salvation Army, the Quakers and, since 1968, the Roman Catholic Church.

The first World Conference on Faith and Order in 1927 in Lausanne considered "the things wherein we agree and the things wherein we differ."[1] This was the first international conference at which theologians from the major traditions of Christianity came together. Their statement on baptism was rather brief:

> *We believe that in Baptism administered with water in the name of the Father, the Son, and the Holy Spirit, for the remission of sins, we are baptized by one Spirit into one body. By this statement it is not meant to ignore the differences in conception, interpretation, and mode which exist among us.*[2]

This was understood as a formulation of "fundamental agreement."[3]

Ten years later, at the second World Conference on Faith and Order in Edinburgh, the representatives from the different churches formulated together the following statement:

> *Baptism is a gift of God's redeeming love to the Church; and, administered with water in the name of the Father, the Son, and the Holy Spirit, is a sign and seal of Christian discipleship in obedience to our Lord's command.*
>
> [Here the text has a footnote with the following contents:]
> *"Baptist delegates desire to add as follows: as regards the above statement which has been passed by their brethren who practice infant Baptism, the Baptists could accept it as applying to the baptism of believers, i.e. of those who are capable of making a personal confession of faith. They believe that children belong to God*

---

1. Final Report, First World Conference on Faith and Order, August 3-21, 1927, quoted in Lukas Vischer, ed., *A Documentary History of the Faith & Order Movement 1927-1963*, Bethany Press, St. Louis, 1963, 27.

2. Ibid., 39.

3. Ibid., 27.

*and that no rite is needed to assure His grace for them. This state-
ment of the Baptists was accepted also by a representative of the
Disciples of Christ on behalf of that body"].*

*It is generally agreed that the united Church will observe
the rule that all members of the visible Church are admitted by
Baptism.*

*In the course of discussion it appeared that there were fur-
ther elements of faith and practice in relation to Baptism about
which disagreement existed. Since the time available precluded
the extended discussion of such points as baptismal regeneration,
the admission of unbaptized persons to Holy Communion, and
the relation of Confirmation to Baptism, we are unable to express
an opinion as to how far they would constitute obstacles to proposals for a united Church.[4]*

The focus here is clearly on the common convictions, which are

- Baptism is a gift of God.

- Baptism is performed with water and in the name of the
  Father, the Son and the Holy Spirit.

In comparison with the previous conference in Lausanne, we
note that while Lausanne understands baptism as being for the
remission of sins, Edinburgh defines it as a "sign and seal of Christian discipleship" and emphasizes obedience to the command of
Jesus Christ as its basis. At the Edinburgh conference the differences on baptism also received a clearer profile through the specific
statement of the Baptists in the footnote, and by the fact that they
are named in the second paragraph.

The third World Conference on Faith and Order in 1952 in
Lund (Sweden) demonstrated a remarkable shift in Faith and Order
methodology. The final report says:

---

4. Final Report, Second World Conference on Faith and Order, August 3-18,
1937, quoted in Vischer, *Documentary History*, 6.

We have seen clearly that we can make no real advance toward unity if we only compare our several conceptions of the nature of the Church and the traditions in which they are embedded. But once again it has been proved true that as we seek to draw closer to Christ we come closer to one another. We need, therefore, to penetrate behind our divisions to a deeper and richer understanding of the mystery of the God-given union of Christ with His Church. We need increasingly to realize that the separate histories of our Churches find their full meaning only if seen in the perspective of God's dealings with His whole people ... Should not our Churches ask themselves whether they are showing sufficient eagerness to enter into conversation with other Churches and whether they should not act together in all matters except those in which deep differences of conviction compel them to act separately? [5]

This text describes what has been called the "Lund principle," indicating the so- called "Christological method" which prevailed within the work of Faith and Order during subsequent decades. It represents a shift from a predominantly comparative methodology to a consensus method.

This method was developed further during the following years. In regard to Baptism, a study was undertaken which resulted in the publication of the book *One Lord, One Baptism*.[6] At the fourth World Conference on Faith and Order in 1963 in Montreal, the reference to this book in the report of Section IV led to a more detailed statement on the common understanding of baptism and to the following recommendations to the churches:

111 The book One Lord, One Baptism *has clearly shown how wide is the agreement amongst the churches with regard to baptism. There attention is focused upon the baptism with which Jesus himself was baptized (Mark 10.38). This began with his acceptance of*

---

5. Final Report, Third World Conference on Faith and Order August 15-28, 1952, quoted in Vischer, *Documentary History*, 85ff.

6. World Council of Churches, Theological Commission on Christ and the Church, *One Lord, One Baptism*, Faith and Order Paper No. 29, SCM Press and Augsburg Publishing House, London, 1961.

solidarity with sinners in his baptism in the Jordan and continued as he followed the path of the Suffering Servant through passion, death and resurrection. The Spirit that came upon Jesus comes also on the Church and unites his people with him in death and resurrection, in and through the baptismal action. Participation in Christ is the central meaning of baptism. Though disagreement remains between those who practise infant baptism and those who practise believer-baptism, all would insist that personal commitment is necessary for responsible membership in the body of Christ. For all, moreover, baptism is related not only to the individual but also to the Church, not only to momentary experience but to life-long growth of participation in Christ. Those who have been raised by the Holy Spirit to new life in Christ are led from baptism to confirmation (or its equivalent) and to Holy Communion. The life is necessarily one of continuing struggle but also of continuing experience of grace. In faith and obedience the baptized live for the sake of Christ, of his Church, and of the world which he loves.

112 We have found general agreement that the following elements should find a place within any comprehensive order of baptism:

(a) an acknowledgement of God's initiative in salvation, of his continuing faithfulness, and of our total dependence on his grace,

(b) a declaration of the forgiveness of sins in and through Christ,

(c) an invocation of the Holy Spirit,

(d) a renunciation of evil,

(e) a profession of faith in Christ,

(f) an affirmation that the person baptized is a child of God and is incorporated into the body of Christ, whereby he becomes a witness to the Gospel.

113 These will precede or follow baptism with water in the name of the Father and of the Son and of the Holy Spirit.

We make some practical recommendations to the churches:

(a) *Baptism is not solely a matter of individual concern, but is intimately connected with the corporate worship of the Church. It should normally be administered during a public service of worship, so that the members of the local congregation may be reminded of their own baptism, and may welcome into their fellowship those who are baptized and whom they are to nurture in the Christian faith.*

(b) *In order to make baptism more prominent in the life of the congregation, the sacrament might well be administered in public on great festival occasions, as was the practice of the Early Church. The use of Easter as one such occasion would emphasize the link between baptism and dying and rising with Christ.*

114 Instruction in the meaning of baptism should be provided regularly and systematically for the whole worshipping community.

115 In addition to instruction in the theological meaning of baptism, the churches must always remind their members that this sacrament, which binds men to Christ in community, brings to an end all human estrangements in both Church and world based on differences of race or class.[7]

BEM on Baptism

On this basis Faith and Order did further work on Baptism during the following years. The major result so far is the document on *Baptism, Eucharist and Ministry* (BEM),[8] also called the "Lima Document" in remembrance of the city of Lima (Peru), where the Faith and Order Commission adopted the final text in 1982.

---

7. Patrick C. Rodger and Lukas Vischer, eds., *The Fourth World Conference on Faith and Order: The Report from Montreal 1963*, Faith and Order Paper No. 42, SCM, London, 1964, 72ff.

8. World Council of Churches, Commission on Faith and Order, *Baptism, Eucharist and Ministry* (henceforth BEM), Faith and Order Paper No. 111, 25th Anniversary Printing, WCC Publications, Geneva, 1982-2007.

BEM: A Convergence Document

BEM represents a new genre of ecumenical theological texts known as "convergence documents." A convergence text is to be distinguished from a consensus text. It tries to formulate what the churches are able to say together; at the same time it looks into the remaining differences among the churches and tries to make proposals as to how their different positions could be brought together. Thus in BEM we find the main text, numbered in paragraphs, which formulates what the churches have in common, while commentaries, inserted in places, point out differences among the churches and reflect on how these differences could be overcome.

Reading this text, therefore, requires that the reader not look primarily at whether this text is in agreement with his or her church's teaching. Rather BEM requires readers to ask: Is this really what we, as Christians from different churches, can say together?

BEM on Baptism: Structure

The section of BEM dealing with baptism is divided into five parts: It begins with the foundation of baptism in the New Testament, namely its institution through Jesus Christ ("The Institution of Baptism") and its theological meaning as it can be discerned from the four gospels and the letters of Paul and other texts in the New Testament ("The Meaning of Baptism"). The third chapter ("Baptism and Faith") discusses the main theological issue which is raised especially in the ecumenical debate between churches which practice infant baptism and churches which do not recognize infant baptism as a true baptism: the relationship between baptism and faith. The fourth chapter takes up questions of "Baptismal Practice"—the baptism of believers and infant baptism as well as the relationship between baptism, chrismation and confirmation. The last chapter deals with liturgical questions ("The Celebration of Baptism").

From this structure we can draw the following conclusions:

- BEM starts from scripture as the common ground for all the churches.

- BEM focuses on a) the difference between churches which baptize only believers and churches which also baptize infants, and b) the difference arising from different practices of chrismation and confirmation as they relate to baptism.

- BEM understands the differences with regard to baptism as differences in baptismal *practice*.

BEM on Baptism: Common Positions

The common starting point for BEM is the institution of baptism by Jesus Christ:

> *Christian baptism is rooted in the ministry of Jesus of Nazareth, in his death and in his resurrection ... St Matthew records that the risen Lord, when sending his disciples into the world, commanded them to baptize (Matt.28:18-20). The universal practice of baptism by the apostolic Church from its earliest days is attested in letters of the New Testament, the Acts of the Apostles, and the writings of the Fathers...*[9]

The meaning of baptism is described as "the sign of new life through Jesus Christ," which "unites the one baptized with Christ and with his people."[10] This fundamental meaning is developed in five aspects, drawing on the texts of the New Testament:

> *A. Participation in Christ's Death and Resurrection ...* *By baptism, Christians are immersed in the liberating death of Christ where their sins are buried, where the "old Adam" is crucified with Christ, and where the power of sin is broken ... Fully identified with the death of Christ, they are buried with him and are raised here and now to a new life in the power of the resurrection of Jesus Christ, confident that they will also ultimately be one with him in a resurrection like his. (Rom. 6:3-11; Col. 2:13, 3:1; Eph. 2:5-6)* [11]

---

9. BEM, "Baptism," par. 1.
10. Ibid., par. 2.
11. Ibid., par. 3.

B. Conversion, Pardoning and Cleansing ... *The baptism administered by John was itself a baptism of repentance for the forgiveness of sins (Mark 1:4). The New Testament underlines the ethical implications of baptism by representing it as an ablution which washes the body with pure water, a cleansing of the heart of all sin, and an act of justification (Heb. 10:22; I Peter 3:21; Acts 22:16; I Cor. 6:11) Thus those baptized are pardoned, cleansed and sanctified by Christ, and are given as part of their baptismal experience a new ethical orientation under the guidance of the Holy Spirit.*[12]

C. The Gift of the Spirit *The Holy Spirit is at work in the lives of people before, in and after their baptism. It is the same Spirit who revealed Jesus as the Son (Mark 1:10f.) and who empowered and united the disciples at Pentecost (Acts 2).*[13]

D. Incorporation into the Body of Christ ... *Through baptism, Christians are brought into union with Christ, with each other and with the Church of every time and place."* [From this aspect BEM draws the conclusion that:] *our common baptism, which unites us to Christ in faith, is thus a basic bond of unity... The union with Christ which we share through baptism has important implications for Christian unity.... When baptismal unity is realized in one holy, catholic, apostolic Church, a genuine Christian witness can be made to the healing and reconciling love of God. Therefore, our one baptism into Christ constitutes a call to the churches to overcome their divisions and visibly manifest their fellowship.*[14]

E. The Sign of the Kingdom *Baptism initiates the reality of the new life given in the midst of the present world... It is a sign of the Kingdom of God and of the life of the world to come. Through the gifts of faith, hope and love, baptism has a dynamic which*

---

12. Ibid., par. 4.
13. Ibid., par. 5.
14. Ibid., par. 6.

embraces the whole of life, extends to all nations, and anticipates
the day when every tongue will confess that Jesus Christ is Lord to
the glory of God the Father.[15]

Concerning the relationship between baptism and faith (part III), BEM states that "Baptism is both God's gift and our human response to that gift … The necessity of faith for the reception of the salvation embodied and set forth in baptism is acknowledged by all churches. Personal commitment is necessary for responsible membership in the body of Christ."[16] Therefore "baptism is related not only to momentary experience, but to life-long growth into Christ."[17] It "has ethical implications which not only call for personal sanctification, but also motivate Christians to strive for the realization of the will of God in all realms of life (Rom 6:9ff.; Gal 3:27-28; 1 Pet 2:21- 4:6)."[18]

Part IV on "Baptismal Practice" takes up, in its first part,[19] the crucial problem in the ecumenical debates about the two principal forms of baptismal practice: the baptism of infants and the baptism of believers.[20] BEM says that both forms are, in one way or another, grounded in the New Testament: the baptism of believers is more clearly testified in the New Testament, but the baptism of infants cannot be excluded either, having taken place in the earliest times: "While the possibility that infant baptism was also practiced in the apostolic age cannot be excluded, baptism upon personal

---

15. Ibid., par. 7.
16. Ibid., par. 8.
17. Ibid., par. 9.
18. Ibid., par. 10.
19. BEM IV.A. in IV, "Baptismal Practice."
20. The expression "baptism of believers" is problematic for two reasons: (1) It is ambiguous on the question whether mentally disabled persons fall under this category, and (2) it implies that infants do not have faith (a position which would be denied by most churches which baptize infants). The expression is used, however, by BEM and, for the sake of brevity, will also be used here to mean "persons who are able to express their own faith." See also BEM, "Baptism," Commentary 12: "When the expressions 'infant baptism' and 'believers' baptism' are used, it is necessary to keep in mind that the real distinction is between those who baptize people at any age and those who baptize only those able to make a confession of faith for themselves."

profession of faith is the most clearly attested pattern in the New Testament documents."[21]

These two different baptismal forms are a result of historical development: "Some churches baptize infants brought by parents or guardians who are ready, in and with the Church, to bring up the children in the Christian faith. Other churches practice exclusively the baptism of believers who are able to make a personal confession of faith."[22] But both sides are of the common opinion that "baptism is an unrepeatable act."[23]

A second difference in the practice of baptism is addressed under the heading "Baptism–Chrismation–Confirmation,"[24] which refers to a difference between the Western churches and the Eastern churches: the Western churches have an additional rite in which the baptized persons confess their faith before they are accepted as full members of the church. This is confirmation. For the Orthodox, baptism cannot be separated from chrismation and is immediately followed by the Eucharist. In other words, baptism and chrismation together–as two sacraments distinguished from one another, but always performed together–effect full membership in the body of Christ. Therefore, the baptized person (the child) immediately takes part in the eucharist.

The difference here is, according to BEM, in the "understanding as to where the sign of the gift of the Spirit is to be found."[25]

According to the authors of BEM, churches can say together that "participation in Christ's death and resurrection is inseparably linked with the receiving of the Spirit. Baptism in its full meaning signifies and effects both." BEM also states: "All agree that Christian baptism is in water and the Holy Spirit."[26]

The last part of the text, "The Celebration of Baptism,"[27] describes the liturgical elements used in the celebration of baptism.

---

21. Ibid., par. 11.
22. Ibid., par. 11.
23. Ibid., par. 13.
24. BEM IV.B. in IV, "Baptismal Practice."
25. Ibid., par. 14.
26. Ibid.
27. BEM, "Baptism," V, "The Celebration of Baptism."

"Baptism is administered with water in the name of the Father, the Son and the Holy Spirit."[28] The text emphasizes the symbolic meaning of liturgical gestures and recommends their practice in order better to express the meaning of baptism through the celebration. For example, "the symbolic dimension of water should be taken seriously and not minimalized. The act of immersion can vividly express the reality that in baptism the Christian participates in the death, burial and resurrection of Christ."[29] Likewise, additional symbolic gestures are recommended[30] and the elements of a "comprehensive order of baptism"[31] are listed. Finally the text recommends that baptism be administered "normally ... during public worship."[32]

BEM on Baptism: Differences and Their Solutions

In general, BEM tries to bring the different sides in each of the two main positions closer to one another. Concerning the difference between believers' baptism and infant baptism, it is important to note that the crucial idea is to understand infant baptism and believers' baptism as two different ways of practicing one and the same baptism. This is developed mainly in Paragraph 11: "In the course of history the practice of baptism has developed in a variety of forms. Some churches baptize infants ... Other churches practice exclusively the baptism of believers who are able to make a personal confession of faith."

A way forward is offered in Commentary 12: "The differences between infant and believers' baptism become less sharp when it is recognized that both forms of baptism embody God's own initiative in Christ and express a response of faith made within the believing community." The commentary continues by explaining the two practices, saying that each of them emphasizes a particular aspect of baptism, namely the corporate faith on the one hand and the person's explicit confession on the other:

---

28. Ibid., par. 17.
29. Ibid., par. 18.
30. Cf. ibid., par. 19.
31. Ibid., par. 20.
32. Ibid., par. 23.

The practice of infant baptism emphasizes the corporate faith and the faith which the child shares with its parents ... Through baptism, the promise and claim of the Gospel are laid upon the child. The personal faith of the recipient of baptism and faithful participation in the life of the Church are essential for the full fruit of baptism. The practice of believers' baptism emphasizes the explicit confession of the person who responds to the grace of God in and through the community of faith and who seeks baptism.

The commentary ends with two concrete proposals, beginning with this one: "Both forms of baptism require a similar and responsible attitude towards Christian nurture. A rediscovery of the continuing character of Christian nurture may facilitate the mutual acceptance of different initiation practices." The second proposal states: "In some churches which unite both infant-baptist and believer-baptist traditions, it has been possible to regard as equivalent alternatives for entry into the Church both a pattern whereby baptism in infancy is followed by later profession of faith and a pattern whereby believers' baptism follows upon a presentation and blessing in infancy. This example invites other churches to decide whether they, too, could not recognize equivalent alternatives in their reciprocal relationships and in church union negotiations."

Concerning the second difference, which is related to the understanding of the gift of the Holy Spirit, BEM simply gives a summary description of the situation[33] and suggests to churches which do not allow children to partake in the eucharist before confirmation that they "may wish to ponder whether they have fully appreciated and accepted the consequences of baptism."[34]

BEM on Baptism: The Way toward Mutual Recognition of Baptism

An extra sub-chapter looks into the way "Towards Mutual Recognition of Baptism."[35] Astonishingly, this chapter looks only into the difference between churches which baptize both infants and

---

33. Par. 14.
34. Commentary 14.
35. BEM, "Baptism," IV.C., par. 15 and 16.

believers and churches which baptize exclusively believers. The difficulties of Oriental and Eastern Orthodox churches in recognizing the baptism of other churches[36] are not taken into consideration.

The chapter emphasizes that mutual recognition of baptism is acknowledged as an important sign and means of expressing the baptismal unity given in Christ. Wherever possible, mutual recognition should be expressed explicitly by the churches."[37] It then makes a concrete proposal:

> *In order to overcome their differences, believer baptists and those who practice infant baptism should reconsider certain aspects of their practices. The first may seek to express more visibly the fact that children are placed under the protection of God's grace. The latter must guard themselves against the practice of apparently indiscriminate baptism and take more seriously their responsibility for the nurture of baptized children to mature commitment to Christ.*[38]

In other words, churches which practice believers' baptism are asked to find ways of making visible the fact that children are also under God's grace, such as in services of child dedication. Churches which practice infant baptism are asked to avoid baptizing children without any engagement on the side of parents and godparents to raise their child in the Christian faith, as tends to happen especially in state churches, or so-called folk-churches.

In addition to the theological proposal that infant baptism and believers' baptism are two practices of one and the same baptism, BEM also gives some very concrete recommendations as to what churches should do—or what they should avoid—in order to express this unity. An example is Paragraph 13, with its statement that baptism is an "unrepeatable act." This is something all the churches agree upon; but it is necessary to add the second sentence, "Any practice which might be interpreted as 're-baptism' must be avoided." Commentary 13 explains why this sentence is there:

36. See Chapter One.
37. Par. 15.
38. Par. 16.

Churches which have insisted on a particular form of baptism or which have had serious questions about the authenticity of other churches' sacraments and ministries have at times required persons coming from other church traditions to be baptized before being received into full communicant membership. As the churches come to fuller mutual understanding and acceptance of one another and enter into closer relationships in witness and service, they will want to refrain from any practice which might call into question the sacramental integrity of other churches or which might diminish the unrepeatability of the sacrament of baptism.

Here BEM makes clear proposals to both sides on this issue, proposals which would help each side more easily accept the other's practice. In the view of BEM, coming closer, or searching for unity, always requires a move from each side.

Critical Evaluation of BEM

BEM points out clearly the main difference between churches which baptize infants and churches which baptize only adults. It understands this difference as emphasizing two different aspects of baptism, aspects which belong somehow together. In summary we can say that BEM points to some fundamental commonalities:

- Understanding baptism as instituted by Jesus Christ.

- Understanding baptism as participation in Christ's death and resurrection.

- Understanding baptism as conversion, pardoning and cleansing.

- Understanding baptism as the gift of the Holy Spirit.

- Understanding baptism as the incorporation into the body of Christ.

- Understanding baptism as the sign of the kingdom.

- The conviction that personal commitment is necessary for responsible membership in the body of Christ.

- The conviction that baptism is a life-long growing into Christ and has ethical implications.

- The conviction that baptism is unrepeatable.

- The conviction that baptism is administered with water in the name of the Father, the Son and the Holy Spirit.

Against this background BEM gives some proposals about what the churches need to do, or where they would need to change, in order to come closer together.

In summary we can say that BEM proposes solutions based on the understanding that the existing differences between the churches in regard to baptism are mainly differences in the *practice* of baptism. This means that the differences have their roots in different historical developments, and therefore should be understood as legitimate differences. The concrete proposals made to the churches aim finally at introducing—and accepting—the different practices as possibilities within *all* the churches.

BEM also points out some other issues such as the symbolic meaning of water and promotes the practice of immersion, although many churches do not have this practice. Furthermore, BEM advocates additional symbolic acts such as the laying on of hands and anointing as well as making the sign of the cross (Paragraph 19). Paragraph 20 gives the liturgical elements which are recommended: "Within any comprehensive order of baptism at least the following elements should find a place: the proclamation of faith in Christ and the Holy Trinity; the use of water; a declaration that the persons baptized have acquired a new identity as sons and daughters of God, and as members of the Church, called to be witnesses of the Gospel."[39]

This shows that BEM follows an inclusive model in which the different traditions are understood as complementary. The criterion of "what goes back to the tradition of the early church" also seems to be applied as a common factor.

---

39. Par. 20.

In a critical evaluation of BEM, two issues become clear from the perspective of the developments in the 25 years after its publication: (1) BEM did not consider seriously enough the difference between the Orthodox churches and the churches from the Western tradition, that is, it did not offer a concrete way towards the mutual recognition of baptism by these two types of churches; (2) BEM did not (and could not) take into consideration the problems and differences which developed during the last 50 years.

These are (a) the question of the baptismal formula as raised by feminist theology and its request for inclusive language; (b) the question of the baptismal elements, raised through the existence of new churches which do not use water; and linked to this, (c) the question of the relationship between water baptism and Spirit baptism raised by Pentecostal and African Independent churches. This question is mentioned, though, in the Lima text on Baptism, Commentary 21: "Some African churches practice baptism of the Holy Spirit without water, through the laying on of hands…" But the document does not go further than recommending that "a study is required concerning this practice and its relation to baptism with water."

THE OFFICIAL RESPONSES TO BEM ON BAPTISM

After studying the text of BEM on baptism, the question is whether it really expresses a convergence. The Faith and Order Commission tried to test this by sending the text to all the member churches of the WCC as well as to the Roman Catholic Church, asking for an official response "at the highest appropriate level of authority."[40] As a guideline for these responses, the Commission formulated the following questions:

The Commission would be pleased to know as precisely as possible

- *the extent to which your church can recognize in this text the faith of the Church through the ages;*

---

40. BEM, "Preface."

- *the consequences your church can draw from this text for its relations and dialogues with other churches, particularly with those churches which also recognize the text as an expression of the apostolic faith;*
- *the guidance your church can take from this text for its worship, educational, ethical, and spiritual life and witness...*[41]

The first question especially has to be examined more closely. It presumes that something exists like "the faith of the Church through the ages," some kind of "core faith" which all the churches share and which has been preserved in all the churches through the ages. The convergences which BEM is trying to work out would lead to this "faith of the Church through the ages," which none of the churches has in its pure or full form.

We will now examine how the churches dealt with this question.

As the analysis of the responses summarizes: "In general the responses of the churches to the section on baptism register gratitude for the work and affirm the impressive degree of agreement and convergence towards consensus."[42] At the same time most of the churches raise some questions, as, for example, "the Baptist Union of Great Britain ... asks whether there are not fundamental assumptions which need exposure and assessment..."[43]

It is illuminating to study more closely which points the churches highlight as being in agreement with BEM and which they highlight as missing in BEM or as not being dealt with appropriately. In the following I will summarize some of the major issues raised by the churches' responses to BEM[44] in a supportive

---

41. Ibid.

42. World Council of Churches, Commission on Faith and Order, *Baptism, Eucharist and Ministry 1982-1990: Report on the Process and Responses*, Faith and Order Paper No. 149, WCC Publications, Geneva 1990, 39, par. 1.

43. Ibid., par. 2

44. The official responses of the churches to BEM are published in six volumes edited by Max Thurian, *Churches Respond to BEM: Official Responses to the "Baptism, Eucharist and Ministry" Text*: Vol. I, Faith and Order Paper No. 129, WCC Publications, Geneva, 1986; Vol. II, Faith and Order Paper No. 132, WCC Publications, Geneva, 1986; Vol. III, Faith & Order Paper No. 135, WCC Publications, Geneva, 1987; Vol. IV, Faith and Order Paper No. 137, WCC Publications, Geneva, 1987; Vol. V, Faith and Order Paper No. 143, WCC Publications, Geneva, 1988; Vol. VI, Faith & Order Paper No. 144, WCC Publications, Geneva, 1988.

or critical way. It has to be noted that some churches point to the same issue but express themselves in different ways. I will try to summarize the issues which have been mentioned without going into excessive detail.

Responses from Orthodox Churches[45]

In general the Orthodox responses appreciate BEM,[46] with the exception of the Church of Greece, which sharply criticizes the request for the "reception" of the BEM text and deems the whole process as "ecclesiologically and theologically unnecessary" and "not foreseen by the stipulations of the WCC's Constitution."[47]

In a positive way, Orthodox churches affirm the "equal status of baptism of believers and baptism of infants."[48] The meaning of baptism as participation in the mystery of Christ's death and resurrection is also stated as "correctly emphasized."[49] Baptism is a gift of God and the human response to that gift.[50] Baptism as a lifelong growth into Christ and the administration with water in the name of the Father and the Son and the Holy Spirit are also highlighted as agreements.[51]

---

45. The Orthodox responses which are analyzed here are the following: Inter-Orthodox Symposium on Baptism, Eucharist and Ministry, in Thurian, *Churches Respond to BEM*, Vol. I, 122-129; Russian Orthodox Church, in Thurian, *Churches Respond to BEM*, Vol. II, 5-12; Bulgarian Orthodox Church, ibid., 13- 23; Finnish Orthodox Church, ibid., 24-29; Armenian Apostolic Church, ibid., 30-31; Greek Orthodox Patriarchate of Alexandria, in Thurian, *Churches Respond to BEM*, Vol. III, 1-3; Romanian Orthodox Church, ibid., 4-14; Orthodox Church in America, ibid., 15-25; Ecumenical Patriarchate of Constantinople, in Thurian, *Churches Respond to BEM*, Vol. IV, 1-6; Church of Greece, in Thurian, *Churches Respond to BEM*, Vol. V, 1-3; Malankara Orthodox Syrian Church (India), ibid., 4-7.

46. See Inter-Orthodox Symposium, 125: "We Orthodox recognize many positive elements in BEM which express significant aspects of the apostolic faith"; see also Bulgarian Orthodox Church, 15; Finnish Orthodox Church, 25; Ecumenical Patriarchate of Constantinople, 1; Romanian Orthodox Church, 4.

47. Church of Greece, 2.

48. Russian Orthodox Church, 7.

49. Finnish Orthodox Church, 26; cf. Romanian Orthodox Church, 5; Orthodox Church in America, 16.

50. Romanian Orthodox Church, 5.

51. Romanian Orthodox Church, 5; Orthodox Church in America, 16.

Concerning baptism, the Orthodox responses raise the following issues as needing further clarification:

- The relationship between baptism and the unity of the church.[52]

- The role of the Holy Spirit in baptism.[53]

- The relationship between baptism and chrismation[54] and eucharist.[55]

- The role of exorcism and renunciation of the Evil One.[56]

- Usage of the terms "sign," "symbol," "sacramental sign."[57]

- Baptism understood as giving "a new ethical orientation" is a reduction of its meaning. Rather baptism is "a beginning of the ontological restoration of man as a new being in Christ."[58]

- Child baptism and adult baptism should not be seen as contradictory.[59]

- Discussion about baptismal formula is missing.[60]

- Infant baptism should be accepted by all.[61]

- The terminology of "adult baptism" is better than "believers' baptism."[62]

---

52. Inter-Orthodox Symposium; Patriarchate of Alexandria; Romanian Orthodox Church; Orthodox Church in America.

53. Inter-Orthodox Symposium; Russian Orthodox Church; Patriarchate of Alexandria, cf. also Romanian Orthodox Church.

54. Inter-Orthodox Symposium; Russian Orthodox Church; Finnish Orthodox Church, Malankara Orthodox Syrian Church.

55. Romanian Orthodox Church; cf. also Finnish Orthodox Church.

56. Inter-Orthodox Symposium; Patriarchate of Alexandria.

57. Inter-Orthodox Symposium; Bulgarian Orthodox Church; Romanian Orthodox Church.

58. Romanian Orthodox Church.

59. Finnish Orthodox Church, 26.

60. Bulgarian Orthodox Church.

61. Bulgarian Orthodox Church; cf. also Romanian Orthodox Church.

62. Finnish Orthodox Church, 26.

- Infant baptism is not appreciated enough.[63]

- The issue of the content of faith is not addressed.[64]

The Response of the Roman Catholic Church[65]

In relation to BEM's section on baptism, the response offers a general appreciation: "We find the text on baptism to be grounded in the apostolic faith received and professed by the Catholic Church."[66] In particular it highlights the following points as "well stated":

- Baptism as gift and work of the trinitarian God.

- Baptism as a sacramental reality (Baptism as a sign, as participation in Christ's death as effect of baptism, gift of the Holy Spirit, Baptism as both God's gift and human response, baptism as unrepeatable, and so on).

A second part of the response gives some "particular comments"[67] related to the different sections of the BEM baptism text. The critical points can be summarized as follows:

- The question of the necessity of baptism for salvation is not dealt with and "clearly requires further common study."[68]

- The doctrine of original sin should be "explicitly incorporated into the discussion on the meaning and effects of baptism."[69]

- Referring to Paragraphs 5 and 6, the response asks for a clarification of the notion of "seal" in relation to Baptism.

- The distinction made in the BEM text between "infants" and "believers" is misleading. "It might have been better if the text spoke of baptism of adults and infants."[70]

---

63. Orthodox Church in America, Romanian Orthodox Church.
64. Orthodox Church in America.
65. Thurian, *Churches Respond to BEM*, Vol. VI, 1-40.
66. Ibid., 9.
67. Ibid., 11-16.
68. Ibid., 12.
69. Ibid.
70. Ibid., 14.

- "There is an absence of a clear concept of sacrament (and sacramentality) in BEM ... The text does not give reasons to show clearly why baptism is an unrepeatable act."[71]

- The Catholic response emphasizes infant baptism as important[72] and points out that confirmation is a distinct sacrament.[73]

Anglican Responses[74]

Among Anglicans there is generally a positive response to BEM, and the section on baptism is considered as representing "what we understand Baptism to be."[75] But the following issues remain as "questions yet to be solved"[76]:

- The term "believers' baptism" is not appropriate.[77]

- Baptism needs to be clearly defined as water baptism.[78]

- Further exploration of confirmation is necessary.[79]

- The issue of re-baptism needs to be treated more deeply.[80]

- The issue of the baptismal formula.[81]

- The terminology of "sacrament" is not clarified in relation to "sign."[82]

- The relation of water baptism to baptism in the Holy Spirit is missing.[83]

---

71. Ibid., 6.

72. Ibid., 14.

73. Ibid., 6ff.

74. Church of England, in Thurian, *Churches Respond to BEM*, Vol. III, 30-79; Anglican Church of Canada, Vol. II, 36-47; Anglican Church of Australia, ibid., 32-35; Scottish Episcopal Church, ibid., 48-56; Episcopal Church (USA), ibid., 57-62; Church of the Province of New Zealand, ibid., 63-68.

75. Episcopal Church (USA), 59.

76. Anglican Church of Australia, 33.

77. Anglican Church of Australia, 33.

78. Anglican Church of Australia, 34.

79. Scottish Episcopal Church, 55.

80. Episcopal Church (USA), 59.

81. Episcopal Church (USA), 59; Anglican Church of Canada, 45.

82. Church of the Province of New Zealand, 64.

83. Church of the Province of New Zealand, 64.

Responses from Methodist Churches[84]

Some Methodists feel suspicious of an overly sacramental understanding of baptism in BEM.[85] In their understanding, the relationship between sign and spiritual reality needs clarification.[86] Since the personal faith of the recipient of baptism is important, confirmation needs to be highlighted as the completion of baptism.[87] Some Methodist churches find that BEM favors believers' baptism too much,[88] and does not pay attention to "original sin."[89] They also miss a discussion of "new birth"[90] and ask for a clarification concerning the relationship between the baptizand and the congregation.[91]

Responses from Lutheran Churches[92]

Lutheran churches in general agree that "baptism is rooted in ministry, death and resurrection of Jesus Christ, that it is administered

---

84. Protestant Methodist Church in Benin, in Thurian, *Churches Respond to BEM*, Vol. IV, 166; Evangelical-Methodist Church: Central Conference in the German Democratic Republic, ibid., 167-172; Evangelical-Methodist Church: Central Conference in the Federal Republic of Germany and West-Berlin, ibi., 173-182; United Methodist Church USA, in Thurian, *Churches Respond to BEM*, Vol. II, 177-199; United Methodist Church, Central and Southern Europe, ibid., 200-209; Methodist Church (UK), ibid., 210-229; Methodist Church in Ireland, ibid., 230-235; Methodist Church of Southern Africa, ibid., 236-244.

85. Methodist Church of Southern Africa, 237; cf. also Methodist Church in Ireland, 232; Methodist Church in the UK, 220 (especially concerned about the lack of clarity about the efficacy of the sacrament). Cf. also United Methodist Church, Central and Southern Europe, 203; a similar concern is behind the statement of Evangelical Methodist Church: Central Conference in the Federal Republic of Germany, 176 and the Central Conference in the German Democratic Republic, 169.

86. Methodist Church of Southern Africa, 237.

87. Methodist Church in Ireland, 231; a similar concern in Evangelical-Methodist Church: Central Conference in the Federal Republic of Germany, 176.

88. Methodist Church UK, 221.

89. United Methodist Church, Central and Southern Europe, 203.

90. United Methodist Church, Central and Southern Europe, 203

91. United Methodist Church, Central and Southern Europe, 204.

92. Lutheran Church in America, in Thurian, *Churches Respond to BEM*, Vol. I, 28-38; North Elbian Evangelical Lutheran Church, ibid.,, 39-53; Lutheran Church of Australia, in Thurian, *Churches Respond to BEM*, Vol. II, 85-98; Evangelical Church of Lutheran Confession in Brazil, ibid., 99-101; Evangelical

according to his command, that it gives forgiveness of sins and new life, that it is administered with water ... and that in all these aspects it is God's operative grace to the sinner, a sacrament on which the faith of the baptized relies and to which he responds."[93] Some Lutheran churches explicitly welcome the rejection in the BEM text of practices which could be considered as re-baptism.[94] In summary they point out that

- Infant baptism needs to be kept as equal to believers' baptism.[95]

- Greater emphasis on conversion and rebirth is necessary.[96]

- Returning to the gift of baptism in repentance is necessary.[97]

- The necessity of baptism for salvation and original sin is mentioned only marginally.[98]

Lutheran Church in Canada, ibid., 102-104; Church of Norway, ibid., 105-122; Church of Sweden, ibid., 123-140; Evangelical-Lutheran Church of Denmark, in Thurian, *Churches Respond to BEM*,Vol. III, 106-115; Evangelical-Lutheran Church of Finland, ibid., 116-127; Lutheran Church in Hungary, ibid., 128-130; Lutheran Church–Missouri Synod, ibid., 131-141; Evangelical Church of the Augsburg Confession of Alsace and Lorraine, ibid., 145-157; Evangelical Lutheran Church of France, ibid., 163-164; Evangelical Lutheran Church in Bavaria, in Thurian, *Churches Respond to BEM*, Vol. IV, 21-41; Estonian Evangelical Lutheran Church, ibid., 42-46; Evangelical Lutheran Church of Hanover, ibid., 47-56; Evangelical Lutheran Church of Iceland, ibid., 57-72; Evangelical Lutheran Church of the Augsburg Confession in Romania, ibid., 81-92; Evangelical Lutheran Church in the Netherlands, in Thurian, *Churches Respond to BEM*, Vol. V, 18-22; Evangelical Lutheran Church in Württemberg, ibid., 23-31; Slovak Evangelical Church of the Augsburg Confession, in Thurian, *Churches Respond to BEM*, Vol. VI, 41-43.

93. Hanover, 48ff.; cf. also Iceland, IV, 58ff.; Württemberg, 23; Bavaria, 27ff.; Missouri Synod, 134; Finland, 117; Denmark, 107ff.; Norway, 109; Sweden, 125ff.

94. Romania, 83; Württemberg, 24; Slovak Evangelical Church of the Augsburg Confession, 41.

95. Württemberg, 24ff.; cf. Estonian Evangelical Lutheran Church, 42 (has the "impression that the baptism of adults is taken as a norm and that more importance was attached to the baptism of adults that to infants' baptism"); Hanover, 49; Denmark, 108; Finland, 119; Canada, 103.

96. Württemberg, 25.

97. Finland, 119; Alsace and Lorraine, 149.

98. Bavaria, 28; cf. also Finland, 119; Norway, 111.

- The priority of baptism as a gift of God should be emphasized; faith is also primarily a gift of God;[99] faith as a response has no constitutive significance for the act of baptism.

- The terminology of "believer's baptism" is not adequate (better "adult baptism").[100]

- Baptism is not a "rite of commitment."[101]

- The role of God's word is unclear.[102]

- The expression "indiscriminate baptism" needs further clarification.[103]

- The word "sign" is too vague to describe the sacrament.[104]

- Baptism as gift of the Holy Spirit is not clearly enough indicated.

Responses from Reformed and Presbyterian Churches[105]

The Reformed and Presbyterian position can be summarized as follows: there is, in general, an appreciation of the BEM document and of its section on baptism. As critical points these churches raise the following issues:

---

99. Bavaria, 29; see. also Estonian Evangelical Lutheran Church, 42; Romania, 85; Finland, 119; Norway, 111; North Elbia, 41.

100. Bavaria, 30; see also Romania, 85; Missouri Synod, 134.

101. Hanover, 50; see also Missouri Synod, 134; Canada,103; North Elbia, 41.

102. Iceland, 59; see also Hanover, 50; Finland, 119; France, 161; Sweden, 126.

103. Canada, 103, and others.

104. Norway, 112.

105. The Reformed and Presbyterian responses which were analyzed are: Presbyterian Church of Rwanda, in Thurian, *Churches Respond to BEM,* Vol. III, 183-185; Presbyterian Church (U.S.A.), ibid., 189-205; Presbyterian Church in Ireland, ibid., 206-221; Church of Scotland, in Thurian, *Churches Respond to BEM,* Vol. I, 86-100; Reformed Church in America, in Thurian, *Churches Respond to BEM,* Vol. II, 141-151; Presbyterian Church in Canada, ibid., 152-159; Presbyterian Church of Wales, ibid., 165-174; Presbyterian Church of New Zealand, ibid., 175-176; Presbyterian Church of Korea, ibid., 160-164; Reformed Church in Hungary, in Thurian, *Churches Respond to BEM,* Vol. V, 161-164; Swiss Protestant Church Federation, in Thurian, *Churches Respond to BEM,* Vol. VI, 75-87; Evangelical Presbyterian Church in Ghana, ibid., 88-103.

- They miss the idea of God's covenant with his people as a model for the understanding of baptism.[106]

- Baptism is not only sign and seal of discipleship, but of the grace of Jesus Christ towards us.[107]

- Infant baptism is not dealt with adequately.[108]

- The use of the terms "sign" and "sacrament" needs more clarification.[109]

- The question of the relationship between baptism and salvation is not dealt with adequately. Baptism is not necessary for salvation (Presbyterian Church in Canada, Presbyterian Church in Ireland).

- Immersion should not be made the exclusive form of baptism (Presbyterian Church in Ireland, Presbyterian Church [U.S.A.]).

- Chrismation should not be seen as a "magic action" (Presbyterian Church of Rwanda, Presbyterian Church in Ireland).

Some churches have, in addition, made the following comments:

- The use of Scripture in general is seen as problematic (Swiss Protestant Church Federation).

- The terminology of "infant baptism" should be avoided (Presbyterian Church [U.S.A.]).

- A clear statement is needed on why baptism is needed only once (Presbyterian, New Zealand).

---

106. See responses from the Presbyterian Church of Rwanda; Reformed Church in America; Presbyterian Church in Canada; Presbyterian Church in New Zealand; Presbyterian Church (U.S.A.).

107. See responses from the Presbyterian Church of Rwanda; Reformed in America; Presbyterian Church in New Zealand; Presbyterian Church (U.S.A.); Presbyterian Church in Ireland.

108. See responses from the Church of Scotland; Presbyterian Church of Wales.

109. See responses from the Church of Scotland; Presbyterian Church of Wales.

- More clarification is needed on the relation between incorporation into Christ and membership in the church (Church of Scotland).

- The nature of the relationship between baptism and faith is ignored (Presbyterian Church in Canada).

- Infant baptism is not given enough justice.[110]

- More clarity is needed on the relation between incorporation into Christ and membership of the church.[111]

- The nature of a "sign" needs to be clarified.[112]

- The term "rite of commitment" is unclear.[113]

- The relation between baptism and salvation needs more elucidation.[114]

- The reference to the Old Testament antecedent of baptism is missing.[115]

- The nature of the relationship between baptism and faith is ignored in BEM.[116]

- There is a lack of attention to covenant theology.[117]

- Baptism is not necessary for salvation, but is the seal of salvation.[118]

- The tension between a sacramental understanding of baptism and a non-sacramental understanding needs more work.[119]

---

110. Scotland, 95; see also Wales, 167.
111. Scotland, 95; United Reformed UK, 107.
112. Scotland, 97; see also Presbyterian Church in Rwanda, 183.
113. United Reformed UK, 104.
114. United Reformed UK, 107.
115. Reformed Church in America, 142ff.
116. Presbyterian Canada, 154.
117. America, 142ff; Presbyterian Church in Canada, 154; Presbyterian New Zealand, 175; Presbyterian Rwanda, 183; Netherlands, 108; Presbyterian USA, 193; Presbyterian Ireland, 209.
118. Presbyterian Church in Canada, 154; Presbyterian Church in Ireland, 208.
119. Presbyterian Church in Wales, 168.

- Baptism as a means of grace is missing.[120]

- The relationship between baptism, forgiveness, conversion and the gift of the Spirit needs deeper exploration.[121]

Responses from Churches Practicing Believers' Baptism[122]

BEM is also welcomed by churches which practice believers' baptism "as a notable milestone in the search for sufficient theological consensus."[123]

These churches accept baptism as participation in Christ's death and resurrection, the washing away of sins, new birth, and in other ways noted as common Christian understandings in BEM.[124] They remark positively on the "significant place accorded to faith within the baptismal reality and the clear recognition of the danger of the indiscriminate baptism of infants."[125] The clear setting of baptism within the lifelong process of preparation, growth and nurture in

---

120. Presbyterian Church in New Zealand, 175; cf. also Presbyterian Church USA, 193; Presbyterian Church in Ireland, 208.

121. Alsace, 166.

122. The responses which were analyzed are: Baptist Union of Great Britain and Ireland, in Thurian, *Churches Respond to BEM.*, Vol. I, 70-77; Baptist Union of Scotland, in Thurian, *Churches Respond to BEM*, Vol. III, 230-245; Baptist Union of Denmark, ibid., 246-253; American Baptist Churches in the USA, ibid., 257-263; Covenant Baptist Churches in Wales, Vol. III, 254-256; Christian Church (Disciples of Christ) in Canada, Vol. III, 264-267; General Mennonite Society (Netherlands), ibid., 289-296; Burma Baptist Convention, in Thurian, *Churches Respond to BEM*, Vol. IV, 184-190; Baptist Union of Sweden, ibid., 200-213; Church of the Brethren (USA), in Thurian, *Churches Respond to BEM*, Vol. VI, 104-114; United German Mennonite Congregations, ibid., 123-129.

123. Baptist Union of Great Britain and Ireland, 70; cf. also Burma Baptist Convention, 185.

124. General Mennonite Society (Netherlands), 290ff.; United German Mennonite Congregations, 125.

125. Baptist Union of Great Britain and Ireland, 70; cf. Baptist Union of Scotland, 233; Baptist Union of Denmark, 247; American Baptist Churches in the USA, 259; Disciples of Christ in Canada, 264; General Mennonite Society, 291.

Christ is also highlighted,[126] as is the significance of immersion.[127] Baptism is seen as unrepeatable.[128]

For the BEM section on baptism, the following critical points are highlighted:

- Baptism is seen too much as something which "gives," "initiates," "effects,"[129] there is a too sacramental understanding of baptism.[130]

- Baptism must be seen as a human act of confession.[131]

- The statement that "re-baptism must be avoided" is problematic.[132]

- There is an ambiguity in the references of BEM to "baptism": is it a shorthand term for initiation or is it just the water rite?[133]

- BEM is wrong in presuming that there is "one baptism."[134]

- Infant baptism is not biblical.[135]

- The existing differences are played down by accepting both practices "side by side."[136]

---

126. Baptist Union of Great Britain and Ireland, 70; cf. Baptist Union of Scotland, 234; Baptist Union of Denmark, 247; United German Mennonite Congregations, 126.

127. American Baptist Churches in the USA, 259; Disciples of Christ in Canada, 264.

128. United German Mennonite Congregations, 126.

129. Baptist Union of Great Britain and Ireland, 70.

130. Baptist Union of Scotland, 234; cf. also Church of the Brethren, 109; United German Mennonite Congregations, 126.

131. General Mennonite Society (Netherlands), 290 .

132. Baptist Union of Great Britain and Ireland, 71; cf. also Baptist Union of Scotland, 235; Baptist Union of Denmark, 249; American Baptist Churches in the USA, 259; Baptist Union of Sweden, 202ff. (accepts the wording, but problematizes the issue); Church of the Brethren, 109.

133. Baptist Union of Great Britain and Ireland, 71.

134. Baptist Union of Scotland, 234; cf. also Baptist Union of Denmark, 248; General Mennonite Society, 292; Baptist Union of Sweden, 201.

135. Baptist Union of Scotland, 235; cf. also General Mennonite Society, 291.

136. General Mennonite Society, 292.

Summary of the BEM Process

What becomes clear from this analysis of the responses to BEM is that in response to the question whether the churches "recognize in this text the faith of the Church through the ages," the criterion for the churches was their own confessional faith. In other words, "the faith of the Church through the ages" was identified with the faith of each church.[137] To put it another way, the churches highlight as positive those passages of BEM which are in agreement with their own convictions, while criticism is expressed on issues where BEM does not correspond with their own confessional standpoint. For example, believer baptist churches criticize the fact that infant baptism is considered on the same level as adult baptism, while churches which practice infant baptism have the feeling that infant baptism is downplayed. Therefore the Lutheran theologian André Birmelé goes as far as to say: "The Lima document is often misunderstood. Although the authors have repeatedly emphasized that they have worked out convergences and in no sense a consensus, the responses of many churches show how this statement has often been heard."[138]

From this it can be concluded that the churches, through the BEM process, did not (yet) overcome the specific theological problems and differences existing between them.[139]

But BEM provided significant material for the churches to study each other's points of view, as well as some starting points for further study on possibilities for the mutual recognition of baptism.

---

137. See for example Church of Norway, 108: "We recognize in this section a number of the central elements for the understanding of baptism which are generally emphasized in our own doctrinal tradition."

138. André Birmelé, "Baptism and the Unity of the Church in Ecumenical Dialogues," in Michael Root and Risto Saarinen, eds., *Baptism and the Unity of the Church*, Eerdmans, Grand Rapids, MI and WCC Publications, Geneva, 1998, 108.

139. See also Eric Geldbach, *Taufe*, Ökumenische Studienhefte 5, Vandenhoeck & Ruprecht, Göttingen, 1996, 147.

Baptism in International Bilateral Dialogues

During the history of Christianity different schisms have occurred, resulting today in the following situation within the ecumenical movement: two groups of churches are facing each other, on the one hand those which have split from one another over certain theological or other issues, and on the other hand churches which are meeting each other for the first time, discovering their differences as a matter of established fact rather than as a result of a split after an earlier common history. Therefore we have to distinguish different starting points for bilateral dialogues; these starting points influence the bilateral dialogues' respective aims. There are bilateral dialogues which deal directly with the healing of a schism, like the bilateral dialogue between the Roman Catholic Church and the Orthodox Church or the dialogue between the Lutherans and the Roman Catholic Church. There are also bilateral dialogues between churches which are not separated by a direct historical split but which have discovered that they have different standpoints and want to get to know each other better, as for example the Roman Catholic Church and the Pentecostals. In this sense, different bilateral dialogues have different perspectives and different goals.

The advantage of a bilateral dialogue over against a multilateral dialogue is that the former can go more deeply into the details of the relationship between the two churches involved.

Here we are interested especially in the question of how the issue of baptism is dealt with in bilateral dialogues. I will distinguish between (1) dialogues between churches which baptize infants and churches which baptize only believers who can speak for themselves; and (2) dialogues between Orthodox and other churches. I will also briefly analyze other bilateral dialogues dealing with the issue of baptism.

BILATERAL DIALOGUES BETWEEN CHURCHES WHICH BAPTIZE INFANTS AND CHURCHES WHICH BAPTIZE ONLY BELIEVERS

Dialogues in this category which address the issue of baptism explicitly are the following:

Baptist–Reformed (1977)[140]

The dialogue partners are representatives of the World Alliance of Reformed Churches (now the World Communion of Reformed Churches) and of the Baptist World Alliance. After various contacts between both organizations since 1969, the dialogue session in 1977 discussed the issue of baptism in the following way:

> *Baptism is being seen in the wider context of the question of mission. Both churches agree that baptism is both an act of God and an act of the human being. They agree on the meaning of baptism as dying and rising with Christ and on its performance with water. They understand baptism as the sacrament of incorporation into Christ.[141]*

The dilemma is the opposition between believers' baptism and infant baptism. Both sides give recommendations to each other:

> *The churches which are convinced that they are entitled only to practice believers' baptism should keep in mind that their practice should not result from a disregard for the priority of God's grace and of the receptive, and not creative, character of human faith, which has to be expressed and confessed, not once for all, but again and again. The churches which are convinced that they are entitled to practice infant baptism should keep in mind that their practice should not result from a disregard of the call for personal faith, which call is involved in God's prevenient grace.*

This dialogue goes as far as to ask the question

---

140. Report of Theological Conversations sponsored by the World Alliance of Reformed Churches and the Baptist World Alliance, 1977, in Harding Meyer and Lukas Vischer, eds., *Growth in Agreement I: Reports and Agreed Statements of Ecumenical Conversations on a World Level. 1972-1982*, Faith & Order Paper No.108, WCC Publications, Geneva, 1984, 139ff. (*Growth in Agreement I is* henceforth quoted as *GiA I.*)

141. Ibid., 141.

whether Christians of Reformed and Baptist convictions who are members in good standing of their churches could recognize one another as both occupying the position of those who have received and responded to the grace of God in baptism as this grace is understood in the New Testament.[142]

All in all this dialogue considers "the Reformed emphasis on the priority of God's grace in baptism and the Baptist accent on man's active participation in the baptismal event...(as) complementary."[143]

It thus becomes clear that the remaining disagreement between Baptists and Reformed should be discussed not primarily in terms of the meaning of baptism and its relation to the work of the Spirit, but rather around the question of how and where it may, in faithfulness to the Scriptural witness, be affirmed that the Holy Spirit is at work.[144]

Disciples–Roman Catholic (1981)[145]

A five-year dialogue between the Disciples of Christ and the Roman Catholic Church was concluded in 1981 with a final report which begins its part on the discussions about baptism with the statement: "By its very nature, baptism impels Christians towards oneness." The report continues to list "important areas in which our understanding and practice of baptism encourage us to speak truly of one baptism."[146] These areas are the biblical roots of baptism: the baptismal rite with water and "in the name of the Father, and of the Son, and of the Holy Spirit," the ordinary administration of baptism by "a duly authorized minister,"[147] the belief, that through baptism one enters into a new relationship with God, the conviction that "rebaptism is contrary to the Gospel"[148] and the necessary role of faith in baptism.

---

142. Ibid., 142.
143. Ibid., 145.
144. Ibid., 146.
145. Disciples–Roman Catholic Conversations, Report 1981, in *GiA I*, 158ff.
146. Ibid., 158.
147. Ibid.
148. Ibid., 159.

The differences are grouped in two parts: "The Relation of Personal Faith to Baptism" and "The Mode of Baptism."[149] The first concerns mainly the fact that the Disciples are convinced "that the rite of baptism should be preceded by a personal confession of faith and repentance,"[150] while Catholics baptize infants. Both sides take a step towards each other by saying: "However, Catholics see the fundamental belief of their church regarding baptism as expressed with new clarity in the revised rite for adult baptism, which includes personal confession of faith." Disciples, meanwhile, "have an increasing appreciation for the place of infant baptism in the history of the Church."[151]

The second area of difference is the Disciples' practice of immersion, in opposition to the Roman Catholic practice of pouring water on the forehead of the child. The report states: "Disciples are coming to recognize the other modes, while retaining a preference for immersion."[152] Finally, Disciples and Roman Catholics "affirm the mutual recognition of baptism administered by Roman Catholics and Disciples."[153]

Baptist–Roman Catholic (1988)[154]

In 1988 the conversations between the Baptist World Alliance and the Vatican Secretariat for Promoting Christian Unity presented a report as a result of five meetings on "Witness to Christ in Today's World." With regard to the issue of baptism, although both sides can see "growing common concern … about authenticity of faith, baptism and Christian witness … there are, however, obvious divergences."[155] While Baptists "insist that the faith response pre-

---

149. Ibid. 159ff.
150. Ibid., 159.
151. Ibid.
152. Ibid., 160.
153. Ibid.
154. "Summons to Witness to Christ in Today's World. A Report on Conversations 1984-1988, Atlanta, USA, 23 July 1988, " in Jeffrey Gros, Harding Meyer, and William G. Rusch, *Growth in Agreement II: Reports and Agreed Statements of Ecumenical Conversations on a World Level, 1982-1998*, Faith and Order Paper No. 187, WCC Publications, Geneva and Eerdmans, Grand Rapids, MI, 2000, 383ff. (*Growth in Agreement II is* henceforth quoted as *GiA II*.)
155. *GiA II*, 383, par. 49.

cede baptism," Catholics "baptize infants."[156] The dialogue partners identify as the "heart of the problem ... the nature of faith and the nature of the sacraments."[157] But this report does not go beyond asking questions which need to be addressed.

Pentecostal–Roman-Catholic (1972-1976; 1985-1989 report; 1998-2006)[158]

This dialogue has had several phases. In 1972-1976 it was led by the Roman Catholic Church with "Leaders of some Pentecostal Churches and Participants in the Charismatic Movement within Protestant and Anglican Churches."[159] With the second phase (1977-1982) it became "exclusively a conversation between the classical Pentecostals and the Roman Catholic Church."[160] It has to be noted that this dialogue is not meant to seek structural unity, but that its purpose is for participants to get to know each other and to promote mutual understanding.[161] The reports of the first, the third, and the fifth phase especially take up the issue of baptism.

The report of the first phase notes:

certain convergences: a) Sacraments are in no sense magical and are effective only in relation to faith. b) God's gift precedes and

---

156. Ibid.

157. *GiA II*, 384, par. 51.

158. Final Report, Dialogue between the Secretariat for Promoting Christian unity and Leaders of Some Pentecostal Churches and Participants in the Charismatic Movement within Protestant and Anglican Churches, 1972-1976, *GiA II*, 713-720, 716ff. (see also *GiA* I, 422-431); "Perspectives on Koinonia": Report from the Third Quinquennium of the Dialogue between the Pontifical Council for Promoting Christian Unity and Some Classical Pentecostal Churches and Leaders, 1985-1989, in GiA II, 740ff; and "On Becoming a Christian: Insights from Scripture and the Patristic Writings," Report of the Fifth Phase of the International Dialogue Between Some Classical Pentecostal Churches and Leaders and the Catholic Church (1998-2006), http://www.vatican.va/roman_curia/pontifical_councils/chrstuni/eccl-comm-docs/rc_pc_chrstuni_doc_20060101_becoming-a-christian_en.html.

159. *GiA I*, 422.

160. *GiA II*, 722.

161. Cf. "On Becoming a Christian: Insights from Scripture and the Patristic Writings," Report of the Fifth Phase of the International Dialogue Between Some Classical Pentecostal Churches and Leaders of the Catholic Church (1998-2006), Introduction, par. 2.

makes possible human receiving ... c)Where paedobaptism is not practiced and the children of believing parents are presented and dedicated to God, the children are this brought into the care of the Christian community and enjoy the special protection of the Lord. d) Where paedobaptism is practiced it is fully meaningful only in the context of the faith of the parents and the community."[162]

Both sides agree that rebaptism in the strict sense of the word is not acceptable; however the problem that the baptism of a person baptized as child is not considered as "baptism" by the Pentecostal side, was not solved.[163]

In the third round of this dialogue, the discussions went deeper: starting with the meaning of baptism, the participants discussed the relationship between "faith and baptism" and between "baptism and church." They looked into "baptismal practice" and the question of "baptism and the experience of the Spirit." While there is agreement about the biblical ground of baptism and its institution by Jesus Christ, Pentecostals and Roman Catholics differ in the understanding of baptism as an ordinance or a sacrament[164] and the practice of infant baptism.[165]

Although there are different understandings within Pentecostalism, there is a difference between Pentecostals in general and Roman Catholics over the question when one "comes to Christ" and over the significance of baptism in this respect.[166] The dialogue group between the two traditions considers further discussion necessary on the question of the effect of baptism.[167] A certain imbalance can be noted in regard to the mutual recognition of baptism: while the Roman Catholic side recognizes the baptism performed by Pentecostals in the name of the Father, Son and Holy Spirit, for

---

162. *GiA I*, 426
163. Ibid., 427
164. *GiA II*, 741, par. 41.
165. Ibid. par. 42.
166. *GiA II*, 742, par. 47.
167. Ibid., par. 51.

Pentecostals unbaptized converts are, in the strict sense, not called "brothers and sisters in Christ."[168] Another imbalance lies in the fact that "Pentecostals do not see the unity between Christians as being based in a common water baptism ... Instead, the foundation of unity is a common faith and experience of Jesus Christ as Lord and Saviour through the Holy Spirit."[169] In other words, for Pentecostals baptism does not have the same significance for the nature of the church and its unity as it has for Roman Catholics.[170]

In terms of the baptismal practice there are more convergences to be found. For both sides, baptism is in water and in the name of the Father, Son and Holy Spirit, and both would agree that "immersion is the most effective visible sign to convey the meaning of baptism,"[171] although Catholics also permit the pouring of water. Both confessional traditions find that "instruction in the faith necessarily follows upon baptism."[172] The dialogue finds "parallels between the Roman Catholic practice of infant baptism and the common practice of infant dedication in Pentecostal churches."[173] While Roman Catholics and Pentecostals "have different understandings of the role of the Spirit in Christian initiation and life," they still may "enjoy a similar experience of the Spirit." [174] In summary, the dialogue finds that "Roman Catholics fear that Pentecostals limit the Spirit to specific manifestations. Pentecostals fear that Roman Catholics confine the Spirit's workings to sacraments and church order."[175]

The fifth period of this dialogue dealt with the issue in the wider context of Christian initiation and took up the question of baptism in the Holy Spirit. Although stating different use of language there is a certain agreement that conversion is linked

---

168. *GiA II*, 743, par.52 and 53.

169. Ibid., 743, par 55.

170. Cf. André Birmelé, "Baptism and the Unity of the Church in Ecumenical Dialogues." In Root and Saarinen, Baptism and the Unity of the Church, 104-129, esp. 123.

171. *GiA II*, 743, par. 57.

172. Ibid., 744, par. 62.

173. Ibid., par. 63.

174. Ibid., par. 65.

175. *GiA II*, 745, par. 68.

> *to a process that includes proclamation of the Word, acceptance of the Gospel, profession of faith, repentance, a turning away from sin and turning to God, the bestowal of the Holy Spirit (Romans 8:9), as well as the incorporation of the individual into the Christian community.*[176]

The difference remains in the theological understanding of infant baptism.

Regarding Spirit baptism the report comes to the conclusion:

> *The most fundamental convergence concerning the theme treated in the present section, about which we can rejoice, is the common conviction within both our communities that Baptism in the Holy Spirit is a powerful action of grace bestowed by God upon believers within the church.*[177]

But

> *While the experience of Baptism in the Holy Spirit seems to have a certain degree of similarity among its recipients, the understanding of it and its place within the series of events by which one becomes a Christian are matters of substantial difference of opinion.*[178]

Evangelical–Roman Catholic (1977-1984)[179]

Note: This dialogue is special, because one side is not a church but rather composed of representatives of different churches and church organizations which "were not official representatives of any international body."[180] This dialogue is therefore not considered in this analysis, but is mentioned for the sake of comprehensiveness.

---

176. "On Becoming a Christian: Insights from Scripture and the Patristic Writings," par. 27.

177. Ibid., par. 260.

178. Ibid., par 261.

179. The Evangelical–Roman Catholic Dialogue on Mission, 1977-1984, in *GiA II*, 399-437, 422ff.

180. *GiA II*, 399.

Mennonite–Roman Catholic (1998-2003)[181]

In the report on the five-year dialogue between the Mennonite World Conference and the Roman Catholic Church the question of baptism is dealt with in the context of the understanding and concept of sacraments, which are called "ordinances" by Mennonites. There is a number of agreements on baptism, such as—as in other dialogues between the Roman Catholic Church and churches which baptize only adults—its biblical grounding, the meaning of baptism as dying and rising with Christ, baptism as a public witness to the faith of the church, the requirement of a public profession of faith and the practice of baptism by affusion or immersion in water and in the name of the Father, the Son and the Holy Spirit.[182] The divergences are related to the practice of infant over against adult baptism. The Catholic Church "accepts Mennonite baptism, which is done with water and in the name of the Trinity, as valid" while "in the Mennonite church, baptism is for those who understand its significance and who freely request it on the basis of their personally owned faith in Jesus Christ." [183] "Mennonites and Catholics differ in part in their understanding of the role of a personal confession of faith as it pertains to baptism."[184]

Baptist–Lutheran (1990)[185]

In the "Message to Our Churches," a summary of a four-year dialogue between the Lutheran World Federation and the Baptist World Alliance, the issue of baptism was discussed in relation to faith and to Christian discipleship. While both sides have "basically

---

181. "Called Together To Be Peace-makers": Report of the International Dialogue between the Catholic Church and The Mennonite World Conference, Assisi, Italy, 1998-2003, in Jeffrey Gros, Thomas F. Best, and Lorelei F. Fuchs, eds., *Growth in Agreement III. International Dialogue Texts and Agreed Statements, 1998-2005*, Faith and Order Paper No. 204, WCC Publications, Geneva and Eerdmans, Grand Rapids, MI, 2007, 235ff. (*Growth in Agreement III is* henceforth quoted as *GiA III*.)

182. *GiA III*, 241, par. 128-132.

183. Ibid., 242, par. 136.

184. Ibid.

185. "A Message to Our Churches," Geneva, Switzerland, 1990, in *GiA II*, 160ff.

the same understanding of faith and discipleship,"[186] they distinguish different emphases. "While Lutherans have emphasized that the response of faith is not our doing nor is faith our possession, Baptists have emphasized the present reality and personal experience of faith."[187] As a main issue the report of the dialogue identifies the question of how faith relates to baptism.[188] Both sides explore together the New Testament witness on baptism.

Baptists regard this New Testament situation as normative, thus finding it impossible to baptize infants. Lutherans, however, have maintained that once the question of children being born into Christian families had to be faced by the growing church, that church rightly modified its view that a personal confession of faith had to precede baptism.[189]

The dialogue also points to the issue of freedom of choice as an anthropological question related to the discussion and to sociological issues related to the notion of a Christian family. Finally the dialogue understands its results as a motivation for closer cooperation and gives a series of concrete practical recommendations for parishes or congregations, including "that both Baptists and Lutherans reject a recent practice by some independent evangelists of encouraging successive baptisms of the same person upon successive conversion experiences" and "that Lutherans continue their efforts to overcome the problem of indiscriminate baptism."[190]

Anglican–Baptist (2000-2005)[191]

In dealing with the issue of baptism in the context of the process of initiation, the report of the "International Conversations between the Anglican Communion and the Baptist World Alliance" during the years 2000–2005 starts by pointing to the difficulties: "Both communities agree that baptism is unrepeatable, and yet

---

186. Ibid., 160, par. 31.

187. Ibid., 161, par. 32.

188. Ibid., par. 33.

189. Ibid., par. 38.

190. Ibid., 165, par. 49.

191. "Conversations around the World. International Conversations between the Anglican Communion and the Baptist World Alliance, McLean, Virginia, USA, 2000-2005," in *GiA III,* 342ff.

draw altogether different conclusions from this affirmation."[192] The report recommends as a first step towards mutual understanding "to abandon a certain 'typecasting.'"[193] As another step it proposes "to recognize that the 'beginning' of the Christian life—or initiation—is not so much a single event, but a process or a journey which may extend over a considerable time."[194] This is further developed by exploring the link of baptism with confirmation and the whole process of initiation.

Disciples–Reformed (1987)[195]

The report of the dialogue between the World Alliance of Reformed Churches and the Disciples Ecumenical Consultative Council is titled "No Doctrinal Obstacles."

While starting with agreement on common convictions concerning baptism and also stating that "in most places, Disciples and Reformed recognize each other as baptized members of the body of Christ and admit one another freely to their respective Eucharistic celebrations,"[196] the report still insists that "Disciples and Reformed should refuse to practice rebaptism."[197] The authors consider that "both forms of baptism embody God's own initiative in Christ and express a personal response of faith made within a believing community."[198]

Reformed–African Instituted (2002)[199]

The dialogue between the World Alliance of Reformed Churches and the Organization of African Instituted Churches is a relatively

---

192. Ibid., 342, par. 40.

193. Ibid., 343, par. 41.

194. Ibid., 343, par. 42.

195. "Disciples of Christ–Reformed Dialogue: No Doctrinal Obstacles, Birmingham, England 4-11 March 1987," in *GiA II*, 182ff.

196. Ibid., 183, par. 24.

197. Ibid., par. 27.

198. Ibid., par. 23.

199. The Final Report: Dialogue between the African Independent or Instituted Churches and the World Alliance of Reformed Churches, Mbagathi, Kenya, 9-14 February 2002, in *GiA III*, 310-318.

new one, begun in 1999. It addressed the issue of baptism briefly in 2002 in Nairobi at the dialogue's third meeting, saying:

> *We agree that the sacraments of baptism and the eucharist are grounded in Scripture and are commended to the church for its spiritual growth. Baptism signifies the entrance of the believer into the community of faith, and his/her engrafting into the body of Christ. In communion, the faithful are fed with Christ himself. The experience of receiving Christ in the sacraments is made possible by the powerful and mysterious action of the Holy Spirit.[200]*

Lutheran–Mennonite (2008)

The bilateral dialogue between the Lutheran World Federation and the Mennonite World Conference is one of those which led to a public event of reconciliation in 2010 at the Assembly of the Lutheran World Federation in Stuttgart, Germany. This is considered a precondition for overcoming their doctrinal differences in the understanding of baptism. The report of the dialogue commission[201] states:

> *In terms of on-going relations between Mennonites and Lutherans, we acknowledge an asymmetry in our approach regarding the question of baptism of newcomers who join our churches from the other tradition. Whereas Lutherans universally recognize baptisms performed in Mennonite churches, Mennonite churches do not generally recognize the baptism of infants performed in Lutheran churches and often require newcomers who have been baptized as infants to be baptized according to Mennonite practice, something that Lutherans would view as rebaptism. At the same time, however, some Mennonite churches do recognize infant baptisms to the extent that they require only a public confession of*

---

200. *GiA III*, 317.

201. Lutheran World Federation and Mennonite World Conference, "Healing Memories: Reconciling in Christ," Report of the Lutheran-Mennonite International Study Commission, 2010, 89, http://www.lutheranworld.org/lwf/wp-content/uploads/2010/10/Report_Lutheran-Mennonite_Study_Commission.pdf.

faith for membership, which completes whatever may have been lacking in the original "water baptism."

They state an agreement in the fact

that baptism cannot be seen as an isolated event. Thus, how baptisms are recognized must be understood within a larger framework that explores how the practice of baptism is related to a larger set of theological doctrines. Since these frameworks are different, Lutherans feel misunderstood by Mennonites when Mennonites assess the Lutheran practice of baptism according to their own framework. Conversely, Mennonites feel misunderstood by Lutherans when Lutherans assess the Mennonite practice according to their own framework...

But a solution still needs to be found:

The members of this study commission hope that neither the Anabaptist-Mennonite rejection of infant baptism nor the condemnation of Anabaptists in Article IX will remain a church-dividing issue. Nevertheless, we have not yet found a way to bridge the divide between the two churches regarding their teaching and practice on baptism ... Among other topics, those conversations will have to address our mutual understandings of the relationship between divine action and human (re)action in baptism.

Summarizing Analysis

Within this group of bilateral dialogues we can distinguish those in which mutual recognition of baptism has been achieved—the dialogues of the Disciples of Christ with different churches in which infant baptism is practiced—and those in which the differences on infant baptism still remain an obstacle. The difficulties in the latter group concern the different emphasis given to the priority of God's grace and to personal faith as well as the relation between faith and baptism. In particular, the dialogues which involve Pentecostals consider the question of the effect of baptism as crucial, but the relationship between baptism and ecclesiology is also important.

Not all of these dialogues make proposals as to how to reach convergence on reaching mutual recognition of baptism. The dialogue between Anglicans and Baptists is interesting in this regard. It proposes considering the beginning of the Christian life as a process rather than a single event. This is clearly an idea which is influenced by the work of the Faith and Order Commission of the World Council of Churches in the second half of the 1990s.[202] This becomes clear when considering the dates of the different dialogues: the Anglican-Baptist was conducted between 2000 and 2005, and is thus the youngest among this group of bilateral dialogues. While the earlier dialogues remain static either stating the differences between the churches or proposing further discussions on specific issues, the proposal of Faith and Order brings a new perspective on a common understanding of baptism as such. It is up to future dialogues to prove whether this is a viable proposal.

Dialogues between Orthodox and Non-Orthodox
Old Catholic–Eastern Orthodox (1985-87)[203]

The dialogue between the Old Catholic and Orthodox Churches on "sacramental teaching" states, in a short text, the common conviction on the understanding of baptism as a God-given sacrament which makes one a member of the church. It is necessary and is administered with threefold submersion in the name of the Father and the Son and the Holy Spirit. Baptism is rebirth, it is joining in one body and becoming a child of God. This includes personal acceptance in faith and conversion. Baptism leads to the gift of the Holy Spirit and to the Eucharist. There are no deep divergences. The question of mutual recognition of baptism is not addressed.

---

202. See Thomas F. Best and Dagmar Heller, eds., *Becoming a Christian: The Ecumenical Implications of Our Common Baptism*, Faith and Order Paper No. 184, WCC Publications, Geneva, 1997.

203. Old Catholic–Eastern Orthodox Dialogue, "Sacramental Teaching," Amersfoort, Netherlands, 3 October 1985 and Kavala, Greece, 17 October 1987, in *GiA II*, 255ff.

Roman Catholic–Eastern Orthodox (1987)[204]

The international joint commission for the dialogue between the Catholic Church and the Orthodox Church published in 1987 a report on "Faith, Sacraments and the Unity of the Church." In this both sides agree on the role of faith as a "presupposition of baptism"[205] and on Christian initiation as a whole, "in which chrismation is the perfection of baptism and the eucharist is the completion of the other two."[206] Although the Roman Catholic side affirms the unity of the three sacraments, it admits that persons who have not yet been confirmed are often admitted to the eucharist. This inversion of the sequence of the three sacraments "calls for deep theological and pastoral reflection."[207] Furthermore, the two churches agree on

1) *the necessity of baptism for salvation;*
2) *the effects of baptism....;*
3) *incorporation into the church by baptism;*
4) *the relation of baptism to the mystery of the Trinity;*
5) *the essential link between baptism and the death and resurrection of the Lord;*
6) *the role of the Holy Spirit in baptism;*
7) *the necessity of water which manifests baptism's character as the bath of new birth.*[208]

Differences remain in the practice of immersion and infusion and in the fact that in the Roman Catholic tradition a deacon can be the ordinary minister of baptism.[209]

---

204. Eastern Orthodox–Roman Catholic Dialogue, "Faith, Sacraments and the Unity of the Church," Bari, Italy, June 1987, in *GiA II*, 660-670.

205. *GiA II*, 662, par. 12.

206. Ibid., 666, par. 37.

207. Ibid., 667, par. 51.

208. Ibid., 667, par. 49.

209. Ibid., par. 50.

Lutheran–Eastern Orthodox (2004)[210]

Within a series of meetings on "The Mystery of the Church," the Lutheran-Orthodox Joint Commission between the Orthodox Church and the Lutheran World Federation dedicated a whole meeting to the theme "Baptism and Chrismation." By comparing the rites of initiation in the two traditions as expressions of their respective theologies, the two groups find a series of agreements, especially concerning the practice of administering baptism with water in the name of the Father, and of the Son, and of the Holy Spirit. Baptism is normally administered by an ordained person, but in cases of emergency can be done by lay people. They agree that baptism is unrepeatable. Both sides compare the liturgical rites, including exorcism, renunciation of the devil and the confession of faith. Both "agree that the third component of Christian initiation is the gift and seal of the Holy Spirit."[211] It is stated that "Orthodox and Lutherans ... found that the three components of Christian initiation are to a large extent included in each other's rites."[212]

The document focuses on comparison and on pointing out the similarities in the baptismal rites, but does not go into the theological discussion of the differences and the question of mutual recognition of baptism.

Summary

These dialogues remain content with identifying the commonalities between the respective traditions, but do not address the question of mutual recognition. There is, however, a bilateral dialogue on a regional level between Orthodox and Protestants in Europe, organized by the Communion of Protestant Churches in Europe (CPCE) and the Orthodox churches, which in its fourth session on "Baptism in the Life of our Churches" recommends to the respective churches "to initiate steps towards the mutual recognition of

---

210. "The Mystery of the Church: Baptism and Chrismation," Lutheran-Orthodox Joint Commission, Twelfth Plenary, Duraù, Romania, 6-15 October 2004, in *GiA III*, 29-32.

211. Ibid., 31, par. 8.

212. Ibid., 32.

Baptism where this is not yet the case."[213] The different understanding of chrismation and confirmation especially is highlighted for further study.

OTHER BILATERAL DIALOGUES IN WHICH THE ISSUE OF BAPTISM WAS ADDRESSED

Anglican–Lutheran (1972)[214]

The Lambeth Conference and the Lutheran World Federation established an official dialogue in 1968. In the so called Pullach Report[215] the issue of baptism is taken up in three paragraphs which confirm the existing common understanding and consensus regarding baptism. This is repeated in the Niagara Report from 1987.[216] Consequently the question of the mutual recognition of baptism is not touched; neither is the question of how baptism could be the basis of unity between the two confessions.

Anglican–Reformed (1984)[217]

The dialogue between the Anglican Communion and the World Alliance of Reformed Churches states clearly that

> *Baptism has not been an issue in dispute between our two traditions, yet our common practice of baptism has not led us into that unity which is stated by St Paul to be the necessary implication of one baptism ... We have to ask whether our failure to draw the proper conclusions from our common baptism is evidence of failure in both our communions to understand fully its meaning.*[218]

---

213. Michael Beintker, Viorel Ionita, and Jochen Kramm, eds., *Baptism in the Life of the Churches: Documentation of an Orthodox-Protestant Dialogue in Europe*, Lembeck, Frankfurt am Main, 2011, 17, par. 7.

214. Anglican- Lutheran Conversations: 1972, Pullach Report, in *GiA I*, 22.

215. Named for the German town of Pullach, where the meeting took place.

216. Anglican–Lutheran Dialogue, "Episcope," Niagara Falls, September 1987, in *GiA II*, 25, par. 64.

217. Anglican–Reformed Dialogue, "God's Reign and Our Unity," Woking, England, January 1984, in *GiA II*, 128ff.

218. Ibid., 128, par. 47.

On this basis the dialogue partners explore the New Testament and come to the conclusion that

> *it has to be confessed that in both our communions many baptized as infants have not in fact been led to make this personal appropriation ... We are agreed, on the one hand, that this situation is a summons to re-examine our baptismal discipline and the care given to the Christian nurture of those baptized as infants. On the other hand we must insist that the call for a second baptism rests on a failure to understand that baptism is primarily the work of God in Christ.*[219]

An issue of difference is the question of membership:

> *Reformed churches have tended to define it primarily as membership in a local congregation, while Anglicans, by the practice of Episcopal confirmation, have emphasized membership in the wider church. These emphases, however, are complementary rather than contradictory and require further exploration by our churches.*[220]

Finally the statement draws the following conclusions:

> *This understanding of our common baptism has very great practical consequences. If we are as realistic about baptism as the apostolic writers are, then we are already by our baptism one body, and the continued separation of our two communions is a public denial of what we are already in Christ. Moreover, there are consequences beyond these ecclesiastical ones. In the one man Jesus we see our common humanity taken up, redeemed and given back to us so that we can share it together—Jew and Gentile, man and woman, slave or free, rich and poor, white and black.*[221]

---

219. Ibid., 130, par. 55.
220. Ibid., 131, par. 57.
221. Ibid., 132, par. 61.

Lutheran–Methodist (1984)[222]

The dialogue between the Lutheran World Federation and the World Methodist Council points out the usual agreements on the administration and meaning of baptism between two churches which practice infant baptism. The dialogue partners find, though, two divergences or disagreements: first the issue of God's prevenient grace and, in consequence, a difference as to how far baptism is necessary for salvation: "Lutherans put a specific emphasis on the necessity of baptism for salvation because baptism is understood as the fundamental application of God's atonement in Christ to the individual."[223] Methodists understand that God's reconciling work has an anticipatory effect, enabling positive response by human beings. Therefore "God's gracious action which bestows salvation upon humankind is not bound to particular human words or actions."[224] The second difference is found in the way in which both sides define the relationship between baptism and membership in the church. "For Lutherans baptism establishes church membership. Most Methodists distinguish between preparatory and full membership. The former is given through baptism, the latter through explicit admission on profession of faith."[225]

Lutheran–Roman Catholic (1984)[226]

The document "Facing Unity"—a conclusion of a second round of bilateral dialogues between the Lutheran World Federation and the Roman Catholic Church—deals with "community in sacraments" and states that "Lutherans and Catholics are conscious that they participate in one and the same *baptism*."[227] Thus "almost everywhere our churches have officially recognized each other's baptism."[228]

---

222. "The Church: Community of Grace," Lutheran–Methodist Dialogue 1979-84, Bossey, Switzerland, June 1984, in *GiA II,* 209ff.

223. Ibid., 210, par. 50.

224. Ibid.

225. Ibid., 210, par. 51.

226. "Lutheran–Roman Catholic Dialogue: Facing Unity," Rome, Italy, 3 March 1984, in *GiA II*, 443-484.

227. Ibid., 461.

228. Ibid., 462.

Reformed–Roman Catholic[229]

The dialogue between the World Alliance of Reformed Churches and the Pontifical Council for Promoting Christian Unity did not specifically address the issue of Baptism. However the Report from the second phase of this dialogue (1984-1990), "Towards a Common Understanding of the Church," makes the following proposal as a step on the way to unity:

> *Our churches should give expression to mutual recognition of baptism. In some countries, the Roman Catholic and Reformed churches have already agreed to accept each other's baptism fully and without reserve, provided that it has been celebrated in the name of the Father, the Son and the Holy Spirit and with the use of water. We believe that such agreements can and should be made in all places without delay. Such an agreement implies that under no circumstances can there be a repetition of baptism which took place in the other church. Mutual recognition of baptism is to be understood as an expression of the profound communion that Jesus Christ himself establishes among his disciples and which no human failure can ever destroy.[230]*

Anglican–Roman Catholic (2006)

In an Agreed Statement by the International Anglican–Roman Catholic Commission for Unity and Mission in 2006 both churches expressed their common understanding of baptism and said officially that:

> *The Anglican Communion and the Catholic Church recognise the baptism each confers. Anglicans and Catholics therefore regard our common baptism as the basic bond of unity between us, even as we recognise that the fullness of eucharistic communion to which baptism should lead is impeded by disagreement concerning some of the elements of faith and practice which we*

---

229. Reformed–Roman Catholic Dialogue, "Towards a Common Understanding of the Church," Second Phase, 1984-1990, in *GiA II*, 780-818.
230. Ibid., 814.

acknowledge are necessary for full, visible communion... Our fundamental baptismal communion gives us the shared responsibility to witness as fully as possible to the Gospel of Christ before the world and to show forth the new life lived by the body of Christ, with the liberation and renewal it brings.[231]

Methodist–Roman Catholic (2011)[232]

The Methodist–Roman Catholic International Commission in 2011 published a text, "Encountering Christ the Saviour: Church and Sacraments," the second chapter of which is dedicated to baptism ("Baptism: Participation in Christ's Death and Resurrection"). The chapter examines commonalities and differences in the practice and understanding of baptism, more specifically the relation of baptism and faith, the understanding of baptism as rebirth, and the relationship of baptism and church. It concludes with the common conviction that "baptism brings us into a fundamental communion with one another in Christ; this communion, though incomplete, is the firm foundation for our shared journey into full communion."[233]

Summary

The mutual recognition of baptism has not been a problem between these churches.[234] Therefore these dialogues are rather a confirmation of their agreement, but also point out some divergences, though these do not prevent the mutual recognition of baptism.

---

231. International Anglican–Roman Catholic Commission for Unity and Mission, "Growing Together in Unity and Mission," at http://www.vatican.va/roman_curia/pontifical_councils/chrstuni/angl-comm-docs/rc_pc_chrstuni_doc_20070914_growing-together_en.html.

232. http://ecumenicalissues.blogspot.com/2011/09/encountering-christ-saviour.html with a link to the document "Encountering Christ the Saviour: Church and Sacrament."

233. Ibid., 27.

234. See also Birmelé, "Baptism and the Unity of the Church in Ecumenical Dialogues," 104-129.

WCC–ROMAN CATHOLIC JOINT WORKING GROUP (2004)[235]

A very specific bilateral dialogue is that between the Roman Catholic Church and the World Council of Churches (WCC-Roman Catholic Joint Working Group or JWG). It is a dialogue between a church and a multilateral institution; in this sense this bilateral conversation is in itself a multilateral dialogue.

On the basis of a statement of Pope John Paul II that "the universal brotherhood of Christians has become a firm ecumenical conviction ... [and this] ... is rooted in recognition of the oneness of baptism"[236] this dialogue sought "to explore the ecclesiological and ecumenical implications of a common recognition of baptism."[237]

This is probably the most comprehensive ecumenical document after BEM on the issue of baptism. Taking as starting point the BEM document on baptism and the fact that baptism "has been claimed as a common bond for Christians,"[238] the document first states the "growing ecumenical convergence on baptism"[239] by showing the convergence in the foundational place of baptism in the church, in the primary aspects of its meaning, the pattern or *ordo* of baptismal initiation and the convergence between the terms sacrament and ordinance used for describing baptism.

It emphasizes "the shared pattern of the early church as a common heritage for the divided churches today,"[240] a pattern which exists in the administration of baptism with water in the name of the Father, the Son and the Holy Spirit and the profession of faith. Differences in understanding are identified as the notion of incorporation into the body of Christ through baptism and the question of church membership through baptism.

---

235. Joint Working Group between the World Council of Churches and the Roman Catholic Church, "Ecclesiological and Ecumenical Implications of a Common Baptism," Kolympari–Chania, Crete, Greece, 6-13 May 2004, in *GiA III*, 559-586.

236. John Paul II, Encyclical *Ut Unum Sint* (1995) 42, quoted in *GiA III*, 559, par. 3.

237. Ibid.

238. Ibid., 561. par. 11.

239. Ibid., 561, ch. 1.

240. Ibid., 562, par. 15.

The document distinguishes three dimensions of the common pattern of baptism: the liturgical water rite; the wider pattern of Christian initiation, including components in addition to the liturgical rite of baptism, and the life-long aspect of baptism pointing to ongoing formation and responsible discipleship.[241] Whether the churches call baptism a sacrament or an ordinance, the realities named with different terminology "bring Christians to the central mysteries of life in Christ."[242] An important "ecclesiological implication" identified in the document is that

> *those Christian communities which agree that baptism means incorporation into the body of Christ, the church, and who agree that the church is one, should belong to one and the same community ... There should be no division among ecclesial communities; baptism should impel Christians to work for the elimination of divisions.*[243]

Baptism is understood as "one of the prerequisites for full communion."[244]

As a concrete proposal towards convergence, the document takes the approach of looking at baptism as "the heart of the process"[245] of Christian initiation and incorporation into the body of Christ. "Baptism is at the heart of the process, both as decisive moment and as model of the entire process."[246]

> *The sacrament of baptism is, in the first meaning of the term, a distinctive water-rite that occurs once in a life-time and cannot be repeated. The ongoing gift of growth in faith and the continual dying and rising in Christ that this entails is truly a living out of the once-for-all encounter of faith with Christ that is given and modeled in the rite of baptism. In this sense Christian life can be*

---

241. Cf. ibid., 563., par. 18.
242. Ibid., 564, par. 24.
243. Ibid., 566, par. 31.
244. Ibid., par. 33.
245. Ibid., 567, par. 34.
246. Ibid.

understood as a "life-long baptism," lasting until final oneness with Christ is attained.[247]

The document then takes a closer look at the divergence between adult baptism and the baptism of infants as well as the theological difference behind this gap, namely the different understanding of the relationship between baptism and faith. Based on the work of the Faith and Order Commission,[248] the document proposes

that the pattern of baptismal initiation has three elements: forma-
tion in faith, baptism in water, and participation in the life of the
community. These elements are present in the rite of water bap-
tism itself for every church, though not in the same way. Likewise
all three elements are present in the life-long process of Christian
discipleship, with its continual formation in faith, recollection
of baptismal grace and promise, and deepening participation in
the life of the church. If we ask about the relation of faith to bap-
tism in reference to the water rite alone, the differences among
the churches remain substantial. When we compare instead the
wider pattern of baptismal initiation and formation in Christ,
more extensive convergence emerges. It is a convergence that is
compatible with and even enriched by the fact that different tradi-
tions emphasize one or other element of the pattern and put them
together in different ways.[249]

The document recommends "that each church, even as it retains its own baptismal tradition, recognize in others the baptism into Jesus Christ by affirming the similarity of wider patterns of initiation and formation in Christ present in every community."[250] From this the document draws the conclusion, that the basic issues

---

247. Ibid., 568, par. 40
248. See Best and Heller, *Becoming a Christian*, 78, referring to Thomas F. Best and Dagmar Heller, eds., *So We Believe, So We Pray: Towards Koinonia in Worship*, Faith and Order Paper No. 171, WCC Publications, Geneva, 1995, 6, par. 4.
249. *GiA III*, 571, par. 52.
250. Ibid., par. 54.

which need to be resolved for overcoming the divergence on infant baptism "are the questions of the nature and purpose of the church and its role in the economy of salvation."[251]

Baptism, despite these differences, is seen as providing "a degree of communion that is real, if imperfect."[252] The document also takes up the ethical implications of baptism, which leads to "the need for a healing of memories between them (i.e. the churches) and reconciliation"[253] and which includes "the call to engage together in the common work of the baptized."[254]

The document emphasizes the "importance of continuing to seek the mutual recognition of baptism as a primary aspect of fostering bonds of unity between separated Christians."[255] It further clarifies that "the mutual recognition of baptism implies an acknowledgement of the apostolicity of each other's baptism," but this does not mean a full recognition of the apostolicity of the other church.[256] What follows is a series of practical recommendations which would help to deepen the bond between churches which exist through baptism.

Summary

This dialogue can, to a certain extent, be understood as a multilateral dialogue, since one of the two sides is a multilateral body. In this sense it can also be considered as a continuation of the work of Faith and Order and BEM. This is confirmed by the heavy use of material from both BEM and follow-up studies of Faith and Order, including the study process resulting in the text *One Baptism: Towards Mutual Recognition*.[257] The dialogue also takes up especially the idea of looking at baptism as part of a wider process

---

251. Ibid., 572, par. 57.
252. Ibid., 573, par. 61.
253. Ibid., 576, par. 73.
254. Ibid., par. 74.
255. Ibid., 578, par. 85.
256. Ibid., 582, par. 98.
257. World Council of Churches, Commission on Faith and Order, *One Baptism: Towards Mutual Recognition; A Study Text*, Faith and Order Paper No. 210, Geneva, World Council of Churches, 2011.

of initiation and the ethical implications of baptism.[258] Finally, it raises the question of apostolicity and the recognition of apostolicity of the respective other church.

Conclusion from the Bilateral Dialogues

As Erich Geldbach, a German Baptist theologian, has pointed out in his analysis of bilateral dialogues, there is a great degree of agreement between the churches concerning the understanding of baptism:

- Baptism is incorporation into the body of Christ.

- Baptism establishes a new relationship with God, it is forgiveness of sins, rebirth, new life.

- Baptism is performed because of Christ's commandment.

- Baptism should not be understood in a magical way.

- Faith is a precondition for baptism.

- Baptism can only be performed in the context of a congregation.

- Baptism is only possible, because God acted beforehand.

- Those who have been baptized need to grow in faith during a lifelong process.

- Re-baptism should be avoided.[259]

- It seems also that most of the churches would agree that baptism is with water and with the trinitarian formula.

But the picture of the bilateral dialogues on the issue of baptism shows that despite many convergences, the differences on infant baptism, and also the difficulties of the Orthodox in recognizing the baptism of others, have still not been resolved. In both the relation between credobaptist churches and paedobaptist churches and

---

258. See ibid., 2, par. 3 and 9-11, par. 41-55; and Best and Heller, *Becoming a Christian*, 88-95.

259. Geldbach, *Taufe*, 127ff.

between Orthodox and non-Orthodox basic theological differences are at stake: on the one hand, the understanding of the relationship between faith and grace and, on the other hand, the question of ecclesiology. The role of the Holy Spirit is also an issue which needs clarification.

CHAPTER 4
BAPTISM IN THEOLOGICAL CONTROVERSY

W HEN WE SURVEY THE OVERALL LANDSCAPE OF THE different confessional traditions on baptism, several lines of division become obvious.

The first is the separation between churches which baptize persons of all ages, including infants, and churches which baptize only believers who can speak for themselves. Behind this division are various theological issues: one is a hermeneutical question of how to understand the biblical sources. Another one is the role of faith in baptism, which is finally related to the understanding of faith as such. The relation between baptism and original sin is a third theological issue. Finally, ecclesiology plays an important role.

The second line of separation is the division existing *within* the groups of churches which baptize infants between those which recognize baptism only within the boundaries of their own church and churches which also recognize baptism performed outside their own boundaries. In fact, this is the division between the Orthodox and non-Orthodox, which is—as we have seen in the first chapter— not a strict line of division, but has been throughout history, until the present, an ambiguity in the attitude of Orthodox churches towards converts from other churches. The issue is again—theologically speaking—ecclesiology. This division includes an additional issue, which is the understanding of baptism as part of the sacraments of initiation.

A third line of division can be identified between churches which distinguish between water baptism and baptism of the Holy Spirit as two separate events and churches which understand baptism of the Holy Spirit as happening *in* the water baptism. The issue here is the relationship between baptism and the Holy Spirit.

During the past several decades a fourth line of division has developed between churches which insist on the trinitarian formula and groups within churches which use other formulas. The issue is twofold: on the one hand it is related to feminist theology and on the other to biblical hermeneutics and the understanding of the Trinity.

Another issue, which is not a direct cause of division but which is a matter of controversy in conversation and given as an additional argument in some divisive discussions, is related to the mode of the water rite: ought baptism to be performed by immersion, or is *affusion (pouring) or aspersion (sprinkling) acceptable?

We will also look at a new and controversial issue which has developed among some local churches in the global South with the introduction of rites from local cultures. This has resulted in discussions about the question of the inculturation of baptism.

Finally, I will mention a new emerging challenge by churches which (re-)baptize everybody who joins them, even if the person was baptized within a church that shares the same theological understanding and practice of baptism.

The Controversy on Infant Baptism

That infant baptism was practiced rather early in history is known from statements made against this practice. One of the earliest such testimonies stems from Tertullian (ca. 150-230 CE), who finds that in infant baptism too much responsibility is put on the shoulders of godparents and sponsors.[1] Clear theological arguments in favor of

---

1. See Joachim Jeremias, *Infant Baptism in the First Four Centuries*, SCM, London, 1960, 81ff.

infant baptism appear very late in the history of the early church, which leads to the conclusion "that infant baptism was so self-evident and unproblematical that any justification of the practice was superfluous"[2] in the early centuries. In the 12th century we know of the first groups to reject infant baptism by referring to the Bible.[3] But only in the 16th century, with the so-called Radical Reformation, is the controversy about infant baptism discussed with theological arguments.

In the following the arguments on both sides will be presented and analyzed according to the underlying theological issues.

INTERPRETATION OF SCRIPTURE

One of the main theological issues in the controversy on infant baptism is the interpretation of scripture. As is clear from the responses to BEM, and as can be seen in church history, one of the main arguments against infant baptism is that it is "not biblical." This argument includes two aspects: first, whether the New Testament actually reports infant baptisms; and second, whether God's command, or the institution of baptism, includes infant baptism. The first aspect is more an historical perspective (see i. below), the second is a theological issue (see ii. below).

i. The New Testament reports explicitly only about baptisms of adults, such as Acts 8:36-38 (Philip and the eunuch), Acts 9:17-19 and Acts 22:12-16 (the baptism of Saul-Paul), Acts 10:44-48, Acts 16:14-15 (Lydia), Acts 16: 29-34 (the jailer), Acts 18:7-8 (Crispus), and Acts 19:1-7 (some disciples).

The biblical arguments on the side of churches which baptize infants refer to passages—in some cases even the same ones quoted *against* infant baptism—which hint indirectly at the fact that children were baptized already in the time of the New Testament. These are passages such as Acts 16:14ff.:

---

2. Edmund Schlink, *The Doctrine of Baptism*, Concordia Publishing, Saint Louis and London, 1972, 137.
3. See above, Chapter Two.

*A certain woman named Lydia, a worshiper of God, was listen-
ing to us ... The Lord opened her heart to listen eagerly to what
was said by Paul. When she and her household were baptized, she
urged us, saying, "If you have judged me to be faithful to the Lord,
come and stay at my home."*

Another such passage is Acts 16:25-34:

*About midnight Paul and Silas were praying and singing hymns
to God, and the prisoners were listening to them. Suddenly there
was an earthquake, so violent that the foundations of the prison
were shaken; and immediately all the doors were opened and
everyone's chains were unfastened. When the jailer woke up and
saw the prison doors wide open, he drew his sword and was about
to kill himself, since he supposed that the prisoners had escaped.
But Paul shouted in a loud voice, "Do not harm yourself, for we
are all here." The jailer called for lights, and rushing in, he fell
down trembling before Paul and Silas. Then he brought them outside and said, "Sirs, what must I do to be saved?" They answered,
"Believe on the Lord Jesus, and you will be saved, you and your
household." They spoke the word of the Lord to him and to all who
were in his house. At the same hour of the night he took them and
washed their wounds; then he and his entire family were baptized
without delay. He brought them up into the house and set food
before them; and he and his entire household rejoiced that he had
become a believer in God.*

Acts 18:8 (Crispus "with all his household") as well as 1 Cor 1:16
(household of Stephanas) are also quoted in this context. All these
texts report that an entire "household" or family was baptized—
which would have included children, slaves and their children.[4]
    While for churches which practice infant baptism these texts
are understood as an indication that infants were already baptized
in early times, for others they indicate something else. A Baptist
theologian, for example, writes:

---

4. See Jeremias, *Infant Baptism*, 20ff.; see also Louis Berkhoff, *Systematic
Theology*, Banner of Truth Trust, Edinburgh, 1979, 634.

> *When we look at the actual examples more closely, we see that in a*
> *number of them, there are indications of saving faith on the part of*
> *all of those baptized. For example, it is true that the family of the*
> *Philippian jailer was baptized (Acts 16:33), but it is also true that*
> *Paul and Silas "spoke the word of the Lord to him and to all that*
> *were in his house" (Acts 16:32). If the Word of the Lord was spoken*
> *to all in the house, there is an assumption that all were old enough*
> *to understand the word and believe it. Moreover, after the fam-*
> *ily had been baptized we read that the Philippian jailer "rejoiced*
> *with all his household that he had believed in God" (Acts 16:34).*
> *So we have not only a household baptism, but also a household*
> *reception of the Word of God and a household rejoicing in faith in*
> *God. These facts suggest quite strongly that the entire household*
> *had individually come to faith in Christ.*[5]

In addition, theologians with a paedobaptist background would point to the fact that in New Testament times, baptisms were naturally baptisms of converts and thus cannot be taken as a model for the situation in later times.

These are just a few examples of the opposite ways of interpreting biblical passages.

ii. Another argument used to defend infant baptism is Acts 2:38f:

> *Peter said to them, "Repent, and be baptized every one of you in*
> *the name of Jesus Christ so that your sins may be forgiven; and*
> *you will receive the gift of the Holy Spirit. For the promise is for*
> *you, for your children, and for all who are far away, everyone*
> *whom the Lord our God calls to him."*

According to the German New Testament scholar Joachim Jeremias "thus in Acts 2:38f, we have before us a witness for the practice of infant baptism in apostolic times."[6] This interpretation is rejected by J. Rodman Williams, who writes:

---

5. Wayne Grudem, *Systematic Theology*, Zondervan, Grand Rapids, 2000, 978, quoted in Simon G. H. Tan, "Reassessing Believer's Baptism in Pentecostal Theology and Practice," *Asian Journal of Pentecostal Studies* 6 (2003): 222.

6. Jeremias, *Infant Baptism*, 41. See also John Murray, *Christian Baptism*, Presbyterian and Reformed Publishing, Phillipsburg, NJ, 1980, 68.

A careful reading of Acts 2: 38-39 and the background of these
verses will show that in the first place, Peter is referring to the gift
of the Holy Spirit, not salvation (contained in the words "repent,"
"be baptized," and "forgiveness of sins"), which is promised to
all whom God "calls to him" (thus who have received salvation).
Hence it is misguided to view baptism of anyone as included in the
promise. Peter's words about children cannot imply infant bap-
tism, since the whole background of repentance and faith calls for
conscious decision, and only in that context can baptism occur
with the resulting promise of the gift of the Holy Spirit. Third,
"your children" is properly understood as "your sons and your
daughters" (v.17)—not your infants—those of responsible age. In
every way to view Peter's words as under-girding the practice of
infant baptism is without warrant.[7]

Churches which baptize infants often also quote texts such as
Mt 18:3; Mk 10:15 or Mt 19:13ff. in order to show Jesus' preference
for children and the inclusiveness of God's kingdom for children.
Others argue that these texts do not speak about baptism.

In the 20th century the issue has been discussed anew by biblical scholars from different confessional backgrounds. The conviction was previously widespread that the primitive church did not
practice infant baptism. However, some scholars with a Lutheran or
Reformed background, such as Joachim Jeremias[8] and others[9] supported the thesis that from the beginning children born before the
baptism of their parents were baptized together with their parents.
Kurt Aland,[10] in opposition to Jeremias, showed that the primitive church did not baptize infants until the 2nd century. Edmund
Schlink therefore came to the conclusion "thus on the basis of the
New Testament infant baptism can neither be excluded nor proved."[11]

---

7. J. Rodman Williams, *Renewal Theology*, vol. 3, *The Church, the Kingdom,
and the Last Things*, Zondervan, Grand Rapids, MI, 1992, 235ff., quoted in Tan,
"Reassessing Believer's Baptism," 225.

8. Jeremias, *Infant Baptism.*

9. See Schlink, *The Doctrine of Baptism*, 131.

10. Kurt Aland, *Did the Early Church Baptize Infants?* Westminster Press,
Philadelphia, 1963.

11. Schlink, *The Doctrine of Baptism,* 136.

What must be noted here is the variety of ways of interpreting scripture, which is the divisive issue in this context. The different interpretation of one and the same text shows that the understanding of infant baptism is determined by one's confessional background. It is a pre-understanding which functions as a kind of prejudice.

Those who insist on the fact that the New Testament teaches only adult baptism apply, as the main interpretive insight, the fact that there are only reports on baptisms of adults. From this starting point all other passages which might indirectly include the possibility of early infant baptisms are interpreted consistently so as not to contradict this main idea. Those theologians who opt for infant baptism apply different hermeneutical keys for the interpretation of scripture. Orthodox and Catholic Christians would claim that scripture and tradition go together. Thus for them the basis for infant baptism is not just the biblical texts, but also the witnesses from the first centuries of the Common Era. The earliest clear references to infant baptism appear around the year 200, for example in the treatise *Against Heretics* of Irenaeus of Lyons.[12] Many centuries later Martin Luther, who in contrast to the Catholic position emphasized *sola scriptura*, interestingly takes experience as an argument for infant baptism: to him history shows that children who received baptism also received the Holy Spirit.[13] Ulrich Zwingli, on the other hand, tries to keep with scripture, arguing for infant baptism by using the hermeneutical key of the foreshadowing of the New Testament message in the Old Testament and trying to establish a parallel between circumcision and baptism.

Thus we can say that for all the churches the historical factor, namely the historical practice of baptism, is an important argument. The problem is that the historical "proofs" are not unequivocal. Therefore, paedobaptist theologians, in order to support their position, also take into consideration indirect biblical indications that God's kingdom includes children.

---

12. See ibid., 132.
13. Cf. above, Chapter One.

BAPTISM AND FAITH

From the discussion about the biblical foundation of infant baptism follows the controversy about the question of the relationship between baptism and faith.

One of the arguments against infant baptism is that, according to the New Testament, baptism requires listening to the gospel, repentance and faith,[14] and that the candidate takes the initiative. Infants, according to this argumentation, are not capable of repentance and faith. Biblical texts on which this argument is based are, for example, Mk 16:16 ("the one who believes and is baptized will be saved"); Acts 10:44-48; Acts 16:14ff. ("A certain woman named Lydia … was listening to us"); Acts 16:31ff. ("'Sirs, what must I do to be saved?' They answered: 'Believe on the Lord Jesus, and you will be saved' … then he and his entire family were baptized without delay."); and Col 2:11ff. ("When you were buried with him in baptism, you were also raised with him through faith in the power of God."); or Eph 4:4-6 ("There is one body and one Spirit, just as you were called to the one hope of your calling, one Lord, one faith, one baptism.").[15]

In fact, as became clear in the BEM process, all churches agree that baptism and faith belong together,[16] but the relationship between the two is understood in different ways.

The church father Augustine (354-430) already argued that "in infant Baptism the sacrament itself takes the place of the missing faith of the person to be baptized"[17] and referred to the representative faith of the church. Thomas Aquinas, in the 13th century, compared the faith of an infant with a man who is asleep: "though he may have the habits of virtue, yet is he hindered from virtuous

---

14. See J. Mark Beach, "Original Sin, Infant Salvation, and the Baptism of Infants," *Mid-American Journal of Theology* 12 (2001): 52.

15. See George R. Beasley-Murray, *Baptism in the New Testament,* Macmillan and Co., London, 1962, 200. Beasley-Murray points out that the three items relate to the baptismal rite and are interrelated in a way, that the passage could be read as "One Lord, the object of faith's confession in baptism."

16. Cf. also Beasley-Murray, *Baptism in the New Testament,* 272: "It is undoubtedly true that in the New Testament it is everywhere assumed that faith proceeds to baptism and that baptism is for faith."

17. Schlink, *The Doctrine of Baptism,* 144.

acts through being asleep."[18] Baptism, in his view, makes acts of faith possible when the child grows up. Martin Luther understood faith as a pure gift of God, "as operation of the Holy Spirit which is received in a completely passive manner."[19] In other words, "Even though faith is accomplished in man's activity, it is not man's work."[20] Therefore even a child has faith, although it cannot produce acts of faith. John Calvin also reckoned with the possibility of the Spirit's activity in infants. "Pointing to the Spirit's activity in John the Baptist in his mother's womb (Luke 1:15) and to the conception of Jesus by the Holy Spirit, Calvin rejects the idea 'that infants cannot be regenerated by God's power, which is as easy and ready to Him as it is incomprehensible and wonderful to us.'"[21] In this understanding faith becomes the effect of baptism, and baptism is the beginning of the Spirit's activity, of which the baptized later on becomes conscious: "Baptism is performed in view of the faith which God will create in the person through Baptism, proclamation, and in answer to intercession."[22]

The opposite understanding is expressed by George R. Beasley-Murray, a Baptist theologian, who points out: "In the New Testament faith *comes* to baptism; the idea of baptism creating faith is not on the horizon."[23]

The issue here is the balance between two major aspects of baptism: baptism as an act of God and baptism as an act of the human being.[24] Generally speaking, churches which baptize infants understand baptism in the first place as an action of God,[25] while churches

---

18. Thomas Aquinas, *Summa Theologica* III, qu. 69, 6. The Summa Theologica of St. Thomas Aquinas Second and Revised Edition, 1920, Literally translated by Fathers of the English Dominican Province Online Edition Copyright © 2008 by Kevin Knight, http://www.newadvent.org/summa/4069.htm#article6

19. Schlink, *The Doctrine of Baptism*, 144.

20. Ibid., 123.

21. Ibid., 144. Schlink is referring to Calvin, *Institutes*, IV, 16, 18.

22. Schlink, *The Doctrine of Baptism*, 169.

23. Beasley-Murray, *Baptism in the New Testament*, 274.

24. See ibid., 275: "So in the doctrine of Sacraments the act of God and the act of man must neither be confounded nor be separated."

25. See World Council of Churches, Commission on Faith and Order, *Baptism, Eucharist and Ministry 1982-1990: Report on the Process and*

which reject infant baptism put more emphasis on the commitment and the initiative of the candidate to be baptized.[26] Both sides, however, see a connection between baptism and salvation and regeneration: while on the side of paedobaptists regeneration is seen as an *effect* of baptism, it is seen as a *precondition* for baptism by churches which do not baptize infants. This different emphasis also explains why many churches which baptize only believers who can speak for themselves do not understand baptism as a sacrament—a means of grace—but speak of baptism as an ordinance and think of it as a confirmation of faith.

Finally we can discern here a different understanding of faith itself in two aspects: On the one side the emphasis is on faith as a decision of the human person, on the other side faith is seen mainly as a gift of God, an act of God within the human person, by grace. And also: on the one side it is an individual act, on the other side the communal aspect of faith is highlighted.[27]

BAPTISM AND ORIGINAL SIN

Historically the increase, and finally the dominance, of infant baptism was influenced by the doctrine of original sin developed in a systematic way by Augustine.[28] In other words, the doctrine of original sin has implications for the understanding of infant baptism.[29] This doctrine refers to Rom 5:12 and expresses the total rupture of the communion between the human being and God.[30] Even children, therefore, are corrupted and live under the power of sin. Consequently baptism as sign and seal of divine redemption from sin has to be administered to them, and is necessary in order to avoid their eternal condemnation.

Responses, Faith and Order Paper No. 149, WCC Publications, Geneva 1990, 44.

26. See Schlink, *The Doctrine of Baptism*, 168ff.

27. Interestingly, an Asian theologian points out that believer's baptism and the individualism expressed in it is a modern Western feature: Tan, "Reassessing Believer's Baptism," 230.

28. See Ralph G. Wilburn, "The One Baptism and the Many Baptisms," *Mid-Stream* 3 (1964): 72-107.

29. See also Beach, "Original Sin, Infant Salvation, and the Baptism of Infants," 50.

30. See for example Origen, hom. Lev. 8, 3; hom Luc. 14, 3-5.

Baptists and other churches which deny infant baptism inherited the doctrine of original sin from Christian history. Some of them hold fast to this doctrine in the sense that all people are accountable before God, but try to distinguish between what this means for children and what it means for adults. Although all persons are born with a corrupted nature, "all those who fail to attain an age of moral competence are exempted from the guilt and consequent damnation that is part of original sin."[31] Therefore baptism administered to them does not make sense and is even seen by some as dangerous.[32]

Others distinguish between original sin and guilt. For example, Stanley J. Grenz affirms original sin as inherited corruption. Guilt, though, is not part of what constitutes original sin, because, according to scripture (Rom 2:6), God judges humans according to their works, and thus it is not the fallen nature which is condemned but sinful actions. "On this basis, we conclude that persons who do not develop the moral potential do not fall under the eternal condemnation of the righteous God." [33]

In modern times the Augustinian understanding of original sin has become problematic. Therefore, modern Protestant theology, in churches which practice infant baptism, has been trying to find new ways of interpreting original sin. Karl Barth, for example, tries to avoid this term as long as it includes the idea of hereditary sin.[34] Paul Tillich and others reject the term as well.[35] But for all of them it is clear that sin is a radical reality which shapes human life independently from human will. Karl Barth, a Reformed theologian, decided to opt for adult baptism, while other Protestant theologians still defend infant baptism as a sign for cleansing from

---

31. Beach, "Original Sin, Infant Salvation, and the Baptism of Infants," 55.

32. Ibid., 53.

33. Stanley J. Grenz, *Theology for the Community of God*, Eerdmans, Grand Rapids, MI and Regent College Publishing, Vancouver, 1994, 2000, 209.

34. Karl Barth, *Church Dogmatics* IV/1, *The Doctrine of Reconciliation*, ed. G.W. Bromiley and T.F. Torrance, T&T Clark International, London and New York, 1956, 500.

35. See Christine Axt-Piscalar, "Sünde VII," in *Theologische Realenzyklopädie 32*, 423ff.

this radical reality of sin,[36] showing inconsistencies in the Baptist argument, for example, that the ground of salvation is different for children and for adults.[37]

The difference between the two positions—infant or adult baptism—is therefore based on a different understanding of how the overall reality of sin can be applied to children and infants.

BAPTISM AND THE ROLE OF THE CHURCH

Another theological difference which plays a role in the controversy about infant baptism is related to ecclesiology: if baptism is understood primarily as God's act, then the church is the instrument of God's action. It is the church which is acting in obedience to God, and in that sense the church's acting is God's acting. But if baptism is mainly understood as a personal commitment of the person being baptized, the church does not necessarily play a role. In this case the church is seen as a human institution, bringing together people with the same experience.

The first option is certainly the case in a highly sacramental understanding of baptism, as in the Orthodox and Catholic churches. Consequently baptism is an act of the church, the church being a human-divine institution. On the opposite side is the view of churches which baptize only adults who can speak for themselves: the focus is on the individual person confessing his or her commitment to Jesus Christ. In many of these churches,[38] therefore, baptism is not related to church membership.

---

36. For example the Reformed theologian J. Mark Beach in "Original Sin, Infant Salvation, and the Baptism of Infants."

37. Ibid., 74.

38. See for example the Pentecostals, as the minutes of the General Assembly of the Church of God Evangel in 1912 show: "Question: Can the Church of God fellowship one who has not taken on the Lord in baptism? Answer: Water baptism is not a door into the church, and is an act of obedience after one has been converted, hence the fellowship is unbroken, provided such a one will be baptized at the first opportunity, and not reject the ordinance." Quoted in Kimberly Ervin Alexander, "Matters of Conscience, Matters of Unity, Matters of Orthodoxy: Trinity and Water Baptism in Early Pentecostal Theology and Practice," *Journal of Pentecostal Theology* 17 (2008): 54.

In summary, it becomes clear that the divergence on infant baptism is based on different interpretations of the Bible which have their roots in different assessments of the doctrine of original sin as well as in different ecclesiologies. This leads to different emphases in the understanding of baptism: while all churches see in baptism a divine aspect (baptism as God's action) as well as a human aspect (baptism as public confession), they emphasize these two aspects in different ways.

The Controversy between Orthodox and Non-Orthodox Churches

Within the group of paedobaptist churches, the Orthodox (Eastern and Oriental) do not recognize baptisms which were performed outside their own churches. In this divergence between Orthodox and non-Orthodox the crucial issue is the understanding of the relationship between baptism and the church and thus the understanding of church in general. The understanding of baptism as part of the sacraments of initiation and the mode of water-baptism[39] also play a role in the divergence.

UNDERSTANDING OF CHURCH

The recognition or non-recognition of baptisms performed in other churches is closely related with the question about the boundaries of the church. In paedobaptist churches baptism is, among other meanings, also understood as reception into the body of Christ, which is the church. Therefore in the early church, baptism immediately led to the eucharist as a sign that the newly baptized person was now a member of the community. This is not just the community of the local parish, but the community of the universal church. In the modern situation, where the church exists in different confessional churches, this raises the question of how these different *churches* are related to the universal *Church* of Jesus Christ.

---

39. See also p. 179f and 190f.

To this question churches respond in nuanced ways. Orthodox churches claim they are the true Church of Jesus Christ:[40]

The Orthodox Church is the true Church in which the Holy Tradition and the fullness of God's saving grace are preserved intact. She has preserved the heritage of the apostles and holy fathers in its integrity and purity. She is aware that her teaching, liturgical structures and spiritual practice are the same as those of the apostolic proclamation and the Tradition of the Early Church.[41]

Nevertheless, Christians outside of the Orthodox Church "retain a certain 'seal' of belonging to the people of God."[42] On this basis the Orthodox Church has different practices of receiving converts from other churches into the Orthodox Church: through baptism, through chrismation, through repentance.[43]

For a better understanding of this practice the Orthodox theologian John Erickson distinguishes "two main lines of approach" in contemporary practice within the Orthodox Church, the "Russian" approach and the "Greek" approach. According to the first approach, mainline Protestants who are baptized in the name of the

---

40. "The Orthodox Church is the true Church of Christ established by our Lord and Saviour Himself, the Church confirmed and sustained by the Holy Spirit, the Church about which the Saviour Himself has said: 'I will build my Church; and the gates of hell shall not prevail against it' (Mt. 16:18)." Bishops' Synod of the Russian Orthodox Church, "Basic Principles of the Attitude to the Non-Orthodox," 2000, par. 1.1. http://www.mospat.ru/en/documents/attitude-to-the-non-orthodox/i/.

41. Ibid., par. 1.18.

42. Ibid., par. 1.11.; see also par. 1.15: "In spite of the rupture of unity, there remains a certain incomplete fellowship which serves as the pledge of a return to unity in the Church, to catholic fullness and oneness."

43. See ibid., par. 1.17: "The existence of various rites of reception (through baptism, through chrismation, through repentance) shows that the orthodox Church relates to the different non-orthodox confessions in different ways. The criterion is the degree to which the faith and order of the Church, as well as the norms of Christian spiritual life, are preserved in a particular confession. By establishing various rites of reception, however, the orthodox Church does not assess the extent to which grace-filled life has either been preserved intact or distorted in a non-orthodox confession, considering this to be a mystery of God's providence and judgement."

triune God are to be received by anointment with chrism, according to the full post-baptismal rite of chrismation. Confirmed Roman Catholics and Eastern Catholics, as well as Oriental Orthodox, are to be received by confession of the Orthodox faith. This practice is based on a distinction made in the 4th century by Basil the Great[44] between heretics, schismatics, and dissidents and goes back to the 95th canon of the Council of Trullo (also called Quinisextum, 691-692), which classifies the non-Orthodox into three groups: (1) those who have to be baptized; (2) those who only have to be anointed; and (3) those who have only to declare their Orthodox faith.[45] The first group are pagans. The second group includes persons who have been baptized in the name of the Father and the Son and the Holy Spirit but whose communities do not have legal priesthood according to the Orthodox understanding and who do not confess the sacrament of anointing. This refers normally to mainline Protestants as the ministry of Protestant churches is not recognized by the Orthodox. Catholics and Orientals who have been anointed in their own church belong to the third category.

The second, or "Greek" approach, is the use of a special rite for the reception of converts. This is different from the rite of the postbaptismal chrismation, although it is also an anointing with chrism. The difference lies in the words related to the rite, which show clearly that it is a rite of reconciliation, with the candidate considered as already belonging to Christ's flock.[46]

As late as the 18th century the Greek church, in principle, baptized converts,[47] even if they came from the Latin (Roman Catholic) church or the non-Chalcedonian (Oriental Orthodox) churches.

---

44. Basil the Great, Epistle 188.

45. Council of Trullo, can. 95, quoted in Vlassios Phidas, "Baptism and Ecclesiology," *Ecumenical Review* 54 (2002): 45.

46. See John Klentos, "Rebaptizing Converts into the Orthodox Church: Old Perspectives on a New Problem," *Studia Liturgica* 29 (1999): 216-234.

47. See Sergiy Hovorun, "Богословские аспекты и практика приема в Православие из инославия" ("The Theological and Practical Aspects of Admission of Non-Orthodox Christians into the Orthodox Church"), V. Международная Богословская Конференция Русской Православной Церкви, *Православное учение о церковних таинствах*, том I, Синодальная Библейско-богословская комиссия Москва, 2009, 349-358.

This was a return to a strict policy stemming from St. Cyprian's principle *extra ecclesiam nulla salus* ("outside the church there is no salvation").

Behind these different practices is the fact that in the canons of various early synods there are two attitudes to be found. The one following Cyprian's strict principle can be based on the Apostolic Canons 46, 47, 50 and 68[48]. The more open attitude is based on Canon 7 of the second Ecumenical Council and on the already quoted Canon 95 of the Quinisextum (Council of Trullo)[49], which permits a certain group of heterodox Christians to be received in the Orthodox Church without baptism.[50]

As an explanation for the earlier practice of a reconciliation rite and in order to find a consistency between the different traditions found in the canons, the idea of *oikonomia* (literally "order of salvation") was found in the 18th century.[51] *Oikonomia* is understood as the way of God to deal with human failure and weaknesses[52] and thus means an exception from the strictly applied *akribia*. "*Akribia* and *oikonomia* are the two poles, which determine the boundaries, within which the activity of the church regarding its own members as well as regarding Christians outside is unfolded."[53] Applied to baptism, this means that *kat'akribian*—according to the meticulous understanding—of Cyprian's position, every non-Orthodox

---

48. The Apostolic Canons or Canons of the Apostles are a collection of 85 decrees from the early church. They were approved by the Council of Trullo in 692 (also called Quinisextum). Fifty of them are included in the Corpus Iuris Canonici of the Roman Catholic Church. The English text can be found on http://www.ccel.org/ccel/schaff/anf07.ix.ix.vi.html.

49. English text can be found on http://www.newadvent.org/fathers/3814.htm

50. Ibid., 355.

51. According to Ioan Sauca, the term "sacramental economy" in its contemporary meaning is linked to Nicodemus of Holy Mountain (1748-1809); see Ioan Sauca, "The Church Beyond Our Boundaries and the Ecumenical Vocation of Orthodoxy," *Ecumenical Review* 56 (2004): 222 n19.

52. See Hamilcar S. Alivizatos, *Die Oikonomia: Die Oikonomia nach dem kanonischen Recht der Orthodoxen Kirche*, ed. Andréa Belliger, Lembeck, Frankfurt am Main, 1998.

53. "Oikonomia in the Orthodox Church: Statement of the Inter-Orthodox Commission for the Preparation of the Holy and Great Council, 1971," German version in *Una Sancta* 28 (1973): 95; translation by the author.

convert would have to be baptized. But *kat'oikonomian*, they would not. From the mid-19th century on this concept was applied as a reason for not baptizing converts.

As Erickson points out, both approaches have their problems. The Russian approach is seen as too much influenced by scholasticism and the idea of "valid orders," while the Greek approach is based on the idea that *kat'akribian,* all non-Orthodox should be baptized, because their baptisms (as are all their sacraments) are considered "null and void."[54] This problematic of the "economic approach" is also discussed by the Romanian Orthodox scholar Ioan Sauca, who insists that this position does not recognize "any sign of ecclesiality outside the Orthodox Church" and is rather new in Orthodoxy. Moreover, he notes, it is "contrary to the Orthodox Theology."[55]

Some contemporary Orthodox theologians keep the idea of *oikonomia,*[56] while others claim "the recognition of the real existence, or even the validity, of baptism given by the ecclesiastical bodies which exist outside of the Orthodox Church,"[57] referring to canon 95 of the Quinisextum.

Finally the problem lies in the fact that on the Orthodox side, there is no clear answer to the question whether non-Orthodox, especially Protestants, are "heretics" in the same way as the term is used in the early church. In other words: "Who are the other Christians and what is the nature of their relationship to the Orthodox Church?"[58] This is the question of the limits of the church, which

---

54. John H. Erickson, "The Problem of Sacramental 'Economy,'" in *The Challenge of our Past: Studies in Orthodox Canon Law and Church History,* St. Vladimir's Seminary Press, Crestwood, 1991, 116.

55. Sauca, "The Church Beyond Our Boundaries," 222. Cf. also below p. 234.

56. For example George Dragas, "The Manner of Reception of Roman Catholic Converts into the Orthodox Church."

57. Vlassios Phidas, "Baptism and Ecclesiology," 46.

58. Sauca, "The Church Beyond Our Boundaries," 219; see also Damaskinos Papandreou, "Zur Anerkennung der Taufe seitens der orthodoxen Kirche unter Berücksichtigung des heiligen und großen Konzils," *Una Sancta* 48 (1993): 51.

needs to be addressed by the Orthodox "with an increasing degree of urgency."[59]

The Roman Catholic Church has a similar understanding to that of the Orthodox: it views itself as the one, holy, catholic and apostolic church, but recognizes baptism performed in other churches as long as it is done in water and the name of the Father, Son and Holy Spirit.[60] This different attitude has an historical background based in the conflicts about the baptism of heretics in the 3rd and 4th centuries.[61] In general the Orthodox have tended to follow Cyprian and his idea that there is no valid baptism outside the church, while the church in the West has followed Rome and Augustine, in whose understanding the effect of the sacrament is independent from the status of the person who baptizes.

It has to be noted though that the Roman Catholic position recognized the validity of trinitarian baptism in water outside the boundaries of the Roman church, but not necessarily its fruitfulness. Therefore during history—especially in the Middle Ages—rebaptisms of Orthodox occurred rather frequently; "conditional baptism" for cases of doubt about the validity of a person's baptism was practiced until the 20th century.[62]

The Reformation churches generally understand that the church is everywhere where the gospel is preached and the sacraments are administered rightly.[63] Therefore they normally recognize the other churches as churches and do not re-baptize converts from other churches.

---

59. Emmanuel Clapsis, "The Boundaries of the Church: An Orthodox Debate," in *Orthodoxy in Conversation: Orthodox Ecumenical Engagements*, WCC, Geneva and Holy Cross Orthodox Press, Brookline, 2000, 117.

60. Pontifical Council for the Promotion of Christian Unity, *Directory for the Application of Principles and Norms on Ecumenism*, Vatican City, 1993, 58: "Baptism by immersion, or by pouring, together with the Trinitarian formula is, of itself, valid."

61. See the historical overview above in Chapter Two.

62. Only in the 16th century did Pope Alexander VI affirm the validity of Orthodox baptism. See http://www.orthodoxresearchinstitute.org/articles/ecumenical/baptism_sacramental_economy.htm

63. CA 7.

BAPTISM AS PART OF THE SACRAMENTS OF INITIATION

In addition to raising the question of the limits of the church, the Orthodox ask how baptism is related and held together with the sacraments of chrismation and eucharist. They understand the sequence of baptism–chrismation–eucharist as the "established order of the initiatory sacraments ... which ... expresses their particular reference to the historic manifestation of the mystery of the divine economy for the salvation of the human race."[64] While the Roman Catholic Church has kept the three sacraments, their sequence nowadays is (in the case of an infant, which is still the prevailing practice) baptism–first eucharist–confirmation. The churches of the Reformation recognize only two sacraments, baptism and eucharist. Confirmation, which is practiced (similarly to the Roman Catholic tradition) at the age of adolescence, is understood as an act of confession and confirmation of one's baptism. Traditionally in the Reformation churches—differently from the Roman Catholic practice—the first eucharist is celebrated after confirmation.

The reason for these differences is to be found in historical developments. In the early church baptism and the eucharist belonged together and were performed together. From the beginning there was obviously also an anointing related to baptism, though in different forms—before and after baptism, either before or after baptism; or even several anointings.[65]

Later on, these three rites were separated in the West, while in the East they were kept together. This had to do with the fact that, from the 3rd century on, as far as we know, the practice of infant baptism grew, especially under the influence of Augustine's doctrine of original sin, in order to secure children from the power of sin. At the same time Christianity spread from the cities to rural areas.[66] Both factors led to baptism being performed more and more by presbyters instead of bishops. In order to preserve the idea

---

64. Phidas, "Baptism and Ecclesiology," 42.

65. See above, Chapter Two.

66. See Kenan B. Osborne, *The Christian Sacraments of Initiation: Baptism, Confirmation, Eucharist*, Paulist Press, New York and Mahwah, 1987; see also Georg Kretschmar, "Firmung," in *Theologische Realenzyklopädie* 11, 197.

that children in remote regions were baptized into the wider community of a certain diocese, the post-baptismal anointing was—in the West—reserved to the bishop. This meant in practice, that children were baptized by a priest right after they were born, but that chrismation was administered later by the bishop and was later called confirmation.[67] This became the general practice in the West by the 11th century.[68]

This practice of separated sacraments was inherited by the churches of the Reformation and other denominations developing in the West, but since the reformers did not recognize confirmation as a sacrament, the threefold initiation was not kept. Confirmation, as practiced nowadays in Protestant churches, has a complex history and reflects different understandings. In general it can be traced to the time of the Reformation, when an examination was required before a person received first communion. Confirmation, therefore, was understood in general as a catechetical act which also functions as the admission to the eucharist.[69] During the period of Pietism and of the Enlightenment two other ideas were added: confirmation as a renewal of the baptismal covenant and confirmation as a coming of age, an act of receiving one's majority and thus certain rights and responsibilities as member of the church.

The separation of baptism and chrismation (confirmation) in the Western church brought about the need to reflect theologically on the meaning and relationship of the two sacraments. A biblical basis for a separate sacrament of confirmation was found in texts in the Acts of the Apostles, such as Acts 9:12, Acts 6:6, and Acts 13:3, but also in Mk 8:23, Mk 10:16 and Lk 13:13.

Confirmation was understood as the gift of the Holy Spirit in the Middle Ages; thus it was the baptism in the Holy Spirit as distinguished from water baptism. For example, Peter Lombard (ca.

---

67. The Latin term *confirmatio* appears for the first time in the 6th century and prevails in the West in the 12th century; see Kretschmar, "Firmung," 197.

68. "Sometime in the eleventh century we find in the west (and only here!) a separated celebration of confirmation as the general practice." Sigisbert Regli, *Firmsakrament und christliche Entfaltung*, Mysterium Salutis, vol. 5, Benziger, Einsiedeln, 1967, 312, transl. In Kenan B. Osborne *Sacraments of Initiation, 117.*.

69. Cf. Karl Dienst, "Konfirmation I," *Theologische Realenzyklopädie* 19, 437-445.

1095/1100-1160) understands confirmation as the gift of the Holy Spirit for strengthening (*ad robur*) the person who had received forgiveness in baptism.[70]

The ecumenical discussion has made clear that this raises questions about the gift of the Holy Spirit in the baptismal water rite, as well as the relationship between water baptism and baptism in the Holy Spirit. It also has to be noted that confirmation as a separate rite is no longer a sacrament related to the eucharist, since the eucharist is given to people who are not (yet) confirmed.

Realizing that this development had led the church astray from the tradition of the early church, in the 20th century the Roman Catholic Church developed a rite of initiation (*ordo initiationis*) which brings these three sacraments together, although they take place at different times in life. For this the Catholic Church refers to various church fathers such as John Chrysostom, Ambrose, and Cyril of Jerusalem, in whose writings examples of ceremonies of baptism taking place over a certain time can be found. For the baptism of adults especially, the unity of water-baptism, confirmation and eucharist is renewed through the Rite of Christian Initiation of Adults.[71] Another new factor is that, from now on, a priest also can perform the confirmation (in the case of adult initiation).

Similar discussions took place in the Anglican tradition. Some theologians in the Anglican churches have argued that baptism bestows forgiveness of sins, while confirmation bestows the Holy Spirit. Others, however, have said that baptism gives full membership in the body of Christ and that the other rites cannot add anything to baptism; therefore confirmation can only be the confession of someone who has been baptized as a child. Based on this argument, children in many provinces of the Anglican Communion are now admitted to the eucharist.

In the Reformation churches chrismation was abandoned because it is not rooted in an institution established by Jesus Christ, which was for Martin Luther one of the main criteria for the

---

70. Peter Lombard, *Sentences* IV, dist. 7, 3.

71. *Ordo Initiationis Christianae Adultorum*, 1972. English text: Rite of Christian Initiation of Adults, Study edition, prepared by the International Commission on English in the Liturgy, Liturgical Press, Collegeville MN, 1988.

identification of a rite as sacrament. Lutherans still have, though, a "signing" of the child on the forehead with the cross immediately after baptism. Instead of chrismation Lutherans introduced confirmation as a personal confirmation of the faith which had been confessed at the baptism of the child by its parents and the congregation. This confirmation was understood as a precondition for receiving the eucharist for the first time (this is changing nowadays) and was understood as the step by which one entered into full membership of the church. The problem is that this can be understood as meaning that baptism is not entrance into full membership in the church. This in turn creates the problem that there is a difference between the Church and the body of Christ!

A modern development: under the influence of the ecumenical movement, there is a move in the Protestant churches (at least in Europe), to correct this theological problem by accepting children to the eucharist. Some Lutherans and Anglicans in the US have even introduced a postbaptismal anointing.[72]

The Controversy on Spirit Baptism

Another controversy around baptism arouse with the appearance of the Pentecostal movement. Pentecostals (except Oneness Pentecostals[73]) make a distinction between Spirit baptism and water baptism. Spirit baptism is the second blessing following regeneration or initial conversion. The model for Spirit baptism is given in the story of Pentecost (Acts 2), and therefore is accompanied by *glossolalia (speaking in tongues) as a proof of the presence of the Spirit.[74] As Koo Dong Yun puts it, in the understanding of most classical

---

72. Dominic E. Serra, "Syrian Prebaptismal Anointing and Western Postbaptismal Chrismation," *Worship* 79 (2005): 329.

73. See above, Chapter One.

74. "We believe that the baptism in the Holy Spirit is the bestowing of the believer with power to be an effective witness for Christ. This experience is distinct from, and subsequent to, the new birth; is received by faith, and is accompanied by the manifestation of speaking in tongues as the Spirit gives utterance, as the initial physical evidence – Luke 24:49; Acts 1:4, 5,8; 2:1-4; 8:16-19; 11:14-17; 19:1-7." Assemblies of God in Australia, *Ministers Manual*, 5.1., "Articles of Faith," quoted in Shane Clifton, "The Spirit and Doctrinal

Pentecostals "one cannot be baptized in the Holy Spirit without the initial-physical evidence, namely, speaking in tongues."[75] Pentecostals understand Spirit baptism as "an empowering for service,"[76] which is different from water baptism, which conveys sacramental grace for salvation.

The gift of the Holy Spirit is, therefore, completely separate from the act of water baptism: "That Baptism of itself confers the Holy Spirit we do not hold."[77]

In contrast to this understanding, the Orthodox tradition and the Roman Catholic Church understand the gift of the Holy Spirit as related to chrismation or confirmation. For their part, Reformation churches understand baptism in the Holy Spirit as identical with water baptism,[78] although exegetes affirm that the New Testament "never affirms that water baptism bestows the baptism of the Spirit."[79]

This controversy finds its roots in the biblical testimony to Spirit baptism. As Robert Menzies shows,[80] the Pentecostal understanding follows the theology of the Holy Spirit found in the works of Luke (Luke–Acts), which differs from that of Paul. "Luke consistently portrays the Spirit as a charismatic or, more precisely, a prophetic gift, the source of power for service."[81] Therefore the "baptism in the Spirit is charismatic rather than soteriological in

---

Developments: A Functional Analysis of the Traditional Pentecostal Doctrine of the Baptism in the Holy Spirit," *Pneuma* 29 (2007): 13.

75. Koo Dong Yun, "Water Baptism and Spirit Baptism: Pentecostals and Lutherans in Dialogue," *Dialog: A Journal of Theology* 43 (2004): 346.

76. Robert P. Menzies, "Luke's Understanding of Baptism in the Holy Spirit: A Pentecostal Dialogue with the Reformed Tradition," *Journal of Pentecostal Theology* 16 (2008): 88.

77. Herbert Clarkson, "The Holy Spirit and the Sacraments," *Baptist Quarterly* 14 (1951-52): 269, quoted in Beasley-Murray, *Baptism in the New Testament*, 277.

78. See Schlink, *The Doctrine of Baptism*, 58.

79. Beasley-Murray, *Baptism in the New Testament*, 275, referring to G. Kittel, "Die Wirkungen der christlichen Wassertaufe nach dem NT," *Theologische Studien und Kritiken* 87 (1914): 25.

80. Ibid.

81. Menzies, "Luke's Understanding of Baptism in the Holy Spirit," 90.

character."[82] Kilian McDonnell and George Montague, two Roman Catholic scholars, agree that in Luke-Acts the prophetic dimension of the Spirit predominates, but they show that the gift of the Spirit cannot be separated from the initiation as a whole.[83]

From a Pentecostal perspective, a clear basis for the distinction between water baptism and Spirit baptism is present in the text of Acts 1:5 (see also Mk 1:8, Mt 3:11, Lk 3:16, Jn 1:33), where Jesus says: "John baptized with water, but you will be baptized with the Holy Spirit not many days from now."[84] For Luke this prophecy was fulfilled on Pentecost (Acts 2), which has no connection with water baptism. Also several other stories of baptisms in Acts clearly separate water baptism from the reception of the Holy Spirit, for example Acts 8:16f. or Acts 19: 1-6.

From a Roman Catholic perspective, Acts 1:5 is interpreted in a different way in relation to Acts 2: it is seen as the scriptural basis for confirmation.[85] Other interpreters understand the texts which distinguish the two baptisms (of water and the Spirit) as exceptions.[86] Therefore Schuyler Brown, a Roman Catholic scholar[87], also shows that it is unlikely that Luke is interested in exalting baptism with the Spirit over water-baptism: for Luke the baptism of the Holy Spirit "represented something from the church's past rather than something that was still experienced within his community,"[88] and "the individuals in Acts who possess the spirit are almost without exception either apostles (Acts 4:8) or persons closely associated

---

82. Ibid., 91.

83. Kilian McDonnell and George Montague, *Christian Initiation and Baptism in the Holy Spirit: Evidence from the First Eight Centuries,* Liturgical Press, Collegeville, 1994.

84. A more exhaustive exegetical analysis of the most important New Testament passages related to Spirit Baptism can be found in James D. G. Dunn, *Baptism in the Holy Spirit: A Re-examination of the New Testament Teaching on the Gift of the Spirit in Relation to Pentecostalism Today,* SCM, London, 1970.

85. Schuyler Brown, "'Water-Baptism' and 'Spirit-Baptism' in Luke-Acts," *Anglican Theological Review* 59 (1977): 143.

86. Ernst Haenchen, *The Acts of the Apostles*, Westminster Press, Philadelphia, 1971, 184. See also Martin Parmentier, "Water Baptism and Spirit Baptism in the Church Fathers," www.pctii.org/cyberj/cyberj3/martin.html.

87. He later became an Anglican.

88. Brown, "'Water-Baptism' and 'Spirit-Baptism' in Luke-Acts," 146.

with the apostles and their work."[89] Luke, in this interpretation, restricts the gift of the Spirit to the early period of the church, "allowing in later periods only the Spirit's continuing guidance of the church through the decision of its leaders, who safeguard the apostolic tradition."[90] For Brown, therefore, baptism with the Holy Spirit is a phenomenon which existed only at a specific time in church history.

Acts 2:37-39 is a text used to prove the connection of water baptism with the gift of the Holy Spirit:[91] "Peter said to them, 'Repent and be baptized, every one of you, in the name of Jesus Christ for the forgiveness of your sins; and you will receive the gift of the Holy Spirit.'" James Dunn, though, shows in his exegesis of this text that "we must distinguish the Spirit from water-baptism."[92]

Acts 10:44-11:18 is an example of the Spirit's coming prior to baptism. The same is the case in Acts 9:17ff. Roman Catholic exegetes interpret these texts as proofs that the laying on of hands is the bestowing of the gift of the Holy Spirit, and belongs, together with baptism, to the integral rite of initiation.[93]

For the Reformation churches, 1 Cor 12:13 is a proof that Spirit baptism and water baptism are one and the same: "For in the one Spirit we were all baptized into one body—Jews or Greeks, slaves or free—and we were all made to drink of one Spirit."[94] Paul, in general, speaks of the soteriological dimension of the Spirit's work.[95] Therefore Edmund Schlink (for example) says: "Baptism in the name of Jesus Christ is at the same time Baptism by the Holy Spirit. It is the common conviction of the primitive Christian church that Baptism takes place by the Holy Spirit and that the Holy Spirit is imparted with Baptism."[96] In a different way, Karl Barth distin-

---

89. Ibid., 147.

90. Ibid., 149.

91. McDonnell and Montague, *Christian Initiation*, 29.

92. James D. G. Dunn, *Baptism in the Holy Spirit*, SCM Press, London, 1970, 100ff.

93. Cf. also Acts 19:6; see McDonnell and Montague, *Christian Initiation*, 38ff.

94. Dunn, *Baptism in the Holy Spirit*, 129 n42.

95. Menzies, "Luke's Understanding of Baptism in the Holy Spirit," 90.

96. Schlink, *The Doctrine of Baptism*, 58

guishes between water-baptism and baptism with the Holy Spirit but insists that they belong together and should not be separated.[97] Beasley-Murray confirms that for Baptists "what is incontestable from the New Testament point of view is the impossibility of dividing *Christ* and his gifts of grace from the *Spirit* whom He has given to his Church."[98] Dunn, on the other hand, understands the Greek term *baptizein* as not necessarily specifying water-baptism, which leads to the conclusion that Paul in 1 Cor 12 does not speak about water baptism.[99]

Tit 3: 5 is also given as a proof for the identity of water baptism and Spirit baptism, as is John 3:5;[100] the latter text is, however, seen by others as a proof of the distinction between water and spirit baptism.[101]

In summary, this controversy is rooted in different interpretations of scripture, based on a different understanding of the role of the Holy Spirit in baptism. In the end this leads to a different understanding of the term "sacrament."

The Controversy over the Baptismal Formula

Another line of divergence seems to develop between churches which insist on baptizing in the name of the Father, the Son and the Holy Spirit, and groups within churches which have changed this formula.[102] There are two main reasons for changing the formula:

---

97. Barth, *Church Dogmatics* IV, 4, 37.

98. Ibid., 275ff.

99. Dunn, *Baptism in the Holy Spirit*, 128ff.

100. Schlink, *The Doctrine of Baptism*, 59.

101. For further texts see McDonnell and Montague, *Christian Initiation*, 46ff., and Dunn, *Baptism in the Holy Spirit*.

102. In fact presently no church has in its official liturgies proposed changes in the baptismal formula. But not all churches explicitly require that baptism has to be administered in the name of the Father, and the Son and the Holy Spirit (see the example mentioned by Ruth C. Duck, *Gender and the Name of God: The Trinitarian Baptismal Formula*, Pilgrim Press, New York, 1991, 190ff.), which allows some freedom in liturgical language. According to Robeck and Sandidge the issue of the language of the baptismal formula is "the most significant church-dividing baptismal issue among Pentecostals." See Cecil M.

a firm concentration on the New Testament, especially among Pentecostals,[103] and the issue of inclusive language.

The first case is related to a development in the early 20th century in the Pentecostal circles, where in 1913 Robert E. McAlister "noted that the apostles had always baptized in the name of Jesus Christ."[104] According to Robeck and Sandidge, this led to painful rifts and has been the most significant church-dividing baptismal issue among Pentecostals.

The second issue is related to a rather complex discussion. One of the main arguments is that "masculine language is related to a patriarchal culture."[105] "Using many masculine images and no feminine images for God sends the message that women are not made in the image of God and thus are less valuable than men."[106] Another argument points to the experience of many worshippers who have been abused, which leaves them with negative reactions to the concept of God as father, especially in important events like baptism. Ruth Duck argues that, for many children, God as "Father" can only have negative connotations.[107] Some are also of the opinion that masculine and paternal imagery for God "supports the patriarchal abuse of power, and particularly the abuse of children by their fathers."[108] A modern theological reflection comes to the conclusion that the masculine language does not fully convey the doctrine of the Trinity.[109]

Some feminists would therefore change the language to female imagery.[110] But for others, this is too simple and does not necessarily

---

Robeck and Jerry L. Sandidge, "The Ecclesiology of Koinonia and Baptism: A Pentecostal Perspective," *Journal of Ecumenical Studies* 27 (1990), 514.

103. For example some Pentecostals changed the formula for other reasons. See Robeck and Sandidge. "The Ecclesiology of Koinonia and Baptism," 514ff.

104. Ibid., 515.

105. Ruth Duck, Patricia Wilson-Kastner, *Praising God: The Trinity in Christian Worship*, Westminster John Knox, Louisville KY 1999, 6.

106. Ibid.

107. Duck, *Gender and the Name of God*, Chapter 2.

108. Duck, *Gender and the Name of God*, 8.

109. Gail Ramshaw, *God Beyond Gender: Feminist Christian God-Language*, Fortress Press, Minneapolis, 1995, 75f.

110. For example Rosemary Radford Ruether, *Women-Church: Theology and Practice in Feminist Liturgical Communities*, Harper & Row, San Francisco, 1985.

help the matter - especially related to the experience of children with their father - since, in some cases, mothers also abuse their children. For some groups, baptism "in the name of the Lord Jesus" is a solution. Others keep to the trinitarian structure of the formula, but change it to "the name of the Creator, Redeemer, Sustainer"[111] or other variations. But this is strongly questioned by people who would say that "Creator, Redeemer, Sustainer" is "misidentifying *how* the God of Jesus Christ is both self-related *(ad intra)* and related to the creation *(ad extra)*."[112] Another solution which also tries to keep the trinitarian structure is proposed by Ruth C. Duck. Referring to the *Apostolic Tradition* (Rome, ca. 215) Duck would introduce a threefold question to the candidate before the administration of the water, using questions which relate to the three persons of the Trinity but are formulated in such a way that they use biblical imagery which goes beyond the father-son-image.[113]

The scriptural background for these discussions is not really clear. In the New Testament we find the trinitarian expression only once, namely in the Great Commandment to baptize "in the name of the Father and of the Son and of the Holy Spirit" (Mt 28:19). In other places there are expressions which talk about baptizing "in the name of the Lord Jesus" (Acts 19:5). Some exegetes take the trinitarian formula as the original one, but others think that "it is more plausible to hold that the simpler formula was the original and that the trinitarian version represents a development of the latter part of the first century and the early part of the second."[114] Some conclude from this that it is evident "that both single and trine immersion were practiced during the Apostolic period."[115] However, for exegetes, it is an open question whether Mt 28 and the other biblical texts are talking about a formula or not.[116] Ruth Duck argues that the trinitarian formula of Mt 28 was not used

---

111. See Duck, *Gender and the Name of God*, 171ff.

112. James F. Kay, "In Whose Name? Feminism and the Trinitarian Baptismal Formula," *Theology Today*, January 1 (1993): 524-533.

113. Duck, *Gender and the Name of God*, 185ff.

114. Wilburn, "The One Baptism and the Many Baptisms," 76.

115. Ibid., 77.

116. See Beasley-Murray, *Baptism in the New Testament*, 83.

during the first centuries, but was more a summary of the theology of baptism.[117]

The trinitarian solutions which change the wording, such as that by Ruth Duck, are, formally speaking, following the distinction made by Karl Barth between the gospel of Jesus Christ and the scriptures that witness to that gospel. The scriptures are not in a one-to-one correspondence with the gospel to which they witness, although they may become vehicles for its conveyance if God so wills. Therefore what is important in this way of thinking is that the trinitarian structure of God is conveyed through the language. The imagery and the exact wording, however, remain open.

Again we find here a different way of using the Bible: Roman Catholics and Orthodox, and most of the mainline Protestant churches, would keep the person-related language of Father, Son and Holy Spirit. They would use the argument that this is the original language found in the Bible. Others would apply here the principle that the Bible does not have to be taken literally, though its intention, and the function of biblical language, has to be kept.

The issue is not, however, just an exegetical one. It is related to the understanding of metaphors. Some understand "father" and "son" as equivocal metaphors, others as "figure[s] of speech."[118]

The Controversy on Immersion, Affusion (Pouring) or Sprinkling

The inner-Orthodox controversy about the reception of heretics and schismatics into the Orthodox Church brought a further issue into the discussion. Already in the 11th century Patriarch Michael Kerularios accused the Western church of deviations and an "unlawful administration of Baptism," including the single immersion.[119] In the 13th century the Patriarch of Constantinople also mentions affusion and aspersion as highly questionable practices. In the 18th

---

117. Duck, *Gender and the Name of God.*

118. See Bryan D Spinks, *Reformation and Modern Rituals and Theologies of Baptism: From Luther to Contemporary Practices*, Ashgate Publishing, Aldershot, UK and Burlington, VT, 2006, 159.

119. See Dragas, "The Manner of Reception of Roman Catholic Converts," 3ff.

century the party advocating for re-baptism of Catholic converts realized that according to the canons (Second Ecumenical Council, Canon 7 and Trullo, Canon 95) heretics could be received without re-baptism only if they had been baptized *correctly*. This was interpreted beyond the traditional understanding which related correct baptism to the triune formula, now related also to triple immersion.[120]

The insistence on immersion is also an issue in discussions between churches which practice infant baptism and credobaptist churches, including Pentecostals. Although there is no wide academic discussion on the issue, a study of websites under the search term "immersion" shows that in particular churches and groups which focus on a literal understanding of the Bible will come to conclusions such as "No other form [than immersion][121] or action is acceptable."[122] According to Robeck and Sandidge, immersion is "the most commonly preferred mode of baptism among Pentecostals worldwide," but it is not the only position taken by Pentecostals.[123]

Thus, in this specific matter, the Orthodox, although baptizing infants, are in agreement with most churches of the credobaptist tradition—but make an exception in the case of imminent danger of death of the candidate.

On the whole we can distinguish four forms of action in the baptismal water rite: submersion (full immersion), immersion with the head dipped with the candidate either standing in water or outside, affusion (pouring of water over the head) and sprinkling water.[124]

Most churches today would agree that baptism by immersion is symbolically the best way of expressing "that in baptism

---

120. See Hovorun, "The Theological and Practical Aspects of Admission of Non-Orthodox Christians," 357.

121. Added by the author.

122. See, for example, http://www.gospelway.com/salvation/baptism_action.php.

123. Robeck and Sandidge, "The Ecclesiology of Koinonia and Baptism," 509.

124. See John Gordon Davies, *The Architectural Setting of Baptism*, Barrie and Rockliff, London, 1962, 23.

the Christian participates in the death, burial and resurrection of Christ."[125] For practical reasons practically all paedobaptist churches (except the Orthodox) remain with the prevailing model, which is either pouring or sprinkling, especially in the case of the baptism of infants; immersion, though, is a possible practice.

From the New Testament it seems that the original practice was immersion, but it is unclear whether it was full or partial immersion.[126] From early sources we get a picture that the prevailing practice in the early church was baptism by immersion. But even early texts such as the *Didache* mention the possibility—in exceptional cases—of pouring water on the head of the candidate. Only in the late Middle Ages did the practice of affusion gradually develop.[127]

In recent discussions within the multilateral ecumenical dialogue in the WCC, this controversy did not play a major role. But it is an issue of controversy within the Pentecostal movement, and it seems that in the encounter with new churches influenced by Pentecostal and charismatic ideas, it will emerge as an issue.

A New Controversy: Inculturation of Baptism

As the ecumenical movement has developed across the whole globe, the question of using local cultural patterns for Christian worship has become more and more an issue for discussion under the term "inculturation."[128] This discussion includes also the baptismal rite. Especially in the Roman Catholic Church, as a world-wide church,

---

125. World Council of Churches, Commission on Faith and Order, *Baptism, Eucharist and Ministry*, Faith and Order Paper No. 111, WCC Publications, Geneva, 1982, "Baptism," par. 18.

126. "Although the descriptions of New Testament baptisms indicate that baptism occurred with both the officiator and the candidate standing in water, they do not state specifically what happened in the act." Grenz, *Theology for the Community of God*, 530.

127. See also Wilburn, "The One Baptism and the Many Baptisms," 82.

128. An overview on the discussion and the distinction of different terms used in this context can be found in Anscar J. Chupungco, *Liturgical Inculturation: Sacramentals, Religiosity, and Catechesis*, Liturgical Press, Collegeville, 1992, 13-31.

the issue has been discussed since the Second Vatican Council.[129] The issue has been taken up in the Lutheran World Federation especially during the 1990s[130] and also in the Anglican Communion.[131]

The Commission on Faith and Order of the World Council of Churches has studied the question in relation to worship in general[132] and in relation to baptism in particular.[133]

The inculturation of baptism has not been a church-dividing issue in the traditional sense of a schism, but the discussion shows that there are controversial attitudes within and between the churches. The study of the Faith and Order Commission observed that "in some regions the use of traditional initiation symbols in baptism by some denominations creates new separations between churches."[134] It seems that, for example, the Roman Catholic Church in some African countries nowadays is much more open to inculturation than some Reformation churches. In Asia, Chang-Bok Chung, for instance, points to the difficulties for the incultura-

---

129. See, for example, Second Vatican Council, *Sacrosanctum Concilium* (Constitution on the Sacred Liturgy), Chapter I, point D, http://www.vatican.va/archive/hist_councils/ii_vatican_council/documents/vat-ii_const_19631204_sacrosanctum-concilium_en.html; see also Anscar J. Chupungco, *Liturgical Inculturations*.

130. See Maren Mattiesen, ed., *Confessing Christ in Cultural Contexts*, Lutheran World Federation Department of Studies, Geneva, 1981; S. Anita Stauffer, *Worship and Culture in Dialogue*, Lutheran World Federation Department for Theology and Studies, Geneva, 1994; S. Anita Stauffer, ed., *Christian Worship: Unity in Cultural Diversity*, Lutheran World Federation Department for Theology and Studies, Geneva, 1996; and S. Anita Stauffer, ed., *Baptism, Rites of Passage, and Culture*, Lutheran World Federation Department for Theology and Studies, Geneva, 1998.

131. See, for example David R. Holeton, *Liturgical Inculturation in the Anglican Communion, including the York Statement "Down to Earth Worship,"* Alcuin/GROW Liturgical Study 15, Grove Books, Nottingham, 1990.

132. Thomas F. Best and Dagmar Heller, eds., *So We Believe, So We Pray: Towards Koinonia in Worship*, Faith and Order Paper No. 171, WCC, Geneva, 1995.

133. Thomas F. Best and Dagmar Heller, eds., *Becoming a Christian: The Ecumenical Implications of Our Common Baptism*, Faith and Order Paper No. 184, WCC, Geneva, 1999.

134. "Becoming a Christian: The Ecumenical Implications of Our Common Baptism: Report of the Consultation," par. 40, in Best and Heller, *Becoming a Christian*, 86.

tion of baptism in the Korean context caused by the missionaries and specific historical circumstances.[135] According to F. Kabasele Lumbala, a Roman Catholic scholar in the Democratic Republic of Congo, "a rite cannot be imported from one culture to another without negotiation and re-arrangements. That is what happened during the first centuries of the church in the West and the East. That is what is happening in Africa today."[136]

Inculturation is necessary because, as Lumbala notes, "[a] message that is not translated into a nation's cultural fabric is not transmitted."[137] The controversial point is finally how far inculturation may go. The use of local rites and other elements from the local culture and the core of the gospel as the global aspect need to be in a relationship which does not obscure the uniqueness of the Christian message, and which at the same time gives enough space for the expression of this same message with means that speak to people in a way which they can understand.

This can happen as a "re-expression of components of Christian worship with elements from a local culture which have an equal meaning, value, and function" (dynamic equivalence), or as an "addition of elements from local cultures to the liturgical *ordo* to enrich its original core" (creative assimilation).[138] The LWF Chicago Statement, whose drafting group also included representatives of the Roman Catholic Church and of the wider ecumenical movement, highlighted four aspects of the relationship between worship and culture, namely transcultural, contextual, counter-cultural and cross-cultural.[139] The transcultural aspect of baptism is to be found in the proclamation of the gospel and the water as well as the *ordo*.[140] Contextualization of baptism is happening in the ways of

---

135. ChangBok Chung, "Baptism in Asia and its Cultural Settings," in Best and Heller, *Becoming a Christian*, 45-50.

136. F. Kabasele Lumbala, "Black Africa and Baptismal Rites," in Best and Heller, *Becoming a Christian*, 39ff.

137. Ibid., 40.

138. "Chicago Statement on Worship and Culture: Baptism and Rites of Life Passage," par. 1.4, in Stauffer, *Baptism, Rites of Passage, and Culture*, 15.

139. Ibid., par.1.3.

140. Ibid., par. 2.1–2.4, in Stauffer, *Baptism, Rites of Passage, and Culture*, 16-19.

teaching baptismal candidates, in the ways of gathering, and in the design of the space for baptism as well as in the use of explanatory symbols. The fact that in Christian baptism all persons, women and men, children and adults, people from all ethnic or class backgrounds, rich or poor, are treated in the same way and stand on equal footing, is an example of the counter-cultural aspect of baptism. The cross-cultural aspect of baptism is expressed in mutual enrichment between churches through music and other elements.

Different emphases on the counter-cultural aspect of the gospel are at the core of the controversies on inculturation. An example of an exaggeration of the counter-cultural aspect of baptism is the attitude of missionaries in the past who linked baptism with the gift of a Christian name, which meant for people in non-Western countries to carry a Western name and thus an alienation from their own culture. But the above-mentioned fact that Christian baptism stands for equality of all people in front of God may in some contexts be counter-cultural, where class, caste or ethnic belonging separate communities from each other.

Theologically this discussion needs to be seen in connection to the question of whether the presence of the Holy Spirit is limited to the church or whether the Spirit is also present in other religions and cultures.

A New Challenge: Baptism as Entry into the Local Congregation

Within the group of churches which baptize only persons who can speak for themselves, some Pentecostal and Independent churches, as we have seen in the first chapter, (re-)baptize every convert, even if he or she comes from other Pentecostal and Independent churches with the same understanding and practice of baptism. Baptism, in this case, is an act of making manifest one's belonging to a specific community. At the same time there seems to be little reflection from theologians within these churches about the consequences of this practice. The idea that baptism cannot be repeated is not reflected upon, nor is the understanding of the church.

This is a challenge for the traditional churches and especially the ecumenical movement. It raises new questions about the understanding of baptism and the question of mutual recognition which will have to be taken up in the future. Traditional churches will ask the following questions: Is baptism repeatable? If it is not repeatable, does the baptism of converts mean that all other baptisms are null and void? Is baptism just the entrance into the local community? What is the relation of the baptism in the local community to baptism in other congregations?

SUMMARY

Looking at the whole of the theological issues in the controversies around baptism, we can say that the differences have their roots in three areas.

The main point in all the controversies is the different interpretation of the scriptural sources. This is mainly a difference between *sola scriptura* and "scripture and tradition." The division, however, is not identical with the controversy on *sola scriptura* on the side of the churches of the Reformation, with Rome as representing "scripture and tradition." In the discussion about baptism, the Reformation churches are not radically applying the principle of *sola scriptura*, and the question of the Church's historical development and heritage seems to be as important for them as for Catholic and Orthodox theology.

In general the interpretation is guided on each side by prejudices which have their roots in the different confessional theologies.

On the one hand, this leads to different ecclesiological presumptions, especially different identifications of the boundaries of the church, but also, in the case of new churches, a vagueness about the relationship of local congregations to Christian communities in general – whether of the same tradition or of another tradition - and the role of baptism in this relationship. On the other hand, the different hermeneutics lead to different understandings of the role of the Holy Spirit. This already played a role in the traditional controversy between East and West and led to the different development, in these two major traditions, of chrismation and confirmation in relation to baptism. But it also becomes important in the new controversy arising with the appearance of the Pentecostal movement and its understanding of Spirit baptism.

Both the ecclesiological issue and the pneumatological one are at the root of possible new separations related to a different understanding of the relationship between gospel and culture.

CHAPTER 5
Toward Mutual Recognition of Baptism

T HE VARIOUS DISCUSSIONS ON BAPTISM—ON MULTILATERAL as well as on bilateral levels—showed that for most churches baptism understood as incorporation into the body of Christ is one of the most important bases for Christian unity. Therefore there is a need not only to overcome the divisions in general, but the divisions related to baptism and its mutual recognition in particular.

A number of theologians from different backgrounds reflected on possibilities for mutual recognition of baptism. Ralph G. Wilburn, from the Disciples of Christ, for example, represents a historical approach by saying: "certain modes and forms of baptism are particularly fitting for some historical situations, but not for others. History in art determines what forms are essential for the faith to possess genuine, cultural integrity. No one form of baptism is valid for all Christian people and for all ages."[1] A different approach is suggested by the Methodist New Testament scholar James D. G.

---

1. Ralph G. Wilburn, "The One Baptism and the Many Baptisms," *Mid-Stream* 3 (1964): 101.

Dunn: he points to the centrality and sovereignty of the Holy Spirit. Thus he asks:

> *Is our discussion of baptism and unity unhelpfully, or even mis-*
> *leadingly, focused? We say baptism is an act of God. But our dis-*
> *putes are all about the humanly devised rubrics which control the*
> *administration of the sacrament. Should our discussion not take*
> *our theology more seriously and orient itself in relation to God's*
> *action? And where God has so acted, baptism is (properly speak-*
> *ing) a secondary consideration—still of major importance, but*
> *secondary.*[2]

Dunn finally thinks the grace of God in a human life should be recognized rather than the proper administration of baptism. From a Baptist perspective, S. Mark Heim proposes as "a more fruitful approach ... to view mutual recognition from the perspective of full Christian initiation,"[3] which involves baptism, personal confession, and participation in the Eucharist. If these three are present in another tradition, recognition should be possible.

Solutions proposed by Orthodox mostly refer to the early church in a general way.[4] By most scholars the *oikonomia* concept is understood as a solution, but there is also a more radical tradition existing which considers persons who are baptized in other churches as Christians, which means that - even according to a meticulous (*kat'akribian*) attitude – they would not have to be (re-) baptized.[5]

In the following chapter we will see how such approaches – and others – have been further developed in multilateral discussions

---

2. James D. G. Dunn, "Baptism and the Unity of the Church in the New Testament," in Michael Root and Risto Saarinen, eds., *Baptism and the Unity of the Church*, Eerdmans, Grand Rapids, MI and WCC Publications, Geneva, 1998, 102.

3. S. Mark Heim, "Baptismal Recognition and the Baptist Churches," in Root and Saarinen, *Baptism and the Unity of the Church*, 163.

4. See Merja Merras, "Baptismal Recognition and the Orthodox Churches," in Root and Saarinen, *Baptism and the Unity of the Church*, 149.

5. See Ioan Sauca, "The Church Beyond our Boundaries and the Ecumenical Vocation of Orthodoxy," *Ecumenical Review* 56 (2004): 211-225.

and how they have resulted in concrete agreements on mutual recognition of baptism between different churches.

The work done by the Commission on Faith and Order of the World Council of Churches in the study process which led to the publication of the BEM document in particular made many churches to reflect on the possibility of recognizing others' baptism. Faith and Order itself continued study work on baptism, especially on the issue of mutual recognition. The Joint Working Group between the Roman Catholic Church and the WCC (JWG) also made some recommendations in this regard. A number of churches came to agreements on mutual recognition of baptism either in a multilateral setting or bilaterally, mostly on the national level. Especially interesting are some bilateral agreements which include Baptists.

Multilateral Developments

Work in the WCC after BEM

The Lima document (BEM) and the process of the churches' responding to it, made clear that there are convergences on baptism between the churches. But these also made clear that more work needs to be done to achieve the goal of mutual recognition of baptism. The analysis of the responses to BEM saw "a hopeful sign that the churches are coming to an understanding of initiation as a unitary and comprehensive process, even if its different elements are spread over a period of time."[6] Therefore from 1993 onwards the Commission on Faith and Order looked again into the issue of baptism, this time with a liturgical approach, going back to the old idea of *lex orandi, lex credendi* ("the rule for prayer is the rule for belief")[7]: there is first praying and worshipping before a doctrine is created.

---

6. World Council of Churches, Commission on Faith and Order, *Baptism, Eucharist and Ministry 1982-1990: Report on the Process and Responses*, Faith and Order Paper No. 149, WCC Publications, Geneva 1990, 112.

7. This idea is attributed to Prosper of Aquitaine (ca. 390-463) who said: "Let us also look at the sacred witness of the public priestly prayers which, handed down by the apostles, are celebrated in the same way in all the world

If we understand doctrine as the result of a reflection on the action of prayer, then doctrine will also have to help improve prayer or worship. On this basis Faith and Order analyzed the pattern of worship within the Christian traditions and came to the conclusion that there is an *ordo* or pattern of worship common to all churches.[8] This pattern is "always marked by pairing and by mutually reinterpretive juxtapositions, roots in word and sacrament held together. It is scripture readings and preaching together, yielding intercessions; and with these, it is *eucharistia* and eating and drinking together, yielding a collection for the poor and mission in the world."[9] And it is founded in the New Testament and the early church.[10]

"Becoming a Christian": The Faith and Order Consultation in Faverges 1997

This basic idea was further developed in a consultation in 1997, held at Faverges, France, in light of the question as to how it would be possible for churches to recognize each other's baptism. The consultation stated:

> *There are two ways in which we may learn to recognize one another's baptism. One is to convert everybody else to our theology and practice. The other is to understand how our baptismal practices*

---

and in every catholic church, so that the rule of praying should establish the rule of believing. For when the leaders of the holy peoples perform the mission entrusted to them, they plead the cause of humankind before the divine clemency, and, sustained by the sights of the whole church, they implore and pray that faith may be given to the unbelieving, that idolaters may be liberated from the errors of their impiety." (*Patrologia Latina* 51: 209-210).

8. See Thomas F. Best and Dagmar Heller, eds., *So We Believe, So We Pray: Towards Koinonia in Worship*, Faith and Order Paper No. 171, WCC Publications, Geneva, 1995.

9. "Towards Koinonia in Worship: Report of the Consultation," in Best and Heller, *So We Believe*, 6.

10. See Gordon Lathrop, "Knowing Something a Little: On the Role of the Lex Orandi in the Search for Christian Unity," in Best and Heller, *So We Believe*, 38-48. See also Gordon Lathrop, "The Water that Speaks: The Ordo of Baptism and its Ecumenical Implications," in Thomas F. Best and Dagmar Heller, eds., *Becoming a Christian: The Ecumenical Implications of Our Common Baptism*, Faith and Order Paper No. 184, WCC Publications, Geneva, 1999, 13-29.

are responses to different pastoral and missionary contexts as well as responses to God's call in Christ.[11]

Faith and Order opted for the latter, and moved forward from two starting points found in BEM, namely a) "baptism is related not only to momentary experience but to life-long growth into Christ"[12] and b) "the awareness that baptism takes place within the community of faith, requires personal confession of faith, and points to and is founded on the faithfulness of God."[13] According to the Faverges report, the basic *ordo* or pattern of worship can also be found in relation to baptism: "this *ordo* of Christian worship includes the great outline of baptism, understood as 'formation in faith and baptizing in water together, leading to participation in the life of the community'" as it can be found in the scriptures.[14] Moreover the report explains:

> *Furthermore, the long process of formation in faith (the catechumenate), baptism and incorporation into community was itself summed up in the central events of the baptismal rite. The renunciations of evil and the confession of faith—the creed—summarized and stood for the whole catechumenate. The reception of candidates into the community, the kiss of peace and the first eucharist, could anticipate the whole Christian life. What is more, the ordo of catechumenate, baptism and incorporation is constantly echoed in the whole Christian existence. In the life-long learning of the faith of Christ the catechumenate continues. In daily dying and rising Christians reclaim their baptism into the death and resurrection of Christ. In repeated reconciliation in the church the baptized are restored to community. In the celebration of worship the church is renewed for the mission of Christ and formed in the patterns of Christian ethics.*[15]

---

11. Best and Heller, *Becoming a Christian*, 76.

12. BEM, "Baptism," par. 9, referred to in Best and Heller, *Becoming a Christian*, 77.

13. Ibid., 77ff.

14. Best and Heller, *Becoming a Christian*, 78ff.

15. Ibid., 79ff.

If churches can understand this pattern as their common basis for baptism this has consequences for the recognition of each other's baptism. Therefore Faith and Order is asking whether the churches could agree that the three elements of the *ordo*—formation in faith, water baptism, life-long growing in the community—are interlinked and overlapping, and thus not fixed to a specific order in time. This would mean accepting that the water rite is performed either at the beginning of a human life or at any later stage, without this implying a difference in the validity of the overall process.[16]

This basic idea has implications for ecumenical discussions. First, it would help also to further the discussion on the inculturation of baptism, which was not taken up in BEM but was dealt with extensively at the Faverges consultation. Faith and Order identified several criteria in order "to discern which cultural elements may help to illuminate the fundamental meaning of baptism and which would otherwise obscure it."[17] Based on insights of the studies on inculturation conducted by the Lutheran World Federation[18] these are the following:

> *The inculturation of baptism needs fidelity to and preservation of the fundamental ordo of baptism as it was developed in the tradition ... No form of incultured baptism can dispense with the basic elements of the baptismal ordo: formation in faith, washing in water and participation in the life of the community.*

The inculturation of baptism will look for gestures, signs and symbols in a specific culture which relate to the essential aspects of baptism, such as its meaning as incorporation into the body of Christ and as conferring a life-long new status.

For the inculturation of the water rite especially the proposed criteria are:

---

16. See the questions which the churches are asked in the report of the meeting "Becoming a Christian" in Best and Heller, *Becoming a Christian*, 82ff.

17. Ibid., 86.

18. See Chapter Four above, p. 193f.

The basic water rite may be embellished in different ways through inculturation, but anything added to the rite should draw attention to its fundamental meaning, illuminating and explicating this rather than obscuring it.

The ritual elaboration of the baptismal rite during the centuries of the early church should be respected, even if these elements are not adopted. Through such respect churches may acknowledge their common origin.

The inculturation of baptism will take into account the role of time and space for the celebration. Christians should be encouraged to baptize on a Sunday or a traditional Christian feast day even if there are cultural pressures against this.

The space and environment for baptism have to be culturally appropriate. For some situations this may mean the use of lakes or rivers, for others the use of baptismal baths or fonts...

Festal vestments can express and enrich the festal character of baptism...

The inculturation of baptism will take into account the role of the minister, the parents and the congregation and will express the community-building potential of baptism.

The community gathered for baptism represents the one holy, catholic and apostolic church into which the candidate is admitted. Thus the inculturation of baptism should transcend any group allegiance and lead into communion with God and with all Christian churches united in a common baptism. Prayers and hymns may be used to express this.

The inculturation of baptism involves the search for language in the formularies which is understood by the people in that specific context...

The inculturation of baptism will look for gestures, signs and symbols in a specific culture which relate to the essential aspects of baptism.[19]

---

19. "Becoming a Christian: Report of the Consultation," par. 39 and 41, in Best and Heller, *Becoming a Christian*, 86ff.

In order to avoid new separations between churches the report recommends that "the inculturation of baptism should happen in mutual respect and mutual accountability to other churches, in such a way that local churches are united in cultural expressions rather than separated."[20]

Secondly, and as a follow-up to indications made by BEM, the idea of the *ordo* of baptism leads to further reflections on the relation of ethics to baptism: baptism is in itself "'moral pedagogy', ethical instruction for the people of God,"[21] and "baptism signifies a special quality of Christian ethics which distinguishes it from other ethical systems and perspectives."[22]

The report of the consultation was published and distributed for open discussion. In some multilateral and bilateral agreements some of these ideas have been taken up;[23] but Faith and Order also continued work on this basis, as we will see below.

The Baptism Study of the Joint Working Group between the Roman Catholic Church and the World Council of Churches

Other substantial work has been undertaken by another important body on the international level, one working in close connection with Faith and Order: the Joint Working Group (JWG) between the Roman Catholic Church and the World Council of Churches. In 2004 it adopted a study document on "Ecclesiological and Ecumenical Implications of a Common Baptism."[24] This study explores the implications of a common recognition of baptism for the Roman

---

20. Ibid., par. 40, in Best and Heller, *Becoming a Christian*, 86.

21. Ibid., 90.

22. Ibid., 91.

23. For example by the Joint working Group between the Roman Catholic Church and the WCC (JWG); see below.

24. Published as Appendix C in: Joint Working Group between the Roman Catholic Church and the World Council of Churches, Eighth Report 1999-2005, WCC Publications, Geneva and Rome, 2005, 45-72. Online at http://www.oikoumene.org/fileadmin/files/wcc-main/documents/p1/8thjointworkinggroup.pdf. Although this text might be considered a bilateral document (Roman Catholic–WCC) it is treated here under the category of multilateral work, because the WCC is a multilateral body.

Catholic side, in relation to the various Christian traditions represented in the WCC.

Stating that a growing mutual recognition of baptism exists among churches this text points out, as a fundamental ecclesiological implication, that

> *if there is one church of Jesus Christ and if baptism is entrance into it, then all those who are baptized are bound to one another in Christ and should be in full communion with one another. There should not be a division among ecclesial communities; baptism should impel Christians to work for the elimination of divisions.*[25]

But taking into consideration the actual situation and the position of the Roman Catholic Church regarding other churches, it also clarifies that

> *churches that share faith in the Trinity and fully recognize one another's baptism may, nevertheless, break communion with each other due to differences about other matters of faith or questions of order. In this case the communion which is the fruit of faith and baptism is impeded. There are churches which consider that a disagreement in faith that is sufficiently serious to be communion-breaking between them and another church makes them unable to admit baptized members of that church to full participation in the eucharist, the normal fulfillment of baptism.*[26]

Based on BEM, as well as on the further work of Faith and Order,[27] the study supports the proposal of the Faith and Order consultation at Faverges: to understand baptism not just as the water rite, but also encompassing the wider process of Christian initiation including the three elements of formation in faith, baptism in water and participation in the life of the community. The

---

25. Ibid., 52, par. 31.
26. Ibid., 55, par. 46.
27. See above.

goal of this is to find "more extensive convergence."[28] Consequently it proposes that

> *each church, even as it retains its own baptismal tradition, recognize in others the one baptism into Jesus Christ by affirming the similarity of wider patterns of initiation and formation in Christ present in every community ... Those churches that practise only believer's baptism could recognize the one baptism in other traditions within their full patterns of Christian initiation, which include personal affirmation of faith. Those churches that normally practise infant baptism could recognize the one baptism within the full pattern of Christian initiation in "believer's churches," even where identical forms of chrismation or confirmation were lacking.[29]*

The document is also aware of the difficulties on the Orthodox side in recognizing baptism in other churches. Therefore the text proposes:

> *When there are obstacles to full communion among different communities, baptism still provides a degree of communion that is real, if imperfect ... Nor do the difficulties that some churches have about recognizing the full sacramental reality of baptism celebrated in churches not in full communion with themselves—difficulties that have to be recognized and respected—deprive baptism of all significance for communion. The position of the Orthodox is a case in point.[30]*

The document highlights the question of apostolicity as one of the main issues to be solved with regard to mutual recognition of baptism:

> *As indicated above, among the issues raised with regard to recognition/reception is the fundamental question of apostolicity*

---

28. JWG, Eighth Report, 57, par. 52.
29. Ibid., 57, par. 54.
30. Ibid., 59, par. 61 and 62.

> ... *The recognition of the apostolicity of the rite and ordo of bap-*
> *tism is a step towards the full recognition of the apostolicity of the*
> *churches in a wider and more profound sense: the full recognition*
> *of the same apostolic faith, sacramental order and mission. Full*
> *recognition of apostolicity, therefore, involves more than the rec-*
> *ognition of baptism.* [31]

Therefore, for the Roman Catholic Church and for the Orthodox the recognition of baptism in other traditions does not auto-
matically imply the sharing of the eucharist.[32]

Finally the text suggests steps to be taken in order "to deepen
ecumenical relationships."[33] These suggestions include (among
others):

- to foster knowledge of the achievement of a significant convergence on baptism;

- to seek a common affirmation that it is illegitimate as well as
unnecessary to perform something that could be understood
as re-baptism;

- to include references to baptism as basis for ecumenical relationship in the theological basis of councils of churches and
other ecumenical bodies;

- to have dialogue concerning the significance and valid celebration of baptism and to consider common baptismal cer-
tificates for us by churches in the same region;

- to study the issue of inculturation;

- not to allow practices to develop which threaten the unity
now shared in respect of the *ordo*, theology and administration of baptism, such as the replacement of the traditional
Trinitarian baptismal formula with alternative wording or
the admission of persons to the eucharist before baptism;

---

31. Ibid., 65, par. 91 and 92.
32. Cf. ibid., 66ff., par. 93-97.
33. Ibid., 68, par. 99-110.

- dialogue with (a) churches which baptize "in the name of Jesus" rather than with the traditional Trinitarian formula, but with water; (b) churches which baptize with the traditional Trinitarian formula, but without water; and (c) churches in which entry into the Christian community is effected without baptismal rites.

This study document clarifies the *implications* of the results of Faith and Order work to that point, especially, the significance of mutual recognition of baptism as an important step on the way to mutual recognition of churches. This process includes clarification and agreement on further issues which are understood differently by different churches.

"One Baptism: Towards Mutual Recognition"

Further work of Faith and Order resulted in 2011 in the publication of the study document "One Baptism: Towards Mutual Recognition."[34]

This text "explores the close relation between baptism and the believer's life-long growth into Christ, as a basis for a greater mutual recognition of baptism."[35] Furthermore, it seeks to address other issues in baptismal understanding and practice which hinder mutual recognition.

It is important to note that this document makes a clear distinction between "Christian initiation" and "baptism":

a) Christian initiation refers to a process that begins with hearing the Gospel and confessing the faith, continues with formation in faith (catechesis), leads to baptism, resulting in the incorporation of the baptized into the Christian community, marked by the sharing of the eucharistic meal. b) Baptism is the central event of this process, in which a believer is incorporated into the body

---

34. World Council of Churches, Commission on Faith and Order, *One Baptism: Towards Mutual Recognition; A Study Text*, Faith and Order Paper No. 210, WCC, Geneva 2011.

35. Ibid., 1, par. 1.

of Christ. *This act includes profession of faith and is "administered with water in the name of the Father, the Son, and the Holy
Spirit."*[36]

The text also recognizes the complex situation concerning the
mutual recognition of baptism among the churches:

*The situation is indeed complex, as the following instances make
clear:*

- *mutual recognition of baptism may reflect a condition of
  full sharing in faith and life among the churches, marked by
  Eucharistic communion, and including common discernment and decision-making, service and mission; or*
- *mutual recognition may exist together with significant
  limitations in sharing, particularly at the eucharistic
  table—raising questions for some about the meaning of
  recognition, if not of baptism itself, or*
- *mutual recognition may exist, but without further shared
  life and mission;*
- *mutual recognition may be lacking, so that some churches
  (or congregations within them) require the baptism of all
  persons seeking membership, even if they have already been
  baptized in another church.*[37]

There are three dimensions to mutual recognition:

It may involve:

- *churches recognizing one another as churches, that is as
  authentic expressions of the One Church of Jesus Christ; or*
- *churches recognizing the baptism of a person from one
  church who seeks entrance into another church; or*
- *persons recognizing one another individually as Christians.*[38]

---

36. Ibid., 2, par. 3.
37. Ibid., 4, par. 11.
38. Ibid., 4, par. 12.

Mutual recognition is understood here as "acknowledgement of apostolicity in the other,"[39] and thus recognition of baptism involves three levels on which apostolicity has to be discerned: "a) discerning the apostolicity of the rite itself... b) discerning apostolicity in the larger pattern of Christian initiation... c) discerning apostolicity in the ongoing life and witness of the church which baptizes and forms the new Christians."[40]

The document then explores the biblical language about baptism, especially that relating to the understanding of baptism as participation in Christ's death and resurrection, the prefiguration of baptism in the Old Testament, the pneumatological and trinitarian aspect of baptism, the new life, reconciliation and the ethical implications of baptism as well as its eschatological dimension.[41] It addresses the issue of different language used by different churches in defining baptism as "sacrament" or "ordinance." It highlights the fact that

> *most traditions, whether they use the term 'sacrament' or 'ordinance', affirm that these events are both instrumental (in that God uses them to bring about a new reality), and expressive (of an already-existing reality). Some traditions emphasize the instrumental dimension, recognizing baptism as an action in which God transforms the life of the candidate as he or she is brought into the Christian community. Others emphasize the expressive dimension.[42]*

The document acknowledges that the different language used represents two "different starting points in understanding baptism." But "they are not mutually exclusive, and may both be regarded as essential for understanding the full meaning of baptism."[43]

---

39. Ibid., 4, par. 14.
40. Ibid., 5, par. 14.
41. Ibid., 5-7, par. 17-25.
42. Ibid., 7ff, par. 30.
43. Ibid., 8, par.. 31.

When looking into the liturgy of baptism the text takes up an issue which has been pointed to in many of the responses to BEM, namely the understanding of "sign" and "symbol". The text clarifies:

> *Some churches have understood water as a "sign," meaning that it points beyond itself to the realities of cleansing and new life in Christ. Other churches have understood water as an "effective sign" or "symbol," meaning that it bears within itself, by faith and through the power of the Holy Spirit, the reality of new life in Christ. With whatever nuances, the churches largely agree that the use of water indicates the believer's entry into a new life made possible by the gospel of divine grace, and pointing towards the fullness of the kingdom to come.*[44]

The use of additional symbols and symbolic actions is supported.[45]

In continuation with "Becoming a Christian," the text "One Baptism: Towards Mutual Recognition" places baptism with water in the name of the triune God within the wider context of Christian initiation, which contains the three elements (1) formation in faith, (2) baptism, and (3) participation in the life of the Christian community. Formation in faith is explained as "a life-long process, ending with that final profession which is the testimony of a Christian death."[46] Baptism is "the central symbolic act within the whole process of Christian initiation."[47] And participation in the life of the Christian community is the daily experience of repenting and turning to Christ.[48]

On this basis the text addresses several closely-related, unsolved issues, namely "baptism as entry into the church," "baptism and the eucharist," and "initiation, church membership and baptism." The paradoxical situation of baptized Christians is mentioned: "while baptism brings Christians into the unity of Christ's body,

---

44. Ibid., 8, par. 36.
45. Ibid., 8ff., par. 37-40.
46. Ibid., 9, par. 43.
47. Ibid., 10, par. 44.
48. Cf. ibid., 10, par. 49.

which is one, the location of baptism within a specific confessional body means that the baptized experience disunity with many other Christians."[49] The text highlights the "dynamic connection between baptism and eucharist,"[50] but also describes the actual current situation, in which some churches "discern apostolicity in another's understanding of baptism," but a common eucharist is still not possible, because "apostolicity is not discerned in the understanding and exercise of ordained ministry."[51]

The relationship between baptism and church membership is described as complex, due to historical developments.[52] But the text proposes:

> *Whenever it is said to be attained, "membership" needs to be understood in light of baptism as entrance into the body of Christ. Through baptism a person is drawn into the mystery of life in Christ. This challenges contemporary understandings of "membership" which sometimes suggest that the church is merely a human institution, rather than the ekklesia (assembly) of believers in communion with the triune God, and thus with one another.*[53]

In a separate chapter the text deals with the question of "Baptism and Faith." It takes seriously what has been confirmed by the BEM study process and the responses to BEM: that "all churches affirm that faith accompanies baptism."[54] According to the document, "the churches affirm the priority of the divine initiative in the process of Christian initiation ... God invites and enables a response in faith."[55] Taking seriously the fact that, even in adult baptism, "faith may take only rudimentary forms"[56] the text proposes that the church welcomes, through baptism, into the community of faith also those, who are too young to articulate their faith.[57]

---

49. Ibid., 11, par. 58.
50. Ibid., 12, par. 59.
51. Ibid., 12, par. 61.
52. Ibid., 12, par. 63.
53. Ibid., 13, par. 65.
54. Ibid., 13, par. 66.
55. Ibid., 13, par. 71.
56. Ibid., par. 73.
57. See ibid., par. 76.

The final chapter summarizes the specific differences in baptismal understanding and practice which are still a barrier to mutual recognition. It combines these with concrete questions to the churches, in order to encourage wider study of these issues.

It has to be noted that this text is understood as "a study document, rather than a convergence text."[58] There is no organized process for official church responses, but an expectation that the text will be studied in various settings both within and between churches.

"One Baptism: Towards Mutual Recognition" develops the idea from the Faverges consultation that there is a common, three-fold pattern of baptism consisting of formation in faith, the water rite, and on-going nurture in faith. The major achievements to be highlighted in this text are twofold. First it clarifies how baptism is related to "life-long growth into Christ"[59] by distinguishing between Christian initiation and the baptismal rite - which at the same time means embedding baptism within the wider context of Christian initiation. Second it analyzes the understanding of baptism as "sacrament" or as "ordinance," leading to the conclusion that the two "are not necessarily incompatible,"[60] but are emphasizing different dimensions of baptism.[61] This brings paedobaptist churches and credobaptist churches closer together.

The fundamental ecclesiological question behind the difficulties of Orthodox churches to recognize other churches' baptism, is dealt with only marginally. But the document does ask the fundamental question:

> On certain conditions some churches recognize a person as a baptized Christian without, however, recognizing either the baptism as it is exercised in that church, or the ecclesial character of that church itself. Some have asked whether this is possible ecclesiologically. With this in mind, the following question is asked: How far does recognition of a person as a baptized Christian imply some

---

58. Ibid., 15, par. 81.
59. BEM, "Baptism," par. 9.
60. WCC, F&O, *One Baptism: Towards Mutual Recognition*, par. 26, 7.
61. See ibid., par. 30, 7ff.

recognition of the baptism which they received, and of the church in which it was performed?[62]

This question is not only a challenge to Orthodox churches, but also to the Roman Catholic Church.

REGIONAL AND LOCAL AGREEMENTS

During the last twenty years, multilateral agreements on mutual recognition of baptism have been signed in a number of countries and regions.

Great Britain

To a certain extent the churches in *Great Britain* were in the forefront of this development. In 1972 the British Council of Churches, with Roman Catholic assistance, studied the theology and practice of baptism. This led to the development of a common baptismal certificate which could be produced in one church as evidence that baptism, with water in the name of the Trinity, had taken place in another.[63]

Australia

In *Australia* theological dialogues between the Roman Catholic Church and the Anglican, Methodist and Presbyterian Churches provided a background for the idea of a common baptismal certificate in 1979.[64] On this certificate the common conviction is

---

62. Ibid., par. 86, 16.

63. Code of Practice for Ecumenical relations in the Anglican-Methodist Covenant, par. 102, 1989-1997, http://www.anglican-methodist.org.uk/Bishops_Code.pdf.

64. See Robert Gribben, "Common Baptismal Certificate: Australia," in Best, *Baptism Today*, 231-233. See also http://www.ncca.org.au/files/Working_Papers_pt2_73-140.pdf, 74: "The following churches have agreed that a certificate stating that a person 'was baptised with water in the name of the Father, Son and Holy Spirit' is evidence of Christian Baptism: the Anglican Church of Australia, the Antiochian Orthodox Church, the Armenian Apostolic Church, the Congregational Federation of Australia, the Greek Orthodox Archdiocese of Australia, the Lutheran Church of Australia, the Roman Catholic Church of Australia, the Romanian Orthodox Church, the Uniting Church in Australia, the Presbyterian Church of Australia."

expressed that baptism is done with water and in the name of the Father, and of the Son, and of the Holy Spirit. The common certificate has been agreed upon by the Anglican Church of Australia, the Catholic Church in Australia, the Antiochian Orthodox Diocese of Australia and New Zealand, the Armenian Apostolic Church, the Congregational Federation of Australia and New Zealand, the Greek Orthodox Archdiocese of Australia, the Lutheran Church of Australia, the Presbyterian Church of Australia, the Romanian Orthodox Church, and the Uniting Church in Australia. From this list it is clear that believers' baptism churches are not able to use this certificate. Although they had been part of the conversations, they would add additional criteria for a baptism to be "authentic."[65] Notably, some Eastern Orthodox churches and an Oriental Orthodox church joined the group of churches which issue a common baptismal certificate.

Chile

A similar development is happening recently in various countries, where churches have signed agreements declaring mutual recognition of their baptisms. Thus an agreement on "Mutual Recognition of Baptism" was signed in *Chile* in 1999 by the Roman Catholic Church, the Orthodox Church of Antioch, the Anglican Church, the Evangelical Lutheran Church, Evangelical Reformed Church, the Methodist Church, the Church of the Brethren and several Pentecostal churches.[66] The document summarizes the commonalities and divergences on baptism, including their different attitudes towards immersion and aspersion, as well as infant baptism. Nevertheless they are able to declare together "the mutual recognition of the baptism celebrated as a sacrament in our churches." The document refers explicitly to the BEM document and the signing churches agree that baptism is performed with water and the Trinitarian formula.

---

65. See Gribben, "Common Baptismal Certificate," 231.
66. http://documentos.iglesia.cl/conf/doc_pdf.
php?mod=documentos_sini&id=594.

This is one of the first agreements involving churches which traditionally do not recognize infant baptism, such as the Church of the Brethren and the Pentecostal churches.

Poland

In *Poland* a declaration entitled "The Sacrament of Baptism—A Sign of Unity" was signed in 2000[67] by the Lutheran Church, the Methodist Church, the Reformed Church, the Roman Catholic Church, the Polish Catholic Church, the Old Catholic Church and the Orthodox Church. It is significant that no believers' baptism church signed the declaration. Three short paragraphs describe the common understanding of baptism and point out that "Baptism is in water and the Holy Spirit; it is administered 'in the name of the Father, and of the Son, and of the Holy Spirit.'" Referring to BEM the document points out that baptism in Christ is "a call for the Churches to overcome their divisions and to manifest visibly their communion." On this basis "the undersigned Churches solemnly recognize the validity of baptism administered by the clergy of those Churches."

Brazil

In *Brazil* it was the Episcopal Anglican Church, the Roman Catholic Church, the Evangelical Lutheran Church, the Presbyterian United Church and the Syrian Orthodox Church which signed an agreement in November 2007. In the document the churches agree that "the Baptism instituted by Christ is fundamentally a free gift of God," and "accept the Baptism as basic link of the unity that is given by the faith in the same Lord." The churches agree that baptism is with water and in the name of the Father, and the Son, and the Holy Spirit, and that baptism is not necessary when a Christian changes affiliation from one church to another.[68] It needs to be noted again that no believers' baptism churches are involved, but an Oriental Orthodox church was able to sign the agreement.

---

67. http://www.ekumenia.pl/index.php?D=42, an English version can be found at http://www.mariavite.org/choecuma.htm#reconn. The author used an unpublished version which was corrected by Renata Nehring and others.

68. Text at http://www.itesc.ecumenismo.com/news/rec%20mutuo.pdf.

Papua New Guinea

In *Papua New Guinea* formal mutual recognition of baptism exists since November 2003 between the Lutherans, the Roman Catholics and the Anglican Church of Papua New Guinea.[69] Again no believers' baptism church is involved, and, in this case, no Orthodox church.

Germany

In *Germany* an agreement on mutual recognition was signed in April 2007 by the Ethiopian Orthodox Church in Germany, the Council of Anglican Episcopal Churches in Germany, the Armenian Apostolic Church in Germany, the Evangelical Old-Reformed Church in Lower Saxony, the European Continental province of the Moravian Church, the Evangelical Church in Germany (EKD), the Evangelical Methodist Church, the Catholic Diocese of the Old-Catholics in Germany, the Orthodox Church in Germany, the Roman Catholic Church, and the Independent Evangelical-Lutheran Church.[70] They "recognize every baptism which has been carried out according to the commission of Jesus in the name of the Father and the Son and the Holy Spirit through the symbolic act of immersion in water or through the pouring of water over the person to be baptized." They mention explicitly that such a baptism is unrepeatable.[71] No believers' baptism church signed the agreement, but, in meantime, the Mennonites expressed their willingness to consider signing. It is significant that all the German dioceses of the Eastern Orthodox churches represented in the Commission of the Orthodox Church in Germany did sign the document.

Other Countries

In other countries discussions on baptism and the possibility of mutual recognition are continuing, for example in the Estonian

---

69. http://www.ask.com/wiki/Anglican_Church_of_Papua_New_Guinea#Ecumenical_relations

70. Text at http://www.oekumene-ack.de/uploads/media/Christian_Baptism.pdf; list of signing churches only in the German version: http://www.oekumene-ack.de/uploads/media/Anerkennung_der_Taufe.pdf.

71. Ibid.

Council of Churches[72] and in the Working Community of Christian Churches (*Arbeitsgemeinschaft Christlicher Kirchen*) in Switzerland.[73]

Summary

In general, these agreements on mutual recognition of baptism are short; they give expression to the formal mutual recognition, and to the basic common understanding, but do not go into theological details. The recognition is stated on the basis of the work done in the ecumenical movement; in some cases BEM is explicitly referred to. It needs to be noted, that practically all these agreements mention that baptism is performed with water and in the name of the Father, and the Son, and the Holy Spirit.

This overview, although incomplete, shows that churches consider it an important ecumenical step either to express officially their existing mutual recognition of baptism or to find ways to overcome the obstacles to mutual recognition. But the fact that only in rare cases churches which reject infant baptism are involved in such agreements shows that mutual recognition of baptism is more difficult in this case. Consequently these documents do not develop new proposals for the solution of specific points of divergence between paedobaptists and credobaptists. Only in very few cases are Oriental Orthodox churches involved in such agreements, while for Eastern Orthodox it seems to be easier to sign such documents.

Bilateral Developments

In the bilateral ecumenical dialogues some concrete, important steps have been taken. We will first have a look at the international level, and then at some forward-leading developments on the national level.

---

72. I am grateful to Dr. Ingmar Kurg, who sent me his presentation to the Theological Commission of the ECC in February 2010.

73. See http://www.agck.ch/de-ch/projekte/taufanerkennung-ausweiten. html. In fact an agreement on mutual recognition of baptism exists in Switzerland already since 1973 between the Reformed, the Roman Catholic and the Old Catholic Churches. The plan is to revise this agreement and to extend it to other churches.

THE INTERNATIONAL LEVEL
Lutherans and Mennonites

A very concrete and practical step has been taken by the Lutheran World Federation and the Mennonite World Conference. In 2010 the Lutheran World Federation approved a statement in which they regret the persecution of Anabaptists by Lutheran authorities.[74] This is based on a dialogue between the LWF and the Mennonites, which led to an in-depth study about the history of the two church families and reflection on how to overcome the condemnations from the Lutheran side, and the inappropriate reactions from the Mennonite side.[75] In this context, they dealt also with the issue of baptism. They

> *acknowledge an asymmetry in our approach regarding the question of baptism of newcomers who join our churches from the other tradition. Whereas Lutherans universally recognize baptisms performed in Mennonite churches, Mennonite churches do not generally recognize the baptism of infants performed in Lutheran churches and often require newcomers who have been baptized as infants to be baptized according to Mennonite practice, something that Lutherans would view as rebaptism. At the same time, however, some Mennonite churches do recognize infant baptisms to the extent that they require only a public confession of faith for membership, which completes whatever may have been lacking in the original "water baptism." Both Mennonites and Lutherans agree that baptism cannot be seen as an isolated event. Thus, how baptisms are recognized must be understood within a larger framework that explores how the practice of baptism is related to a larger set of theological doctrines. Since these frameworks are different, Lutherans feel misunderstood by Mennonites when Mennonites assess the Lutheran practice of baptism according*

---

74. http://www.lwf-assembly.org/uploads/media/Mennonite_Statement-EN.pdf.

75. Lutheran-Mennonite International Study Commission, Report, *Healing Memories: Reconciling in Christ*, The Lutheran World Federation and The Mennonite World Conference, 2010, online at: http://www.lutheranworld. org/lwf/wp-content/uploads/2010/10/Report_Lutheran-Mennonite_Study_ Commission.pdf.

to their own framework. Conversely, Mennonites feel misunder-
stood by Lutherans when Lutherans assess the Mennonite practice
according to their own framework. Clearly, both sides experience
great anguish in this conflict since the deepest convictions of their
faith seem to be at stake and each side can easily feel misunder-
stood by the other. The members of this study commission hope
that neither the Anabaptist/Mennonite rejection of infant baptism
nor the condemnation of Anabaptists in Article IX [of the Confes-
sio Augustana][76] will remain a church-dividing issue. Neverthe-
less, we have not yet found a way to bridge the divide between the
two churches regarding their teaching and practice on baptism.
Further conversations are needed, perhaps especially among our
MWC and LWF member churches.[77]

In summary, we have here the example of a concrete act of repentance which brings a paedobaptist church and a believer's baptism church closer together; but the theological obstacles to mutual recognition of baptism are left to further dialogue.

Baptists and the Community of Protestant Churches in Europe (CPCE)

On the European level, an official dialogue took place 2002 - 2004 between the European Baptist Federation (EBF) and the Community of Protestant Churches in Europe (CPCE, formerly the Leuenberg Church Fellowship). The results of these conversations are published in the communiqué "The Beginning of the Christian Life and the Nature of the Church: Results of the Dialogue between the CPCE and the EBF."[78] This is based on the understanding of baptism as a "bond of unity" among Christians; it states that "for this reason, the churches recognize every baptism that has been carried

---

76. Addition by the author.

77. Ibid., 89.

78. Communiqué "The Beginning of the Christian Life and the Nature of the Church: Results of the Dialogue between the CPCE and the EBF," in Wilhelm Hüffmeier and Tony Peck, eds., *Dialogue between the Community of Protestant Churches in Europe (CPCE) and the European Baptist Federation (EBF) on the Doctrine and Practice of Baptism*, Leuenberg Documents Vol. 9, Lembeck, Frankfurt am Main, 2005, 9-29.

out in accordance with the gospel and they rejoice over every person who is baptized."[79]

Referring to the bilateral dialogue between Baptists and Lutherans both sides affirm that they have basically the same understanding of faith:

> *In baptism into the name of the triune God, the Christian church celebrates the victory of the love of God over human godlessness and over all the powers of evil which have been given entrance into life by our unbelief, our lack of love and our loss of hope for this world. Death is swallowed up in Victory ... but thanks be to God who gives us the victory through Jesus Christ our Lord (1 Cor. 15:54ff). Baptism is therefore also a place where human beings can say a "yes" of faith to the God who has already said yes to them in the victory of love.*[80]

Baptism is understood as "the sign and central event of initiation, or the beginning of the Christian life."[81] Baptism, therefore, belongs together with "repentance and initial Christian nurture, until the point is reached where a person can make his or her own grateful response of 'yes' to God, is commissioned for service in the world, and shares in the Lord's Supper for the first time." Thus baptism is the focus of the wider process of initiation.

Both sides further affirm that baptism is unrepeatable. Therefore "the point at issue can only be the validity of the baptism that someone has already received."[82]

The document's approach is based on the conviction that the different baptismal practices result from different emphases: In infant baptism the responsibility of the parents, sponsors and the congregation for the spiritual growth of the baptizand is stressed; while Baptists emphasize the individual aspect of baptism. The authors propose an understanding of initiation as a process: "If Christian initiation is understood as a process in which baptism

---

79. Ibid., 18.
80. Ibid., 19.
81. Ibid., 19.
82. Ibid., par. 9, 22.

is only one moment, then some Baptists will be able to recognize infant baptism as a valid part of that process, as long as it is followed later by a faith which is owned personally by the person baptized." But

> *many Baptists, however, will want to recognize the initiation of other Christians into Christ and the church, regardless of the form of baptism. Without recognizing infant baptism, they will affirm that Christians baptized only as infants have been incorporated into the body of Christ, when they discern in their lives the one Spirit, one body, one hope, and one faith which God grants (Eph. 4:3-8).* [83]

On this basis the document states: "All baptisms are recognized by our churches which, following the command of Jesus Christ (Matt. 28:19), are performed in accordance with the Gospel." To clarify what a baptism "carried out in accordance with the Gospel" means, the document mentions "baptizing in the name of the Father and the Son and the Holy Spirit, with the symbolic action of effusion with water or immersion in water."[84] But it is clear that further examination is required. Thus, despite remaining difficulties, the document comes to the conclusion that "regardless of our present disagreements over water-baptism, the recognition that all Christians are immersed into the life, death and resurrection of Jesus Christ is, however, a powerful expression of the unity of the church already given in Christ."[85]

The remaining disagreements are described in the following way:

> *The CPCE churches can recognize that the Baptist practice only to baptize believers who are asking for baptism and who have made a confession before baptism, is a proper practice of baptism according to the gospel. But the churches of the CPCE also claim*

---

83. Ibid., par. 9, 22.
84. Ibid., par 11, 23.
85. Ibid., par.11, 23.

for themselves that the baptism of infants of Christian parents is a possibility which is in accord with the Gospel. When the baptism of believers is performed in Baptist communities of those who have already been baptized as infants, the CPCE churches perceive this as a denial of the validity of this sacrament. For this reason they must reject this practice, which in their view constitutes an inadmissible rebaptism, as an administration of the sacrament which is not according to the Gospel.

Baptist Churches feel obliged by their understanding of the biblical testimony only to practise the baptism of believing disciples as being according to the gospel. Many Baptist Churches cannot accept infant baptisms which have been performed in other churches as valid baptisms. This is especially the case when an infant baptism has not been followed by a Christian upbringing. Therefore they do not understand those baptisms as re-baptisms when they baptize those who have been baptized as infants.[86]

Thus this document finds two aspects to be considered in order to move forward: first, a common understanding of the process of Christian initiation, in which different forms of baptism could have different, but valid, places;[87] and second—based on the first aspect—focusing on the question of the validity of infant baptism might help Baptists not to (re-)baptize, but rather to receive, through a confession of faith, converts who have been baptized as infants.[88]

THE NATIONAL LEVEL
Waldensians and Baptists in Italy

One of the earliest examples of mutual recognition of baptism between a church which traditionally rejects infant baptism and paedobaptist churches can be found in Italy: in 1990 the Waldensians/Methodists[89] and the Baptists in Italy adopted a common

---

86. Ibid., par. 4 and 5, 26ff.

87. Cf. ibid., par. 10, 28.

88. Cf. ibid., par. 11, 29.

89. Although these are two distinct churches, they are considered here as one side in a bilateral dialogue, because already in 1975 the Waldensians and the Methodists in Italy joined in an "alliance of integration."

"Document on Mutual Recognition."[90] This document covers mutual recognition of each other as churches in general. But— since baptism is one of the major controversial issues between the two churches—the text includes an important section dealing with baptism.

The two sides first state their mutual agreement in many fundamental aspects of the faith, and their response to the gospel in witness and service. They mention especially:

> *salvation by grace alone and its adoption by faith; the centrality of the biblical word ... the two big signs and seals of God's work in the life of the church, baptism and holy supper; the Christian life as a life in freedom and love; the church as called forth by the Holy Spirit through the word of grace ... the Christian calling to mission, i.e. to proclaim the gospel to each creature in words and in life, by making known Christ as liberation, hope and salvation of the world and by witnessing to the kingdom of God, which moves us forward to answer for a just, peaceful, free and brotherly world.*[91]

The issue of baptism is approached in a very careful way. The document asks first:

> *Is it possible, to find an agreement, which on the one hand does not imply a capitulation of one side to the other and which on the other hand allows to set up a comprehensive, complete and unlimited communion between our churches and their members by emphasizing that what is "essential according to the*

---

90. This document is unfortunately not published in English. The original Italian text has the title "Documento sui reciproco riconoscimento fra chiese battise metodiste valdesi in Italia" in *Sinodo des 1990 delle chiese valdesi e metodiste: Session straordinaria*, 1.-4. November 1990, 14-22. A German version is accessible in Cornelia Nussberger, ed., *Wachsende Kirchengemeinschaft: Gespräche und Vereinbarungen zwischen evangelischen Kirchen in Europa*, Texte der Ev. Arbeitsstelle Ökumene Schweiz No. 16, Bern, 1992, 155-167.

91. Translation by the author from the German version in Nussberger, *Wachsende Kirchengemeinschaft*, 157.

Gospel" in each position and in this way not hurting and force any conscience?[92]

This is an attempt to find a solution whereby none of the actors has to give up their own identity.

The text then lists as points which are "necessary and sufficient" for agreement concerning baptism that (a) baptism is "an essential part of the Christian revelation"; (b) according to the testimonies from the first Christian congregations baptism has its place between conversion and a life in the imitation of Christ (Acts 2:38; 2 Cor 5:17); (c) baptism is not just a sign or symbol, but is closely linked with the forgiveness of sins, with the association with Christ as well as with the reception of the Holy Spirit; (d) water baptism can be a response to spirit baptism or an expression of the wish for spirit baptism; (e) the "normal and usual form" of baptism is the baptism of adults on the grounds of a personal confession of faith, but in the New Testament the baptism of infants is neither prohibited nor clearly witnessed to; (f) the Reformation based the theology of baptism in a new way on the Bible, but kept the baptism of infants despite the critic of the Anabaptists, who considered the baptism of infants as not permitted and therefore not valid.

On this basis the document states that today the Waldensians and the Methodists are able to appreciate the value of the critique of Anabaptists and Baptists against the baptism of infants. "Therefore they welcome with joy and thankfulness the witness of the Baptist congregations concerning believers' baptism."[93] They themselves also baptize adults—but not only. However "they are not of the opinion that an infant baptism which has been performed in the context of a believing family and a confessing church would be an act of disobedience to the Word of God."[94] On the other hand, Baptists today are able to agree with some theological statements concerning infant baptism, such as the priority of God's grace in baptism. But they don't feel they have the right to recognize the practice of infant baptism.

---

92. Ibid., 159.
93. Ibid., 161.
94. Ibid., 161.

Here, there is still a deep difference between these two (or three) churches which needs further discussion. But it is crucial that this difference is not considered as an obstacle for full communion.[95] This is possible for two reasons: first, because there is an agreement on the close connection between baptism and confession of faith, and on the fact that no one's baptismal faith can substitute for another's. Both forms of baptism are based on the priority of grace, which is especially underlined by the practice of infant baptism. While infant baptism also emphasizes the significance of God's covenant, as well as the responsibility of the family and the congregation for a baptized person, believers' baptism emphasizes the personal decision "to respond to God's call."

But the second, crucial and forward-leading reason why differing practices of baptism are not an obstacle for full church communion is found in the New Testament, where "greater store is set on the fruits of baptism than on its form."[96] Therefore the Baptists declare their readiness to "accept a person in every respect as member of their community, if in this person the reality of the fruits of baptism can be found, independently of the form and time of the performance of baptism. The existence of the fruits shows, that thanks to the work of the Spirit the essence of baptism is present in this person."

The Waldensians and Methodists confirm the same about members of Baptist congregations.

What is important in this agreement is that, although the difference in understanding and practice of baptism is not really overcome, the two churches have found a way to accept each other mutually. They have done this by emphasizing as the criterion for validity the fruits of baptism rather than its form.[97]

95. Cf. Ibid., 162.
96. Ibid., 163.
97. See also André Birmelé, "Baptism and the Unity of the Church in Ecumenical Dialogues," in Root and Saarinen, *Baptism and the Unity of the Church*," 121.

Lutherans and Baptists in Bavaria

A recent convergence document was published in 2009 on the local level in Bavaria (Germany), between the Lutheran Church in Bavaria and the Bavarian regional association of the Union of Evangelical Free Churches in Germany (Baptists). Bearing the title "Learning from One Another—Believing Together"[98] this document was produced on a local level within Germany, but it is meant for wider reception on the national level. It is presented here because it proposes a different way to overcome the divergence between infant baptism and believers' baptism.

The document refers to the Italian agreement between Baptists and Waldensians/Methodists but deliberately tries to find another solution, because its authors "see a danger of inappropriately reducing faith to a matter of ethics in a way which does not solve the theological problems."[99]

Consequently this document discusses the issue of original sin, of justification and the understanding of church, as questions which underlie the differences on baptism. They find that the Baptist critique of "original sin" does not reflect Lutheran teaching[100] and they "agree on the fundamental aspects of the doctrine of justification."[101] Neither the differences in the emphasis on the charismatic and institutional aspects of the church nor the forms of ministry in the churches are considered an obstacle for mutual recognition.[102]

In addition to the understanding of baptism according to the biblical witness, the crucial point of convergence—and this is new in a dialogue with a church which practices only believers' baptism—is the fact that "faith and baptism belong together (Col 2:12) but they may be separated in time."[103] Consequently, the two sides find that their different emphases on *gratia praeveniens* (prevenient

---

98. English version online at http://www.gftp.de/press/public/weitere/Bavarian%20Baptists%20and%20Lutherans%20Final%20Report.pdf.
99. Ibid., 5.
100. Ibid., 6.
101. Ibid., 9.
102. Ibid., 11 and 12.
103. Ibid., 13.

grace or "grace coming before") and on *gratia adveniens* (advenient grace or "grace coming swiftly to the lost person"), as expressed through infant baptism or adult baptism, both belong to baptism and "are not mutually exclusive."

> *The difference in accentuation with regard to the aspect of grace in baptism is expressed in the choice of a different moment for its administration. Whereas Lutherans see an expression of the prevenient grace of God which precedes all human action and of the gift of both temporal and eternal life in the baptism of the immature infant which is to be confirmed personally at confirmation, Baptists underline the close link between faith and baptism by selecting a time following a decision of faith. In this way, God confirms that the person baptised has personally appropriated the gospel and opens up for this person the possibility of being called to give account of their faith. What the Lutheran tradition expresses in baptism and confirmation is combined into one for the Baptists.*[104]

In order to proceed towards mutual recognition of baptism, the document proposes:

> *On the way to a mutual recognition of baptism, it seems helpful to reflect on the nature of Christian initiation as the process of becoming a Christian. Both Church traditions are of the view that initiation into the Christian life should be understood not merely as an event at a particular point in time but also as a process— either between baptism and confirmation or between conversion and baptism. The initiation process is complete when, in the form of a personal response to the call of Christ to discipleship, the person also accepts responsibility for discipleship and the baptised person is prepared to openly declare their faith.*[105]

---

104. Ibid., 16.
105. Ibid., 16.

Baptists and Lutherans come to the conclusion that they can recognize both understandings of baptism as "different but legitimate interpretations of the one gospel."[106]

The authors of the document give specific recommendations to both sides in the dialogue. The first concerns requests from persons who have been baptized as infants, and would now like to be baptized in a Baptist church, because they have only now developed an awareness of what it means to "believe." Here the document says firstly:

> *However, the basic consensus reached between the two churches is considered to be sufficiently firm for the Lutheran side to be able to imagine tolerating isolated cases of such baptisms for pastoral reasons, provided that this practice no longer constitutes the regular form of ecclesial action in Baptist congregations. The Baptist side can imagine conducting such baptisms in a way that expresses a recollection of baptism.*[107]

Secondly "the Baptists recommend to their congregations that they resist problematic requests for baptism which question the uniqueness of baptism as presented in the gospel" and "the Lutherans recommend to their congregations, in the case of a confirmation candidate who has not previously been baptised, that the link between baptism and confirmation should be liturgically expressed so that the central role of baptism is fully evident."[108]

A crucial recommendation is given to the Baptist congregations "to (further) develop forms of entry into the congregation which do not absolutely restrict to believer's baptism the desire of persons to join a congregation who were baptised as infants."[109] And "the Lutheran side reminds its congregations that, as a consequence of their baptismal practice, special emphasis should be

---

106. Ibid., 17.
107. Ibid., 18 (italics by the author).
108. Ibid.
109. Ibid.

given to working with children and young people to lead them to the Christian faith."[110]

This document is a further development of the proposals made by BEM, and by the further work of Faith and Order on baptism. It represents a considerable step towards mutual recognition, by making it possible for the two sides to continue their different practices, but on the basis of a common understanding: namely, that baptism and the confession of faith belong together but may be separated in time, as long as both are understood as elements within an overall process of initiation.

The reception of this document within the wider context of Germany as a whole is still to be awaited.

Baptists, Methodists and Mission Covenant in Sweden
An interesting case is the merger in 2012 of three churches, the Baptist Union, the Mission Covenant Church and the United Methodists in Sweden into one church, called with the preliminary name *Gemensam Framtid* (Common Future). Concerning baptism they agree in their Basic Document that there are different baptismal practices existing within their community.[111]

Other Agreements on the National Level
On the national level we find especially agreements between Catholic bishops' conferences and their ecumenical partners, such as in the Netherlands, the Philippines, Australia, Slovakia, and the USA.

The Netherlands In the Netherlands the Catholics signed three declarations of the same content with three Protestant Churches in the late 1960s. As these three Protestant churches in 2004 united into one, this is now one declaration considered as valid between the Roman Catholic Church and the new Protestant Church in the Netherlands.[112]

---

110. Ibid.
111. http://gemensamframtid.se/wp-content/uploads/2011/10/GF-teologisk_grund_111010.pdf, par. 26.
112. Text in the appendix.

The Philippines Already in 1972 in the Philippines, the Roman Catholic Church and the Lutheran Church signed an agreement in which they recognized "that each Church administers the same baptism of Christ and that our respective ordinances and traditions comply with the biblical institution of baptism in their essential aspects."[113] Therefore a Roman Catholic Archdiocese emphasizes on its website that for Lutherans, "the baptism is not to be repeated under any circumstances, not even conditionally."[114] A similar agreement exists between the Roman Catholic and the Episcopal Church in the Philippines.[115]

Australia In Australia, Catholics and Lutherans signed a formal document on the mutual recognition of baptism in 2001[116] on the basis of an "Agreed Statement" on the common understanding of baptism from 1977.[117] In this the use of water and the Trinitarian formula are considered essential for the validity of baptism.

Slovakia In the same year Catholics and Lutherans in Slovakia signed a similar "Agreement on Holy Baptism."[118] They consider a baptism valid if it is done in "an intention that agrees with Christ's intention" and they agree on the essential signs of immersion in water or pouring water on the candidate's head with either an active ("I baptize you") or passive ("N. is baptized") baptismal formulation including the Trinitarian formula. They confirm the continuing validity of baptism, and reject baptizing "those who have

---

113. http://catholicchurch.ph/filer/14-1_091.pdf

114. See http://www.lingayen-dagupan.org/ArchBishop/appendix.html.

115. Mentioned on the website of the Roman-Catholic Archdioces of Lingayen-Dagupan, unfortunately without a date, http://www.lingayen-dagupan.org/ArchBishop/appendix.html

116. Text at http://www.lca.org.au/doctrinal-statements--theological-opinions-2.html.

117. Text at http://www.catholic.org.au/index.php?option=com_content&view=article&id=1668:lutheran-church-roman-catholic-church&catid=106:ecumenical-dialogues-and-relations&Itemid=391.

118. The original Slovak text is published at http://www.kbs.sk/do_pdf/index.php?cid=1117713909. I am referring to an unpublished English translation provided by Jonathan Sorum and Ondrej Prostrednik.

already been validly baptized." These agreements are considered "a sufficient basis for mutual recognition of Baptism."

USA In the USA a text "These Living Waters: Common Agreement on Mutual Recognition of Baptism" was signed between the U.S. Conference of Catholic Bishops and several Reformed churches (the Christian Reformed Church in North America, Presbyterian Church USA, Reformed Church in America, United Church of Christ) in 2010 and 2011. [119]

Spain In Spain, mutual recognition was expressed in 2011 between the Spanish Episcopal Conference (Roman Catholic) and the Spanish Reformed Episcopal Church.[120]

Egypt In Egypt the Coptic Orthodox Church in 2001 signed a Pastoral Agreement with the Greek Orthodox Patriarchate of Alexandria; this mutual recognition of baptism was agreed on the basis of the official dialogues on Christology between the Eastern and the Oriental Orthodox churches.[121]

Summary
As with the multilateral agreements on the national level, the bilateral declarations mentioned here are short and keep to the formal recognition of each other's baptism, without discussing the theological details. Most of these are bilateral agreements with the local Roman Catholic church and do not involve believers' baptism churches, which means that there are no major theological differences in the understanding of baptism.

---

119. Text at http://www.pcusa.org/media/uploads/worship/pdfs/common_agreement_baptism.pdf and at http://www.ncccusa.org/pdfs/commonbaptism.pdf.
120. See http://www.zenit.org/article-31829?l=english.
121. The text of this agreement could not be found. But it is mentioned at http://orthodoxwiki.org/Pastoral_Agreement_between_the_Coptic_Orthodox_and_Greek_Orthodox_Patriarchates_of_Alexandria_(2001).

The few cases of bilateral dialogues including believers' baptism churches have produced some interesting forward-leading agreements and proposals. These are, concretely, two approaches:

- to consider rather the fruits of baptism than its practice;

- to reflect together on the processual aspect of baptism as becoming a Christian rather than on the water event in an isolated way, and thus agree on the elements included in this process, which can be separated in time.

The first dialogue, which is the Italian agreement, was seen by Erich Geldbach as forward-leading,[122] but it did not find any followers. On the contrary, newer agreements, such as the one from Bavaria, find that this approach is in the theological perspective not going far enough. It seems thus, that the second approach is more promising.

Looking at the Orthodox churches, there seems to be some openness to sign agreements of mutual recognition. But more theological reflection is necessary. An interesting case in this regard is an agreed statement on "Baptism and 'Sacramental Economy'" issued by the North American Orthodox-Catholic Theological Consultation in 1999. It has the status of a "proposal" and is therefore different from the other documents mentioned above. But it has an important potential for the future mutual recognition of baptism, by highlighting the common teaching about the understanding of baptism and by stating the following: "The fact that our churches share and practice this same faith and teaching requires that we recognize in each other the same baptism and thus also recognize in each other, however 'imperfectly,' the present reality of the same Church. By God's gift we are each, in St. Basil's word, 'of the Church.'"[123] The document shows that such mutual recognition would be "fully consistent with the perennial teaching of both churches." It also shows that the theory of sacramental economy

---

122. Ibid., 187.
123. http://www.orthodoxresearchinstitute.org/articles/ecumenical/baptism_sacramental_economy.htm, III. A. 3.

"does not represent the tradition and perennial teaching of the Orthodox Church."[124] Whether this proposal will be adopted by the respective churches is to be awaited.

This is an example for a solution involving the Orthodox side which would go beyond the "sacramental economy" idea—but only related to the Roman Catholic Church. The two churches recognize in each other the same faith and teaching about baptism and therefore can talk about being "*of* the church."[125] A next step would be to explore whether such an agreement would also be possible between Orthodox and Protestant churches.

On the whole this chapter shows that a beginning is made by churches to recognize their baptism mutually. For the difficulty of credobaptist churches to recognize the baptism of paedobaptist churches several different approaches for a solution have been found. It still needs to be seen how far they can be received by a wider range of churches, including Pentecostals.

Perspectives for Further Work

The overview has shown a certain imbalance in regard to mutual recognition of baptism. A majority of paedobaptist churches nowadays do not have any major problem to recognize the baptism performed in other churches, while many credobaptist churches do not see themselves in a state to sign agreements on mutual recognition of baptism with churches which baptize infants. A similar imbalance exists in the case of relations between Orthodox and other infant baptism churches. But existing multilateral agreements on the local level show that it seems to be easier for Orthodox churches to sign such agreements than it is for credobaptist churches.

This observation, though, should not lead to the understanding that only those churches which have difficulties to sign such agreements have to re-visit critically their own tradition. The situation remains a challenge for *all* churches to rethink their own theology in a critical way in an ecumenical perspective.

---

124. Ibid., II, B.
125. Italics added.

For further considerations on the way towards mutual recognition of baptism we need in a first step to analyze more closely the few agreements, in which credobaptist churches are involved. This is the case in the Lutheran-Mennonite dialogue on the international level and the conversations between CPCE and the European Baptist Union. But even more interesting in this regard are the Italian agreement between Waldensians/Methodists and Baptists, and the agreement in Bavaria between Lutherans and Baptists.

From the Lutheran-Mennonite dialogue it is clear that baptism cannot be discussed separately from other doctrinal issues. But it needs to be clarified, which ones these are. At the same time this dialogue shows also that the mutual recognition of baptism is related to a healing of memories and reconciliation on the wider background of the history—at least in cases where direct relationships in the past led to separation and enmity.

A new approach was found in the agreement between Waldensians/Methodists and Baptists in Italy by emphasizing the fruits of baptism instead of its form. It shows that a move away from the emphasis on the baptismal rite might lead forward.

The discussions on the European level between Lutherans and Reformed on the one side and Baptists on the other shows that the approach proposed by Faith and Order in emphasizing the aspect of baptism as a life-long process seems to be considered as a helpful step.[126] The reception of converts who were baptized as infants into a Baptist church *could* happen with a confession of faith, which is considered as a completion of the first step of initiation taken in (infant) baptism.

In a similar way the Bavarian agreement is based on the Faith and Order discussions. It confirms that baptism and faith belong together, but that the water rite and the confession of faith can be separated in time.

In conclusion it is necessary for mutual recognition of baptism between credobaptists and paedobaptists to move away from

---

126. This is also confirmed in the British conversations between Anglicans and Baptists; see Faith and Unity Executive Committee of the Baptist Union of Great Britain and The Council for Christian Unity of the Church of England, *Pushing at the Boundaries of Unity: Anglicans and Baptists in Conversation*, Church House Publishing, London, 2005, 41.

a static understanding of baptism to a dynamic one in which the different aspects, expressed in different ritual acts are understood as belonging together although not performed at the same time.

The progress made in these examples of dialogues has been possible by focusing on theological aspects from a liturgical perspective. And study of the question from this perspective has to be continued. But at the same time it is necessary to return to systematic theological reflections in order to make progress in the search for mutual recognition of baptism.

As Fernando Enns has pointed out,[127] the question cannot be reduced to the issue of converts being (re-)baptized or not, but the question needs to be seen in the wider horizon of ecclesiology. Mennonites recognize other confessions as church of Jesus Christ, although they cannot recognize infant baptism practiced in those churches. On this basis many Mennonites agreed to receive converts from the Lutheran church only with a personal confession of faith in front of the congregation. In any case the wish of the person has to be respected.[128] This means a certain degree of recognition of the baptism performed according to the Lutheran tradition. This is a feature which also appears in the Bavarian agreement between Lutherans and Baptists: the question whether a convert should be (re-)baptized or not is left to the person him- or herself. It also has to be considered whether in case of a Lutheran who had been baptized as adult, recognition on the side of believers' baptism churches is possible.

According to Enns there is a *consensus* between Mennonites— here taken as an example for believers' baptism churches in general—and the other churches in the understanding of baptism, but a *divergence* remains in the understanding of "sacrament" and a

---

127. Fernando Enns, "Die gegenseitige Anerkennung der Taufe als bleibende ökumenische Herausforderung: Konsens, Divergenzen und Differenzen," in Fernando Enns, Martin Hailer, and Ulrike Link-Wieczorek, eds., *Profilierte Ökumene: Bleibend Wichtiges und jetzt Dringliches*, Festschrift für Dietrich Ritschl, Beih. zur Ökumenisch Rundschau 84, Lembeck, Frankfurt am Main, 2009, 133.

128. Ibid., 141.

difference exists in the practice of baptizing people who have been baptized as infants but ask now for a believer baptism.[129]

It has to be noted that all the discussions related to mutual recognition of baptism include traditional believers' baptism churches. In dialogues with Pentecostals mutual recognition has not been discussed yet, and Pentecostals have not been part of agreements on mutual recognition to my knowledge.

In the case of Orthodox and their attitude towards converts from other churches, the question of the apostolicity of other churches and thus the boundaries of the church remain an issue to be clarified further.

Therefore what in all these cases needs to be considered further is the following reflection: Thus far the discussions about mutual recognition of baptism took their starting point from the reception of converts from one church into another. In other words: the discussions focused on the recognition of the baptism of a specific person. Although most of the statements we examined state in general a mutual recognition, there are no further reflections about the implications of such recognition. Do these agreements on mutual recognition of baptism mean that believers of other churches who remain members of their respective churches are recognized as baptized members of the body of Christ? And consequently what are the implications for the mutual recognition of churches as churches?

As Enns states, "The mutual recognition as church and the recognition of baptism imply each other mutually."[130] A similar observation is made by the Orthodox theologian Gennadios of Sassima (Limouris): "Logically, mutual recognition of *Baptism* leads to mutual recognition of *members*, as mutual recognition of members leads to the full communion … Thus, Baptism and membership in the body of the Church, of every Church, are interrelated through the bond of the incorporation of baptized persons 'into the Body of Christ.'"[131] These statements hint at the fact that in both cases

---

129. Ibid., 135.
130. Ibid., 153.
131. Gennadios of Sassima, "Baptism in the Life of the Orthodox Church," in Michael Beintker, Viorel Ionita, and Jochen Kramm, eds., *Baptism in the*

ecclesiological questions still need to be taken into consideration in a deeper way.

And in this regard the ecumenical situation regarding baptism looks different compared with what we stated above: On the side of believers' baptism churches Fernando Enns claims that

> *a total agreement in doctrine is not a precondition for mutual recognition of baptism ... Therefore for churches of the baptist tradition the only question for discussion is whether the fact of a Christian being baptized according to the rite of infant baptism can be recognized ... if it is recognized that—according to Scripture—the water-rite is only considered as a part of the wider initiation event of baptism to which necessarily the personal confession of faith is added, then the theological preconditions for (mutual) recognition of baptism are given.*[132]

The mutual recognition of *churches* already exists in that case and should make the mutual recognition of *baptism* possible.

On the side of the Orthodox churches it seems to be the other way round. While a certain recognition of baptism is possible—as we have seen in the discussions and in concrete agreements—Metropolitan Gennadios of Sassima, for example, is of the opinion that between Orthodox and Protestants there is no "common understanding of both Baptism and membership." The consequence is that "we must place our understanding of Baptism in the dynamic perspective of the ontological relationship between Christ and His Church, which is fully manifested in the holy Eucharist."[133] This question needs also to be taken up with the Roman Catholic Church, which on the one hand recognizes all baptisms which are performed with water and with the trinitarian formula, but at the same time does not admit to the eucharist believers from churches which are considered as not being in the apostolic tradition.

Life of the Churches: Documents of an Orthodox-Protestant Dialogue in Europe, Leuenberg Documents, vol. 12, Otto Lembeck, Frankfurt am Main, 2011, 96.

132. Enns, "Die gegenseitige Anerkennung der Taufe," 155ff; translation by the author.

133. Gennadios, "Baptism in the Life of the Orthodox Church," 97.

The other divergences which have been mentioned in chapter Four of this book have also to be taken into consideration. It seems that the controversy on Spirit baptism was an issue of discussion only in the Roman Catholic–Pentecostal dialogue, but has, so far, not been part of any agreement on mutual recognition of baptism. The issue of the baptismal formula has never been part of an official dialogue, as far as I can see. But the fact that in many, if not most, of the official agreements on mutual recognition the churches involved agree on the trinitarian formula shows that the issue is mainly discussed within churches and not between churches. It is still an open question in which way this will become a church-dividing issue. The controversy on immersion, affusion or sprinkling seems to be an issue of past disputes, and has not been a major separating issue in the contemporary official dialogues. It might well be an issue in the future, if Pentecostal or Independent churches enter more into official ecumenical dialogue. The same is true for the question of inculturation of baptism and the question of baptism as entry into the local congregation.

A FINAL REFLECTION

As a general consideration it seems to me important that the churches in the future find a way to re-discover the common study of the Bible. For the issue of baptism one of the basic texts on which most churches agree as the fundament for understanding baptism as a bond of unity[134] is Eph 4: 1-6. While often in ecumenical discussions only vv.4-6 are quoted, it is important to read the whole passage:

> *I therefore, the prisoner in the Lord, beg you to lead a life worthy of the calling to which you have been called, with all humility and gentleness, with patience, bearing with one another in love, making every effort to maintain the unity of the Spirit in the bond of*

---

134. The analysis of the different bilateral dialogues and agreements shows that paedobaptist churches in general agree to understand baptism as a bond of unity; during the last decades also traditional credobaptist churches such as Baptists and Mennonites have agreed on this, while Pentecostals (see Roman Catholic Pentecostal dialogue) do not.

peace. There is one body and one Spirit, just as you were called to the one hope of your calling, one Lord, one faith, one baptism, one God and Father of all, who is above all and through all and in all.

Central in this appeal is "to maintain the unity of the Spirit in the bond of peace." Unity, thus, belongs centrally to the calling of Christians. And central for unity is peace. Peace can be achieved, according to Paul, through humility, gentleness, patience, and bearing with one another in love. These four qualities describe in the context of this text what it means to be a Christian, or in other words they describe the ethical consequences of baptism.

Therefore, the crucial question is: What do these qualities mean for the ecumenical dialogue and for the unity of the church?

I will try to give some ideas only looking at two of the four: humility and love. Humility is a central category in the gospel, as it is expressed in the most impressive way in the letter to the Philippians: "Let the same mind be in you that was in Christ Jesus: who though he was in the form of God, did not regard equality with God a something to be exploited, but emptied himself, taking the form of a slave, being born in human likeness, and being found in human form, he humbled himself and became obedient to the point of death—even death on a cross" (Phil 2:5-8). For the ecumenical dialogue, would this not mean to reckon with the possibility that my own church could be corrected, and that the same Spirit which is at work in my church might also be at work in other churches? Would it not mean to reckon with the possibility that the different understandings of other Christians –their understandings of baptism, of the church—could also be true?

The other notion is love—*the* central commandment in the Bible, identified with God himself (1 John). Love is not related to sentimentality. Love means to be engaged in a relationship with the other, to care for the other, to take the other seriously, but also to accept the other as he or she is. For the ecumenical dialogue and for the search for unity, would this not mean to accept the other church despite the differences?

This is not a call for an ecumenism of just being friendly with each other. It is rather a call for taking each other seriously, which means to discuss the differences in an open and honest way, but on the background of humility and love as just described. It is not a call for an ecumenism which would recognize and accept any group. It is rather a call for taking humility and love of Christ as criteria for discernment for the recognition of others: where there—or even *if* there—is a life led "worthy of the calling to which you have been called, with all humility and gentleness, with patience, bearing with one another in love, making every effort to maintain the unity of the Spirit in the bond of peace," this is *because* there is "one body and one Spirit ... one Lord, one faith, one baptism, one God and Father of all, who is above all and through all and in all."

This means finally the churches have to become more conscious of the fact that the one baptism is a baptism into the body of Christ, which is not just identical with a confessional or local church but is a universal entity that goes beyond human understanding.

Bibliography

Books[1]

Aland, Kurt. *Did the Early Church Baptize Infants?* Westminster Press, Philadelphia, 1963.

Alivizatos, Hamilcar S. *Die Oikonomia: Die Oikonomia nach dem kanonischen Recht der Orthodoxen Kirche.* Edited by Andréa Belliger. Lembeck, Frankfurt am Main, 1998.

Amanze, James N. *A History of the Ecumenical Movement in Africa.* Pula Press, Gaborone, Botswana, 1999.

Anderson, Allan H. *African Reformation: African Initiated Christianity in the 20th Century.* Africa World Press, Trenton, NJ, 2001.

Andronikof, Constantin. *Des mystères sacramentels.* Les Editions du Cerf, Paris, 1998.

Barth, Karl. *The Teaching of the Church regarding Baptism.* SCM Press, London, 1948.

Barth, Karl. *Church Dogmatics* IV,1, " The Doctrine of Reconciliation." Edited by G. W. Bromiley and T. F. Torrance, T&T Clark International, London and New York, 1956.

Beasley-Murray, George R. *Baptism in the New Testament.* Macmillan and Co., London, 1962.

---

1. Anthologies of ecumenical documents are in the Ecumenical Documents section below. Russian-language articles cited this Bibliography by English titles are taken from unpublished versions prepared for conference use. They are denoted by an asterisk.

Berkhoff, Louis. *Systematic Theology*. Banner of Truth Trust, Edinburgh, 1979.

Best, Thomas F., and Dagmar Heller, eds. *So We Believe, So We Pray: Towards Koinonia in Worship*. Faith and Order Paper No. 171. WCC Publications, Geneva, 1995.

Best, Thomas F., and Dagmar Heller, eds. *Becoming a Christian: The Ecumenical Implications of Our Common Baptism*. Faith and Order Paper No. 184. WCC Publications, Geneva, 1999.

Best, Thomas F., ed. *Baptism Today: Understanding, Practice, Ecumenical Implications*. Faith and Order Paper No. 207. WCC Publications, Geneva and Liturgical Press, Collegeville, MN, 2008.

Brock, Sebastian Paul. *The Holy Spirit in the Syrian Baptismal Tradition*. Enlarged 2nd ed. The Syrian Churches Series 9, edited by Jacob Vellian. Jyothi Book House, Kottayam, Kerala, India, 1998.

Buchanan, Colin. *Infant Baptism and the Gospel: The Church of England's Dilemma*. Darton, Longman & Todd, London, 1993.

Chupungco, Anscar J. *Liturgical Inculturation: Sacraments, Religiosity, and Catechesis*. Liturgical Press, Collegeville, MN, 1992.

Davies, John Gordon. *The Architectural Setting of Baptism*. Barrie and Rockliff, London, 1962.

Duck, Ruth. *Gender and the Name of God: The Trinitarian Baptismal Formula*. Pilgrim Press, Cleveland, 1991.

Duck, Ruth, and Patricia Wilson-Kastner, *Praising God: The Trinity in Christian Worship,* Westminster John Knox, Louisville KY, 1999.

Dunn, James D. G. *Baptism in the Holy Spirit: A Re-examination of the New Testament Teaching on the Gift of the Spirit in Relation to Pentecostalism today*. Studies in Biblical Theology, 2nd ser., vol. 15. SCM Press, London, 1970.

Felmy, Karl Christian. *Orthodoxe Theologie: Eine Einführung*. Wissenschaftliche Buchgesellschaft, Darmstadt, 1990.

Felton, Gayle Carlton. *The Gift of Water: The Practice and Theology of Baptism Among Methodists in America*. Abingdon Press, Nashville, 1992.

Ferguson, Everett. *Baptism in the Early Church: History, Theology and Liturgy in the First Five Centuries*. Eerdmans, Grand Rapids, MI, 2009.

Fiddes, Paul, ed. *Reflections on the Water: Understanding God and the World Through the Baptism of Believers*. Regent's Study Guides 4. Smyth & Helwys, Macon, GA, 1996.

Finn, Thomas M. *The Liturgy of Baptism in the Baptismal Instructions of St. John Chrysostom*. Catholic University of America Press, Washington, DC, 1967.

Finn, Thomas M. *Early Christian Baptism and the Catechumenate: Italy, North Africa, and Egypt*. Liturgical Press, Collegeville, MN, 1992.

Fisher, J. D. C. *Christian Initiation: Baptism in the Medieval West: A Study in the Disintegration of the Primitive Rite of Initiation*. SPCK, London, 1965.

Garrett, James Leo. *Systematic Theology: Biblical, Historical, and Evangelical*, vol. 2. Eerdmans, Grand Rapids, MI, 1995.

Geldbach, Erich. *Taufe*. Bensheimer Hefte 79, Ökumenische Studienhefte 5. Vandenhoeck & Ruprecht, Göttingen, 1996.

Grenz, Stanley J. *Theology for the Community of God*. Eerdmans, Grand Rapids, MI and Regent College Publishing, Vancouver, 1994, 2000.

Grudem, Wayne. *Systematic Theology*. Zondervan, Grand Rapids, MI, 2000.

Haenchen, Ernst. *The Acts of the Apostles*. Westminster Press, Philadelphia, 1971.

Heyer, Friedrich. *Konfessionskunde*. De Gruyter, Berlin and New York, 1977.

Heyer, Friedrich, ed. *Die Kirche Armeniens*. Die Kirchen der Welt, vol. 18. Evangelisches Verlagswerk, Stuttgart, 1978.

Holeton, David R. *Liturgical Inculturation in the Anglican Communion, Including the York Statement "Down to Earth Worship."* Alcuin/GROW Liturgical Study 15. Grove Books, Nottingham, 1990.

Jeremias, Joachim. *Infant Baptism in the First Four Centuries*. SCM Press, London, 1960.

Johnson, Maxwell E. *The Rites of Christian Initiation: Their Evolution and Interpretation*. Liturgical Press, Collegeville, MN, 2007.

Kuntima, Diangienda. *L'histoire du Kimbanguisme*. Editions Kimbanguistes, Kinshasa, 1984.

Lange, Christian, Clemens Leonhard, and Ralph Olbrich, eds. *Die Taufe: Einführung in Geschichte und Praxis*. Wissenschaftliche Buchgesellschaft, Darmstadt, 2008.

Lumbala, F. Kabasele. *Celebrating Jesus Christ in Africa: Liturgy and Inculturation*. Orbis Books, Maryknoll, NY, 1998.

Mattiesen, Maren, ed. *Confessing Christ in Cultural Contexts*. Lutheran World Federation, Geneva, 1994.

McBeth, H. Leon. *A Sourcebook for Baptist Heritage*. Broadman Press, Nashville, 1990.

McDonnell, Kilian, and George T. Montague. *Christian Initiation and Baptism in the Holy Spirit: Evidence from the First Eight Centuries*. Liturgical Press, Collegeville, MN, 1994.

Meyendorff, John. *Initiation à la théologie byzantine*. Editions du Cerf, Paris, 1975.

Murray, John. *Christian Baptism*. Presbyterian and Reformed Publishing, Philipsburg, NJ, 1980.

Oosthuizen, C. G. *Baptism in the Context of the African Indigenous/Independent Churches (A.I.C.)*. University of Zululand, Kwadlangezwa, South Africa, 1985.

Osborne, Kenan B. *The Christian Sacraments of Initiation: Baptism, Confirmation, Eucharist*. Paulist Press, New York and Mahwah, NJ, 1987.

Ositelu, Rufus Okikiolaolu Olubiyi. *African Instituted Churches: Diversities, Growth, Gifts, Spirituality and Ecumenical Understanding of African Initiated Churches*. Lit Verlag, Hamburg, 2002.

Pomazansky, Michael. *Orthodox Dogmatic Theology*. St. Herman of Alaska Brotherhood, Platina, CA, 1983.

Porter, Stanley E. and Anthony Cross, eds. *Dimensions of Baptism: Biblical and Theological Studies*. Journal for the Study of the New Testament Supplement no. 234. Sheffield Academic Press / T&T Clark, London and New York, 2002.

Rahner, Karl. *Grundkurs des Glaubens*. Herder Verlag, Freiburg im Breisgau, 1976.

Ramshaw, Gail. *God beyond Gender: Feminist Christian God-Language*, Fortress Press, Minneapolis, 1995.

Regli, Sigisbert. *Firmsakrament und christliche Entfaltung*. Mysterium Salutis, vol. 5. Benziger, Einsiedeln, 1967.

Riggs, John Wheelan. *Baptism in the Reformed Tradition: An Historical and Practical Theology*. Westminster John Knox, Louisville, KY and London, 2002.

Root, Michael, and Risto Saarinen, eds. *Baptism and the Unity of the Church*. Eerdmans, Grand Rapids, MI and WCC Publications, Geneva, 1998.

Roy, Kevin. *Baptism, Reconciliation and Unity*. Paternoster Press, Carlisle, UK, 1997.

Ruether, Rosemary Radford. *Women-Church: Theology and Practice of Feminist Liturgical Communities*. Harper & Row, San Francisco, 1985.

Schlink, Edmund. *The Doctrine of Baptism*. Concordia Publishing, Saint Louis and London, 1972.

Schmemann, Alexander. *Of Water and the Spirit*. St. Vladimir's Seminary Press, Crestwood, NY, 1974.

Schneider, Theodor. *Zeichen der Nähe Gottes: Grundriss der Sakramententheologie*. Matthias Grünewald, Mainz, 1992.

Simon, Benjamin. *Afrikanische Kirchen in Deutschland*. Lembeck, Frankfurt am Main, 2003.

Spinks, Bryan D. *Reformation and Modern Rituals and Theologies of Baptism: From Luther to Contemporary Practices*. Ashgate Publishing, Aldershot, UK and Burlington, VT, 2006.

Stauffer, S. Anita, ed. *Christian Worship: Unity in Cultural Diversity*. Lutheran World Federation, Geneva, 1996.

Stauffer, S. Anita, ed. *Baptism, Rites of Passage, and Culture*. Lutheran World Federation, Geneva, 1998.

Wainwright, Geoffrey. *Worship with One Accord: Where Liturgy and Ecumenism Embrace*. Oxford University Press, New York and Oxford, 1997.

Whitaker, Edward Charles. *Documents of the Baptismal Liturgy*. SPCK, London, 1960.

Williams, J. Rodman. *Renewal Theology*. Vol. 3, *The Church, the Kingdom, and the Last Things*. Zondervan, Grand Rapids, MI, 1992.

Wood, Susan K. *One Baptism: Ecumenical Dimensions of the Doctrine of Baptism*. Liturgical Press, Collegeville, MN, 2009.

Essays[2]

Albrecht, Daniel. "Witness in the Waters: Baptism and Pentecostal Spirituality." In Best, *Baptism Today*, 147-168.

Alexander, Kimberly Ervin. "Matters of Conscience, Matters of Unity, Matters of Orthodoxy: Trinity and Water Baptism in Early Pentecostal Theology and Practice." *Journal of Pentecostal Theology* 17 (2008): 48-69.

Alexopoulos, Stefanos. "Gestalt und Deutung der christlichen Initiation im mittelalterlichen Byzanz. " In Lange et al., *Die Taufe*, 49-66.

Axt-Piscalar, Christine. "Sünde VII: Reformation und Neuzeit." *Theologische Realenzyklopädie* Vol. 32, 400-436.[3]

Beach, J. Mark. "Original Sin, Infant Salvation, and the Baptism of Infants." *Mid-American Journal of Theology* 12 (2001): 47-79.

---

2. In these references, references for books already listed in the section above are given here in abridged form.

3. All references to entries from *Theologische Realenzyklopädie* (*TRE*) are from the following edition: *Theologische Realenzyklopädie*, ed. by Gerhard Krause und Gerhard Müller, Vol 1-36, De Gruyter, Berlin, 1977-2004, Studienausgabe 1993-2006.

Berlis, Angela. "Heute leben aus der Taufe: Theologische Reflexionen in praktischer Perspektive." *Ökumenische Rundschau* 53 (2004): 282-297.

Birmelé, André. "Baptism and the Unity of the Church in Ecumenical Dialogues." In Root and Saarinen, *Baptism and the Unity of the Church*, 104-129.

Bobrinskoy, Boris. "Baptism: Sacrament of the Kingdom." In Best, *Baptism Today*, 3-14.

Bradshaw, Paul. "Baptism in the Anglican Communion." In Best, *Baptism Today*, 55-71.

Brock, Sebastian Paul. "The Transition to a Post-Baptismal Anointing in the Antiochene Rite." In Bryan D. Spinks, ed., *The Sacrifice of Praise: Studies on the Themes of Thanksgiving and Redemption in the Central Prayers of the Eucharistic and Baptismal Liturgies*. In Honour of Arthur Hubert Couratin. Edizioni Liturgiche, Rome, 1979, 215-228.

Brown, Dale. "The Brethren." In Merle D. Strege, ed., *Baptism and Church: A Believers' Church Vision*. Sagamore Books, Grand Rapids, MI, 1986, 29-37.

Brown, Schuyler. "'Water-Baptism' and 'Spirit-Baptism' in Luke-Acts." *Anglican Theological Review* 59 (1977): 135-151.

Buchinger, Harald. "Baptism and the Anointing with Myron in the Syrian tradition in the 3rd-4th Centuries."* In V. Международная Богословская Конференция Русской Православной Церкви, *Православное учение о церковних таинствах*, том I, Синодальная Библейско-богословская комиссия, Москва, 2009, 220-233.

Chung, ChangBok. "Baptism in Asia and its Cultural Settings." In Best and Heller, *Becoming a Christian*, 45-50.

Clapsis, Emmanuel. "The Boundaries of the Church: An Orthodox Debate." In *Orthodoxy in Conversation: Orthodox Ecumenical Engagements*. WCC Publications, Geneva and Holy Cross Orthodox Press, Brookline, 2000, 114-126.

Clarkson, Herbert. "The Holy Spirit and the Sacraments." *Baptist Quarterly* 14 (1951-52): 265-270.

Dienst, Karl. "Konfirmation I." *Theologische Realenzyklopädie* 19, 437-445.

Dragas, George. "The Manner of Reception of Roman Catholic Converts into the Orthodox Church, with Special Reference to the Decisions of the Synods of 1484 (Constantinople), 1755 (Constantinople), and 1667 (Moscow)." Paper presented at the Orthodox/Roman Catholic Dialogue (USA) in 1998. http://jbburnett.com/resources/dragas_baptism.pdf.orebookbrowse.com/dragas-baptism-pdf-d13434776.

Dunn, James D. G. "Baptism and the Unity of the Church in the New Testament." In Root and Saarinen, *Baptism and the Unity of the Church*, 78-103.

Enns, Fernando. "Die gegenseitige Anerkennung der Taufe als bleibende ökumenische Herausforderung: Konsens, Divergenzen und Differenzen." In Fernando Enns, Martin Hailer, and Ulrike Link-Wieczorek, eds., *Profilierte Ökumene: Bleibend Wichtiges und jetzt Dringliches*, Festschrift für Dietrich Ritschl, Beih. Ökumenische Rundschau 84. Lembeck, Frankfurt am Main, 2009, 127-158.

Erickson, John H. "The Problem of Sacramental 'Economy.'" In *The Challenge of our Past: Studies in Orthodox Canon Law and Church History.* St. Vladimir's Seminary Press, Crestwood, 1991, 115-132.

Erickson, John H. "Reception into the Orthodox Church." *Ecumenical Review* 54 (2002): 66-75.

Ferguson, Everett. "Christian and Jewish Baptism According to the Epistle of Barnabas." In Porter and Cross, *Dimensions of Baptism*, 207-223.

Feulner, Hans-Jürgen. "The Sacraments of Baptism and Holy Chrism in the Western Tradition prior to the VIIIth Century."* In V. Международная богословская конференция русской православной церкви, *Православное учение о церковних таинствах*, том I. Синодальная Библейско-богословская комиссия, Москва, 2009, 257-279.

Fiddes, Paul. "The Baptism of Believers." In Best, *Baptism Today*, 73-80.

Gennadios, Metropolitan of Sassima. "Baptism in the Life of the Orthodox Church." In Michael Beintker, Viorel Ionita, and Jochen Kramm, eds., *Baptism in the Life of the Churches: Documents of an Orthodox-Protestant Dialogue in Europe.* Leuenberg Documents, vol. 12. Lembeck, Frankfurt am Main, 2011, 79-97.

George, Kondothra M. "Sacramental Theology in the Malankara Tradition."* In V. Международная Богославская Конференция Русской Православной Церкви, *Православное учение о церковних таинствах*, том III, Синодальная Библейско-богословская комиссия, Москва, 2009, 571-585.

Gribben, Robert. "Common Baptismal Certificate: Australia." In Best, *Baptism Today*, 231-233.

Heim, S. Mark. "Baptismal Recognition and the Baptist Churches." In Root and Saarinen, *Baptism and the Unity of the Church*, 150-163.

Heller, Dagmar. "Baptism the Basis of Church Unity? The Question of Baptism in Faith and Order." *Ecumenical Review* 50 (1998): 480-490.

Heller, Dagmar. "Baptism into the Body of Christ: An Exploration of its Ecumenical Implications." 2010. http://doc.rero.ch/record/20538?ln=fr.

Hovorun, Sergiy (Cyril). "Богословские аспекты и практика приема в Православие из инославия" ("The Theological and Practical Aspects of Admission of Non-Orthodox Christians into the Orthodox Church").* In V. Международная Богославская Конференция Русской Православной Церкви, *Православное*

учение о церковних таинствах, том I, Синодальная Библейско-богословская комиссия, Москва, 2009, 349-358.

Kay, James F. "In Whose Name? Feminism and the Trinitarian Baptismal Formula." *Theology Today* 1 (1993): 524-533.

Kittel, Gerhard. "Die Wirkungen der christlichen Wassertaufe nach dem Neuen
Testament." *Theologische Studien und Kritiken* 87 (1914): 25-53.

Klentos, John. "Rebaptizing Converts into the Orthodox Church: Old Perspectives on a New Problem." *Studia Liturgica* 29 (1999): 216-234.

Kretschmar, Georg. "Firmung." *Theologische Realenzyklopädie* 11, 192-204.

Küppers, Werner. "Altkatholizismus." *Theologische Realenzyklopädie* 2, 337-344.

Kurien, Jacob. "The Baptismal Liturgy of the Malankara Orthodox Syrian
Church." In Best, *Baptism Today*, 23-27.

Lange, Christian. "Gestalt und Deutung der christlichen Initiation in der Alten
Kirche." In Lange et al., *Die Taufe*, 1-28.

Lathrop, Gordon. "Knowing Something a Little: On the Role of the Lex Orandi
in the Search for Christian Unity." In Best and Heller, *So We Believe, So We Pray*,
38-48.

Lathrop, Gordon. "The Water that Speaks: The Ordo of Baptism and its Ecumenical Implications." In Best and Heller, *Becoming a Christian*, 13-29.

Lumbala, F. Kabasele. "Black African and Baptismal Rites." In Best and Heller,
Becoming a Christian, 36-40.

Menzies, Robert P. "Luke's Understanding of Baptism in the Holy Spirit: A Pentecostal dialogues with the Reformed Tradition." *Journal of Pentecostal Theology*
16 (2008): 86-101.

Merras, Merja. "Baptismal Recognition and the Orthodox Churches." In Root
and Saarinen, *Baptism and the Unity of the Church*, 138-149.

Miller, Marlin E. "The Mennonites." In Merle D. Strege, ed., *Baptism and Church:
A Believers' Church Vision*. Sagamore Books, Grand Rapids, MI, 1986, 15-28.

Moore-Keish, Martha. "Baptism in the Presbyterian and Reformed Tradition." In
Best, *Baptism Today*, 63-71.

Nüssel, Friederike. "Baptism and Baptismal Order in the Life of the Protestant
Church." In Michael Beintker, Viorel Ionita, and Jochen Kramm, eds., *Baptism
in the Life of the Churches: Documents of an Orthodox-Protestant Dialogue in
Europe*. Leuenberg Documents, vol. 12. Lembeck, Frankfurt am Main, 2011,
125-147.

Oduro, Thomas. "Water Baptism in African Independent Churches: The Paradigm of Christ Holy Church International." In Best, *Baptism Today*, 181-191.

Papandreou, Damaskinos. "Zur Anerkennung der Taufe seitens der Orthodoxen Kirche unter Berücksichtigung des heiligen und grossen Konzils." *Una Sancta* 48 (1993): 48-53.

Parmentier, Martin. "Water Baptism and Spirit Baptism in the Church Fathers." *Cyberjournal for Pentecostal-Charismatic Research.* www.pctii.org/cyberj/cyberj3/martin.html .

Phidas, Vlassios. "Baptism and Ecclesiology." *Ecumenical Review* 54 (2002): 39-47.

Pobee, John. "Baptismal Recognition and African Instituted Churches." In Root and Saarinen, *Baptism and the Unity of the Church*, 164-182.

Puglisi, James F. "Rite(s) of Baptism in the Catholic Church: A Theological-Pastoral Commentary." In Best, *Baptism Today*, 29-43.

Robeck, Cecil Jr. and Jerry L. Sandidge. "The Ecclesiology of *Koinonia* and Baptism: A Pentecostal Perspective." *Journal of Ecumenical Studies* 27 (1990): 504-534.

Sauca, Ioan. "The Church Beyond our Boundaries and the Ecumenical Vocation of Orthodoxy." *Ecumenical Review* 56 (2004): 211-225.

Scouteris, Konstantin. "Baptism and Original Sin."* In V. Международная Богословская Конференция Русской Православной Церкви, *Православное учение о церковних таинствах*, том I, Синодальная Библейско-богословская комиссия, Москва, 2009, 328-337.

Serra, Dominic E. "Syrian Prebaptismal Anointing and Western Postbaptismal Chrismation." *Worship* 79 (2005): 328-341.

Short, Howard E. "The Christian Church (Disciples of Christ)." In Merle D. Strege, ed., *Baptism and Church: A Believers' Church Vision*. Sagamore Books, Grand Rapids, MI, 1986, 71-84.

Sinclair-Faulkner, Tom. "A Church Historian's Response." In Ross Thomas Bender and Alan P. F. Sell, eds., *Baptism, Peace, and the State in the Reformed and Mennonite Traditions*. Calgary Institute for the Humanities, Waterloo, ON, 1991, 210-232.

Slough, Rebecca. "Baptismal Practice among North American Mennonites." In Best, *Baptism Today*, 89-98.

Spinks, Bryan D. "Taufe VI: Neuzeit." *Theologische Realenzyklopädie* 32, 710-719.

Tan, Simon G. H. "Reassessing Believer's Baptism in Pentecostal Theology and Practice." *Asian Journal of Pentecostal Studies* 6 (2003): 219-234.

Tashjian, Mesrob. "The Sacrament of Holy Baptism in the Armenian Apostolic Church." In Best, *Baptism Today*, 15-21.

Truscott, Jeffrey A. "The Rite of Holy Baptism in the *Lutheran Book of Worship*." In Best, *Baptism Today*, 45-54.

Tuilier, André. "Didache." *Theologische Realenzyklopädie* 8, 731-736.

Ulrich, Jörg. "Taufe IV : Mittelalter." *Theologische Realenzyklopädie* 32, 697-701.

Wahle, Stephan. "Gestaltung und Deutung der christlichen Initiation im mittelalterlichen lateinischen Westen." In Lange et al., *Die Taufe*, 29-48.

Watkins, Keith. "Baptismal Understanding and Practice in the Christian Church (Disciples of Christ)." In Best, *Baptism Today*, 109-114.

Westerfield Tucker, Karen B. "The Initiatory Rites of the United Methodist Church." In Best, *Baptism Today*, 99-107.

Wilburn, Ralph G. "The One Baptism and the Many Baptisms." *Mid-Stream* 3 (1964): 72-107.

Winkler, Gabriele. "The Original Meaning of the Prebaptismal Anointing and its Implications." In Maxwell E. Johnson, ed., *Living Water, Sealing Spirit: Readings on Christian Initiation*. Liturgical Press, Collegeville, MN, 1995, 58-91.

Yarnold, Edward J. "Taufe III: Alte Kirche." *Theologische Realenzyklopädie* 32, 674-696.

Yun, Koo Dong. "Water Baptism and Spirit Baptism: Pentecostals and Lutherans in Dialogue." *Dialog: A Journal of Theology*, 43 (2004): 344-351.

Primary Sources and Documents

The following is a selected list of the major primary sources quoted and discussed in this book.

Holy Bible. The New Revised Standard Version. Nelson, Nashville, 1989.

Early Church

Agathangelos. *History of the Armenians*. Translated with commentary by Robert W. Thomson, State University of New York Press, Albany, NY, 1976.

Ambrose of Milan. *On the Sacraments*. In *Ambrosius, De Sacramentis. De Mysteriis. Über die Sakramente. Über die Mysterien*, Josef Schmitz, ed., Herder, Freiburg-Basel-Wien, 1990.

Ambrose of Milan. *On the Mysteries*. In *Ambrosius, De Sacramentis. De Mysteriis. Über die Sakramente.Über die Mysterien*, Josef Schmitz, ed., Herder, Freiburg-Basel-Wien, 1990. English translation online available on http://www.newadvent.org/fathers/3405.htm

Augustine of Hippo. "Contra Iulianum libri VI" (P.L., XLIV, 640 sqq.), engl.:*The Works of Saint Augustine: A Translation for the 21st Century,* ed. J. E. Rotelle, New City Press, New York, 1990-, Vol. I.

Clement of Alexandria. *The Tutor* [*Paidagogos*]. In John Ferguson, Clement of Alexandria, Twayne Publishers, 1974, 68-105

Cyril of Jerusalem. *Mystagogical Catecheses.* In Cyrill von Jerusalem. *Mystagogicae Catecheses. Mystagogische Katechesen,* Georg Röwekamp, ed., Herder, Freiburg-Basel-Wien, 1992

Didache. In *Didache (Apostellehre), Barnabasbrief,Zweiter Klemensbrief, Schrift an Diognet,* Klaus Wengst, ed., Wissenschaftliche Buchgesellschaft, Darmstadt, 1984, 66-91.

Ephrem the Syrian. *Hymns on Virginity.* In *Ephrem the Syrian: Hymns,* translated by Kathleen E. McVey, Paulist Press, Mahwah NJ, 1989, 261-473.

Epistle of Barnabas. In *Didache (Apostellehre), Barnabasbrief, Zweiter Klemensbrief, Schrift an Diognet,* Klaus Wengst, ed., Wissenschaftliche Buchgesellschaft, Darmstadt, 1984, 138-202. English translation online available on http://www. earlychristianwritings.com/barnabas.html.

Hippolytus of Rome. *Apostolic Tradition, in* Gregory Dix, ed., *The Apostolic tradition of St. Hippolytus,* Alban Press, London 1992. An online English translation available on www.bombaxo.com/hippolytus.html.

John Chrysostom. "Baptismal Instructions." In *St. John Chrysostom, Baptismal Instructions,* translated and annotated by Paul W. Harkins, Newman Press, New York, 1963

Justin of Rome (Martyr). *First Apology.* In *Ante-Nicene Fathers,* Vol. 1. Edited by Alexander Roberts, James Donaldson, and A. Cleveland Coxe, Christian Literature Publishing Co., Buffalo, NY, 1885. Online translation available on www. earlychristianwritings.com/text/justinmartyr-firstapology.html.

Justin of Rome (Martyr), Dialogue with Trypho, in *Iustini Martyris Dialogus cum Tryphone,* ed. Miroslav Marcovich, Walter de Gruyter, Berlin, 1997.

Nicholas Cabasilas. *The Life in Christ.* St. Vladimir's Seminary Press, Crestwood, 1974.

The Shepherd of Hermas. In Martin Leutzsch and Ulrich Körtner, eds., *Papiasfragmente. Hirt des Hermas,* Wissenschaftliche Buchgesellschaft, Darmstadt, 1998. Online translation available on http://www.textexcavation.com/shepherdhermas.html

Tertullian. *De Baptismo.* in B. Luselli, Q. Septimi Florentis Tertulliani De Baptismo, Turin 2 1968. English transation online available on http://www.newadvent.org/fathers/0321.htm

Theodore of Mopsuestia. "Homilies to Catechumens." In *Theodore of Mopsuestia*, Frederick G. McLeod, ed., Routledge, London, 2009

Middle Ages

Aquinas, Thomas. *Summa Theologica. In J.P. Migne, ed., Thomae Aquitanis summa theologica.* Paris 1861. English translation online available on http://www.newadvent.org/summa/

Gelasian Sacramentary. In *Liber sacramentorum romanae eclesiae ordinis anni circoli*, L. Eizenhöfer, ed., Rom, ³1981.

Reformation

Calvin, John. *Institutes of the Christian Religion*, Translated by Henry Beveridge, Eerdmans, Grand Rapids MI, 1989, see also www.reformed.org/master/index. html?mainframe=/books/institutes/

Confessio Augustana. http://www.ccel.org/ccel/schaff/creeds3.iii.ii.html

Luther, Martin. *The Large Catechism.* Translated by F. Bente and W.H.T. Dau, Published in: *Triglot Concordia: The Symbolical Books of the Ev. Lutheran Church,* Concordia Publishing House, St Louis, 1921, pp. 565-773, online on http://www. godrules.net/library/luther/50luther1.htm; see also http://www.iclnet.org/pub/ resources/text/wittenberg/luther/catechism/web/cat-13a.html

Luther, Martin. "Sermon on John 1:32-34." In: E. Theodore Bachmann and Helmut T. Lehmann, eds., *Luther's Works*, American Edition, Muhlenberg Press, Philadelphia, 1960, vol. 22, 174.

Luther, Martin. "The Order of Baptism (1523)," in E. Theodore Bachmann and Helmut T. Lehmann, eds., *Luther's Works*, American Edition, Muhlenberg Press, 1960, vol. 53, 96-101.

Orthodoxy

"Basic Principles of the Attitude to the Non-Orthodox." Bishops' Synod of the Russian Orthodox Church, 2000. www.mospat.ru/en/documents/ attitude-to-the-non-orthodox/i/.

Roman Catholic Church

Catechism of the Catholic Church (CCC). Second edition revised in accordance with the official Latin text, Libreria Editrice Vaticana, Vatican City, 2000. Online see http://www.vatican.va/archive/ENG0015/_INDEX.HTM

Directory for the Application of Principles and Norms on Ecumenism. Pontifical Council for the Promotion of Christian Unity. Vatican City, 1993.

Rite of Christian Initiation of Adults (RCIA). Study edition, prepared by the International Commission on English in the Liturgy, Liturgical Press, Collegeville, MN, 1988. Online www.catholicliturgy.com/index.cfm/FuseAction/ DocumentContents/Index/2/SubIndex/40/Documentindex/539.

Dogmatic Constitution on the Church (*Lumen Gentium)*). Second Vatican Council, 1964, online on http://www.vatican.va/archive/hist_councils /ii_vatican_council/documents/vat-ii_const_19641121_lumen-gentium_ en.html.

Decree on Ecumenism (*Unitatis Redintegratio),* Second Vatican Council. Online on http://www.vatican.va/archive/hist_councils/ii_vatican_council/documents/ vat-ii_decree_19641121_unitatis-redintegratio_en.html().

Anglican Communion
The Book of Common Prayer according to the Use of the Episcopal Church. 1979. http://www.bcponline.org/.

Articles of Religion. http://anglicansonline.org/basics/thirty-nine_articles.html.

Methodism
Wesley, John. "Treatise on Baptism." In *The Works of John Wesley,* ed. Thomas Jackson, 14 vols., CD-ROM edition, Providence House, Franklin, TN, 1994 vol. 10.

Believers' Baptism Churches
Church of the Brethren. *Manual of Organization and Polity.* Church of the Brethren General Board, Elgin, IL, 1979.

Mennonite Brethren General Conference. Decisions of the Mennonite Brethren General Conference 1963. www.directionjournal.org/article/?509.

Schleitheim Confession. www.anabaptists.org/history/schleith.html.

Simons, Menno. *Foundation of Christian Doctrine,* 1539. In John C. Wenger, ed., *Complete Writings of Menno Simons.* Herald Press, Scottdale PA, 1974, 103ff.

Simons, Menno. *Christian Baptism.* In John C. Wenger, ed., *Complete Writings of Menno Simons.* Herald Press, Scottdale PA, 1974, 227ff.

Pentecostals
Assemblies of God in Australia. *Ministers' Manual,* 5.1., "Articles of Faith." Quoted in Shane Clifton, "The Spirit and Doctrinal Developments: A Functional Analysis of the Traditional Pentecostal Doctrine of the Baptism in the Holy Spirit," *Pneuma* 29 (2007): 5-23, 13.

Ecumenical Documents

"Becoming a Christian: The Ecumenical Implications of Our Common Baptism; Report of the Consultation." In Best and Heller, eds., *Becoming a Christian: The Ecumenical Implications of Our Common Baptism.* Faith and Order Paper No. 184. WCC Publications, Geneva, 1999, 74-97.

Final Report of the First World Conference on Faith and Order, Lausanne 1927. In Lukas Vischer, *A Documentary History of the Faith and Order Movement 1927-1963*. Bethany Press, St. Louis, MO, 1963, 40-74.

Final Report of the Third World Conference on Faith and Order, Lund 1952. In Lukas Vischer, *Documentary History*, 85-130.

The Fourth World Conference on Faith and Order: The Report from Montreal 1963. Edited by Patrick C. Rodger and Lukas Vischer. Faith and Order Paper No. 42. SCM Press, London 1964.

Gros, Jeffrey, Harding Meyer, and William G. Rusch. *Growth in Agreement II: Reports and Agreed Statements of Ecumenical Conversations on a World Level, 1982-1998*. Faith and Order Paper No. 187. WCC Publications, Geneva and Eerdmans, Grand Rapids, MI, 2000.

Gros, Jeffrey, Thomas F. Best, and Lorelei F. Fuchs, eds. *Growth in Agreement III: International Dialogue Texts and Agreed Statements, 1998-2005*. Faith and Order Paper No. 204. WCC Publications, Geneva and Eerdmans, Grand Rapids, MI, 2007.

Meyer, Harding, and Lukas Vischer, eds. *Growth in Agreement I: Reports and Agreed Statements of Ecumenical Conversations on a World Level, 1972-1982*. Faith and Order Paper No. 108. WCC Publications, Geneva, 1984.

Thurian, Max, ed. *Churches Respond to BEM: Official Responses to the "Baptism, Eucharist and Ministry" Text*, Vol. I. Faith and Order Paper No. 129. WCC Publications, Geneva, 1986.

Thurian, Max, ed. *Churches Respond to BEM: Official Responses to the "Baptism, Eucharist and Ministry" Text*, Vol. II. Faith and Order Paper No. 132. WCC Publications, Geneva 1986.

Thurian, Max, ed. *Churches Respond to BEM: Official Responses to the "Baptism, Eucharist and Ministry" Text*, Vol. III. Faith and Order Paper No. 135. WCC Publications, Geneva, 1987.

Thurian, Max, ed. *Churches Respond to BEM: Official Responses to the "Baptism, Eucharist and Ministry" Text*, Vol. IV. Faith and Order Paper No. 137. WCC Publications, Geneva, 1987.

Thurian, Max, ed. *Churches Respond to BEM, Official Responses to the "Baptism, Eucharist and Ministry" Text*, Vol. V. Faith and Order Paper No. 143. WCC Publications, Geneva, 1988.

Thurian, Max, ed. *Churches Respond to BEM: Official Responses to the "Baptism, Eucharist and Ministry" Text*, Vol. VI. Faith and Order Paper No. 144. WCC Publications, Geneva, 1988.

Vischer, Lukas, ed. *A Documentary History of the Faith and Order Movement 1927-1963*. Bethany Press, St. Louis, MO, 1963.

World Council of Churches, Theological Commission on Christ and the Church. *One Lord, One Baptism*. Faith and Order Paper No. 29. SCM Press and Augsburg Publishing House, London, 1961.

World Council of Churches, Commission on Faith and Order. *Baptism, Eucharist and Ministry*. Faith and Order Paper No. 111. WCC Publications, Geneva, 1982.

World Council of Churches, Commission on Faith and Order. *Baptism, Eucharist and Ministry 1982-1990: Report on the Process and Responses*. Faith and Order Paper No. 149. WCC Publications, Geneva 1990.

World Council of Churches, Commission on Faith and Order. *One Baptism: Towards Mutual Recognition; A Study Text*. Faith and Order Paper No. 210, Geneva, WCC Publications, 2011.

International Bilateral Dialogues

Report of Theological Conversations sponsored by the World Alliance of Reformed Churches and the Baptist World Alliance, 1977. In *Growth in Agreement I*, 132-151.

Disciples-Roman Catholic Conversations, Report 1981. In *Growth in Agreement I*, 154-166, 158ff.

"Summons to Witness to Christ in Today's World": A Report on Conversations 1984-1988. Atlanta, GA, 23 July 1988. In *Growth in Agreement II*, 373-385.

Final Report. Dialogue between the Secretariat for Promoting Christian Unity and Leaders of Some Pentecostal Churches and Participants in the Charismatic Movement within Protestant and Anglican Churches, 1972-1976. In *Growth in Agreement II*, 713-720 (also *Growth in Agreement I*, 422-431).

"Perspectives on *Koinonia*." Report from the Third Quinquennium of the Dialogue between the Pontifical Council for Promoting Christian Unity and Some Classical Pentecostal Churches and Leaders, 1985-1989. In *Growth in Agreement II*, 735-752.

"Report on Becoming a Christian: Insights from Scripture and the Patristic Writings." Report of the Fifth Phase of the International Dialogue Between Some Classical Pentecostal Churches and Leaders and the Catholic Church (1998-2006). http://www.vatican.va/roman_curia/pontifical_councils/chrstuni/eccl-comm-docs/rc_pc_chrstuni_doc_20060101_becoming-a-christian_en.html.

"Called Together To Be Peace-makers." Report of the International Dialogue between the Catholic Church and The Mennonite World Conference, Assisi, Italy, 1998-2003. In *Growth in Agreement III*, 206-267.

"Baptist-Lutheran Dialogue: A Message to Our Churches." Geneva, Switzerland, 1990. In *Growth in Agreement II*, 155-175.

"Conversations around the World": International Conversations between the Anglican Communion and the Baptist World Alliance. McLean, VA, 2000-2005. In *Growth in Agreement III,* 319-374.

"Disciples of Christ-Reformed Dialogue: No Doctrinal Obstacles." Birmingham, England, 4-11 March 1987. In *Growth in Agreement II,* 178-186.

The Final Report: Dialogue between the African Independent or Instituted Churches and the World Alliance of Reformed Churches. Mbagathi, Kenya, 9-14 February 2002. In *Growth in Agreement III,* 310-318.

"Healing Memories: Reconciling in Christ." Report of the Lutheran-Mennonite International Study Commission, The Lutheran World Federation and The Mennonite World Conference. 2010, 89 . http://www.lutheranworld.org/lwf/wp-content/uploads/2010/10/Report_Lutheran-Mennonite_Study_Commission.pdf.

Old Catholic-Eastern Orthodox Dialogue. "Sacramental Teaching." Amersfoort, Netherlands, 3 October 1985; Kavala, Greece, 17 October 1987. In *Growth in Agreement II,* 254-263.

Eastern Orthodox-Roman Catholic Dialogue. "Faith, Sacraments and the Unity of the Church." Bari, Italy, June 1987. In *Growth in Agreement II,* 660-670.

"The Mystery of the Church: Baptism and Chrismation." Lutheran-Orthodox Joint Commission, Twelfth Plenary, Duraù, Romania, 6-15 October 2004. In *Growth in Agreement III,* 29-32.

Anglican-Lutheran Conversations: 1972. Pullach Report. In *Growth in Agreement I,* 14-34.

"Anglican-Lutheran Dialogue: *Episcope.*" Niagara Falls, September 1987. In *Growth in Agreement II,* 11-37.

"Anglican-Reformed Dialogue: God's Reign and Our Unity." Woking, England, January 1984. In *Growth in Agreement II,* 114-154.

"The Church: Community of Grace." Lutheran-Methodist Dialogue 1979-84, Bossey, Switzerland, June 1984. In *Growth in Agreement II,* 200-218.

Lutheran-Roman Catholic Dialogue: "Facing Unity." Rome, Italy, 3 March 1984. In *Growth in Agreement II,* 443-484.

Reformed-Roman Catholic Dialogue: "Towards a Common Understanding of the Church," Second Phase, 1984-1990. In *Growth in Agreement II,* 780-818.

International Anglican–Roman Catholic Commission for Unity and Mission. "Growing Together in Unity and Mission," http://www.vatican.va/roman_curia/pontifical_councils/chrstuni/angl-comm-docs/rc_pc_chrstuni_doc_20070914_growing-together_en.html.

Methodist-Roman Catholic Dialogue: "Encountering Christ the Saviour: Church and Sacraments." http://ecumenicalissues.blogspot.com/2011/09/

encountering-christ-saviour.html with a link to the document "Encountering Christ the Saviour: Church and Sacrament."

Joint Working Group between the World Council of Churches and the Roman Catholic Church. "Ecclesiological and Ecumenical Implications of a Common Baptism." Kolympari–Chania, Crete, Greece, 6-13 May 2004. In *Growth in Agreement III*, 559-586.

Joint Working Group between the Roman Catholic Church and the World Council of Churches. Eighth Report 1999-2005. WCC Publications, Geneva and Rome, 2005.

Code of Practice for Ecumenical Relations in the Anglican-Methodist Covenant. Paragraph. 102, 1989/1997. http://www.anglican-methodist.org.uk/Bishops_Code.pdf.

Lutheran World Federation. Statement : Action on the Legacy of Lutheran Persecution of "Anabaptists." Lutheran World Federation, 2010.

http://www.lwf-assembly.org/uploads/media/Mennonite_Statement-EN.pdf.

Lutheran World Federation and Mennonite World Conference. "Healing Memories: Reconciling in Christ." Report of the Lutheran-Mennonite International Study Commission, 2010. http://www.lutheranworld.org/lwf/wp-content/uploads/2010/10/Report_Lutheran-Mennonite_Study_Commission.pdf.

Community of Protestant Churches in Europe (CPCE) and Eastern Orthodox Churches. Communiqué: "Fourth CPCE-Eastern Orthodox Consultation on Baptism in the Life of our Churches." Vienna 2008. In Michael Beintker, Viorel Ionita, and Jochen Kramm, eds., *Baptism in the Life of the Churches: Documentation of an Orthodox-Protestant Dialogue in Europe.* Leuenberg Documents, Vol. 12. Lembeck, Frankfurt am Main, 2011, 14-18.

Regional Agreements
Community of Protestant Churches in Europe (CPCE) and European Baptist Federation (EBF). Communiqué: "The Beginning of the Christian Life and the Nature of the Church. Results of the Dialogue between the CPCE and the EBF." In Wilhelm Hüffmeier and Tony Peck, eds., *Dialogue between the Community of Protestant Churches in Europe (CPCE) and the European Baptist Federation (EBF) on the Doctrine and Practice of Baptism.* Leuenberg Documents, Vol. 9. Lembeck, Frankfurt am Main, 2005, 9-29.

Michael Beintker, Viorel Ionita, and Jochen Kramm, eds., *Baptism in the Life of the Churches: Documentation of an Orthodox-Protestant Dialogue in Europe.* Leuenberg Documents, Vol. 12. Lembeck, Frankfurt am Main, 2011.

Local Bilateral Conversations
Faith and Unity Executive Committee of the Baptist Union of Great Britain and The Council for Christian Unity of the Church of England. *Pushing at the*

Boundaries of Unity: Anglicans and Baptists in Conversation. Church House Publishing, London, 2005.

Local Agreements

Australia: Report of the Commission on Faith and Unity of the National Council of Churches in Australia. http://www.ncca.org.au/files/Working_Papers_pt2_73-140.pdf.

Australia: The Mutual Recognition of Baptism: Roman Catholic and Lutheran Churches in Australia, reviewed July 2001. http://www.lca.org.au/doctrinal-statements--theological-opinions-2.html.

Bavaria, Germany: "Learning from One Another – Believing Together." Convergence Document of the Bavarian Lutheran-Baptist Working group (BALUBAG), 2009. English version at http://www.gftp.de/press/public/weitere/Bavarian%20Baptists%20and%20Lutherans%20Final%20Report.pdf.

Brazil: Information about mutual recognition of baptism in Brazil. http://clericalwhispers.blogspot.com/2007/11/brazil-churches-agree-on-mutual.html, http://archive.livingchurch.org/news/news-updates/2007/11/27/brazilian-churches-agree-on-mutual-recognition-of-baptism. Also: http://www.itesc.ecumenismo.com/news/rec%20mutuo.pdf

Chile: Agreement on "Mutual recognition of Baptism" in Chile, 1999. http://documentos.iglesia.cl/conf/doc_pdf.php?mod=documentos_sini&id=594.

Egypt: Pastoral Agreement between the Coptic Orthodox and Greek Orthodox Patriarchates of Alexandria, 2001. http://orthodoxwiki.org/Pastoral_Agreement_between_the_Coptic_Orthodox_and_Greek_Orthodox_Patriarchates_of_Alexandria_(2001).

Germany: Agreement on mutual recognition of baptism in Germany, 2007. http://www.oekumene-ack.de/uploads/media/Christian_Baptism.pdf (German original: http://www.oekumene-ack.de/uploads/media/Anerkennung_der_Taufe.pdf).

Italy: "Documento sui reciproco riconoscimento fra chiese battise metodiste valdesi in Italia" (Document on mutual recognition of Baptist, Methodist, and Waldensian churches in Italy.) In Sinodo des 1990 delle chiese valdesi e metodiste. Session straordinaria, 1.-4. November 1990, 14-22. A German version is accessible in: Cornelia Nussberger, ed., *Wachsende Kirchengemeinschaft: Gespräche und Vereinbarungen zwischen evangelischen Kirchen in Europa*. Texte der Ev. Arbeitsstelle Ökumene Schweiz Nr. 16, Bern 1992, 155-167.

Netherlands: Declaration concerning the mutual recognition of baptism by the synod of the Protestant Church in the Netherlands and the episcopacy of the Roman Catholic Church in the Netherlands. http://www.protestantchurch.nl/site/uploadedDocs/Dooperkenning(1).pdfm.

North America: Agreed statement on "Baptism and 'Sacramental Economy'" issued by the North American Orthodox-Catholic Theological Consultation in

1999. http://www.orthodoxresearchinstitute.org/articles/ecumenical/baptism_sacramental_economy.htm

Papua New Guinea: Agreement on mutual recognition of baptism in Papua New Guinea, 2003. http://www.ask.com/wiki/Anglican_Church_of_Papua_New_Guinea#Ecumenical_relations

Philippines: Agreement on Baptism between the Lutheran Church in the Philippines and the Roman Catholic Church in the Philippines, 1972. http://catholic-church.ph/filer/14-1_091.pdf.

Poland: "The Sacrament of Baptism – a Sign of Unity." Poland, 2000. http://www.ekumenia.pl/index.php?D=42 and English version at http://www.mariavite.org/choecuma.htm#reconn.

Slovakia: "Agreement on Holy Baptism" between Lutherans and Catholics in Slovakia, 2001. http://www.kbs.sk/do_pdf/index.php?cid=1117713909.

Spain: "Spanish Anglicans, Catholics reach accord on baptism, 2011." http://www.zenit.org/article-31829?l=english.

Sweden: Basic Document of "Gemensam Framtid" in Sweden. http://gemensamframtid.se/wp-content/uploads/2011/10/GF-teologisk_grund_111010.pdf

Switzerland: Project for mutual recognition of baptism in Switzerland. http://www.agck.ch/de-ch/projekte/taufanerkennung-ausweiten.html.

United States of America: "These Living Waters: Common Agreement on Mutual Recognition of Baptism." Signed between the U.S. Conference of Catholic Bishops and several Reformed churches, 2010-2011. http://www.pcusa.org/media/uploads/worship/pdfs/common_agreement_baptism.pdf. Also at http://www.ncccusa.org/pdfs/commonbaptism.pdf.

Others: Christ Holy Church International. http://gntcs.org/Christ_Holy_%20Church.html.

Glossary

Ablution	cleansing or washing of a person's body or parts of the body. The term is especially used for religious rites.
Acolyte	A male lay person with specific liturgical tasks
Adiaphora	(greek adiaphora: indifferent things) In the Christian context: Matters which are not regarded as essential to faith.
Affusion	(Latin: *affusio* – pouring on) Baptismal practice, in which water is poured on the head of the candidate
Anabaptists	Literally: 're-baptizers'. This term was used in the 16th century for naming the groups which appeared in the Radical Reformation, from which the Mennonites descended.
Anointing	A ritual in which oil or other substances are poured or smeared on parts of the human body. In Christianity anointing are in some confessional traditions related to the sacraments of baptism, chrismation and anointing of the sick.
Baptistery	Chapel with a font for baptisms either next to a church or within a church building.
Canon	In church law a canon is a specific paragraph or article in a law document or in the decisions of synods and councils.
Caritas	love (of the neighbor)
Catechesis	The education in Christian faith, orginally during the preparation period for baptism.

Catechism	(Greek: *katechesis* – teaching, instruction) "Catechism" describes the act of the baptismal instruction; the contents of the baptismal instruction and also the book which contains this contents. In the last sense it is a summary of the Christian faith, used for teaching purposes. Catechisms in form of questions and answers were developed especially in the West from the 16th century onwards.
Catechumen	Candidate for baptism
Catechumenate	Preparation period for catechumens before baptism, during which the candidates were taught in faith.
Character indelebilis	A spiritual mark in a person, which cannot be removed.
Chrism	(in the East called Myron, cf. below) A mixture of oil and fragrances, which is consecrated (in the Roman Catholic Church) by a diocesan bishop and his priests and used for the sacrament of confirmation, in the early church and in the Orthodox churches called chrismation.
Chrismation	One of the seven sacraments in the Orthodox and Roman Catholic churches. It is an anointing with chrisma (Myron). Originally (and still in the Orthodox churches) chrismation was liturgically linked with baptism.
Credobaptist church	A church which baptizes only persons who can confess their faith (cf. Creed)
Deacon	(Greek: *diakonos* – servant, helper) A person who holds the ministry of the diaconate. The Christian use of the term goes back to Acts 6:1-7, where seven deacons were chosen in order to care for the poor of the community. In the early church the deacon was one of the three ministers, together with the bishop and the presbyter. In addition to social tasks and the function of a helper first to the bishop, later to the presbyter, he had also a liturgical function. In the course of history the diaconate developed in different ways in the different church traditions. While in the Orthodox churches the deacon has purely a liturgical function, the Roman Catholic Church has recently re-discovered the social aspects of this ministry. In many Protestant churches deacons have purely social- diaconical functions.

Disciplina arcani	(lat. Arcanum: secret) The principle to restrict the access to certain rituals only to initiated persons.
Enthusiasts	The English translation of the German term *Schwärmer*, which was used by Martin Luther and other reformers to describe the representatives of the radical branch of the Reformation, especially as far as they referred to visions or prophesies and other supranatural revelations.
Ephphetha	(= be opened) Rite for the 'opening of the senses'. The name is taken from Mk 7:32-37, the story of the healing of a deaf man
Epiclesis, epicletic	Prayer to the Holy Spirit with the special request to be present and to transform people or the elements of a sacrament.
Eucharist	(Greek: eucharistia: thanksgiving) A wide spread term for the sacrament of the Last Supper or Holy Supper, instituted by Jesus Christ before his death.
Exorcism	Religious practice of evicting demons or bad spirits from a person or a place. This can be done by addressing God or by addressing the spirits
Glossolalia	Speaking in tongues. Speaking with words and syllables with no comprehensive meaning. It is mentioned in the New Testament and practiced nowadays mainly by Pentecostals and charismatic groups, where it is meant to be a spiritual gift, initiated by the presence of the Holy Spirit.
Heretic	A person who holds a theological opinion which is different from the officially recognized doctrine of the church (different from 'schismatic').
Immersion	Baptismal practice, by which a person is immersed into the water with his/her whole body, sometimes except the head.
Initiation	The introduction of an external person into a community
Martyr/Martyrdom	(Greek: *martys* – witness; *martyria* – testimony) Generally a martyr is someone who gives a (written) testimony. During history the term *martyrdom* has been used for the act of suffering persecution or death for renouncing to betray one's faith conviction as a specific way of giving witness to Jesus Christ.

Myron	(cf. chrism) Eastern term for 'chrism'. In the Orthodox churches it is consecrated by the patriarch.
Mystagogy	The interpretation of mysteries
Neophyte	(Greek: *neophytes* – the newly born) A newly baptized person; a convert or in general a beginner in faith.
Non-credal (churches)	Churches that do not use a formulated creed.
Paedobaptist churches	Churches which baptize infants.
Postbaptismal anointing	Anointing after the water rite.
Prebaptismal anointing	Anointing before the water rite.
Presbyter	(greek 'presbyteros': elder) In the New Testament 'presbyter' is a ministry, related to a bishop, in English 'priest'. In some Protestant churches today 'presbyters' is the term for the members of the parish council.
Scrutinies	Celebrations within the context of the catechumenate, including a testing of the candidates.
Sponsors	Another term for 'godparents'. A sponsor is meant for spiritual support of the baptismal candidate.
Submersion	Baptismal practice, by which a person is completely immersed in the water with the whole body
Tonsure	Cutting some hair during the rite of baptism (Oriental and Eastern Orthodox); shaving a part of the hair of a monk. In the West this part of the head remained shaved (this custom was abandoned after the Second Vatican Council); in the East a monk after the tonsure stops cutting his hair.

Index

Persons

Institutions

Biblical texts